C000121198

THE (GOSPEL) OF

MATTHEW

THE KING IS COMING

The King is Coming !

Ed Hindson

Advancing the Ministries of the Gospel

AMG *Publishers*

God's Word to you is our highest calling

TWENTY-FIRST CENTURY
BIBLICAL COMMENTARY SERIES®

THE GOSPEL OF

MATTHEW

THE KING IS COMING

EDWARD
HINDSON
AND

JAMES
BORLAND

GENERAL EDITOR
MAL COUCH

To John MacArthur Jr.
Pastor, Grace Community Church
Sun Valley, California

For a wonderful example of biblical exposition,
theological insight, and pastoral ministry.

Twenty-First Century Biblical Commentary Series®

Mal Couch, Th.D., and Ed Hindson, D.Phil.

The New Testament has guided the Christian Church for over two thousand years. This one testament is made up of twenty-seven books, penned by godly men through the inspiration of the Holy Spirit. It tells us of the life of Jesus Christ, His atoning death for our sins, His miraculous resurrection, His ascension back to heaven, and the promise of His second coming. It also tells the story of the birth and growth of the church and the people and principles that shaped it in its earliest days. The New Testament concludes with the book of Revelation pointing ahead to the glorious return of Jesus Christ.

Without the New Testament, the message of the Bible would be incomplete. The Old Testament emphasizes the promise of a coming Messiah. It constantly points us ahead to the One who is coming to be the King of Israel and the Savior of the world. But the Old Testament ends with this event still unfulfilled. All of its ceremonies, pictures, types, and prophecies are left awaiting the arrival of the "Lamb of God who takes away the sin of the world!" (John 1:29).

The message of the New Testament represents the timeless truth of God. As each generation seeks to apply that truth to its specific context, an up-to-date commentary needs to be created just for them. The editors and authors of the Twenty-First Century Biblical Commentary Series have endeavored to do just that. This team of scholars represents conservative, evangelical, and dispensational scholarship at its best. The individual authors may differ on minor points of interpretation, but all are convinced that the Old and New Testaments teach a dispensational framework for biblical history. They also hold to a pretribulational and premillennial understanding of biblical prophecy.

The French scholar René Pache reminded each succeeding generation, "If the power of the Holy Spirit is to be made manifest anew among us, it is of primary importance that His message should regain its due place. Then we shall be able to put the enemy to flight by the sword of the Spirit which is the Word of God."

William Hendriksen said of Matthew's gospel, "This gospel has been called 'the most important book in the world' (Renan) and 'the most successful book ever written' (Goodspeed). Besides being important and successful, it is also truly beautiful. Reading it from beginning to end at one sitting is a thrilling experience. The book is simply irresistible."

Craig Blomberg observes that of the four gospels, "Matthew was usually the most popular in the first several centuries of the church's history. It contains the greatest quantity of Jesus' teaching, including his most famous sermon (the Sermon on the Mount). . . . Matthew also contains the greatest number of links to Judaism and the Old Testament."

John Walvoord referred to Matthew's gospel as "a bridge between the Old and New Testaments [which] fittingly introduces the books that follow. Matthew deals primarily with the life of Jesus Christ as fulfilling Old Testament prophecies relating to the coming King." Thus, Matthew focuses on both the first and second comings of Christ, with the assurance that in both cases, indeed the King is coming!

Contents

Foreword

The Gospel of Matthew is the most Jewish of all the Gospels. In its inspired pages, we see Jesus of Nazareth on display as the "King of the Jews." From the opening genealogy to the Great Commission, Jesus is at center stage in this masterful biography of the Messiah.

Matthew, the tax collector turned disciple, writes to Jewish believers and unbelievers alike. For the believers, he emphasizes the legitimacy of Jesus as the long-awaited Jewish Messiah. For the unbelievers, he portrays the One who is the Savior of all people everywhere. His arguments are cogent, his style is vibrant, and his portrayal of Christ is magnificent.

The early church was so impressed with the Gospel of Matthew that it was always placed first in their list of canonical books. It was the perfect bridge to the Old Testament and the ideal introduction to the New Testament. In its powerful pages, we are introduced to the One who is the fulfillment of the prophecies of the Hebrew Scriptures. We are given a glimpse of the Savior through Jewish eyes as He challenges His own people to know and love God with all their hearts, souls, and minds.

We are also introduced to some of Jesus' most prominent sermons, parables, and miracles. Matthew provides a personal record of such important messages as the Sermon on the Mount (chaps. 5–7), the Parables of the Kingdom (chap. 13), and the Olivet Discourse (chaps. 24–25). He also provides an eyewitness account of such significant events as the transfiguration, the triumphal entry, the crucifixion, and the resurrection.

Matthew also helps us understand the dispensational transition from the era of law to that of grace. He explains the character and nature of the ministry of John the Baptist as the last of the prophets. He takes us to Caesarea Philippi, a Gentile area, where Jesus announces that He will build His church, and then he lets us listen as the risen Savior challenges His disciples to "go . . . and make disciples of all the nations" (28:18–20).

Matthew also gives special attention to the rejection of Jesus by the Jewish leaders. He exposes the religious blindness of his fellow countrymen, and He demonstrates Jesus' superior understanding of the person of God, the intent of the law, and the proper application of biblical truth. The evangelist is especially critical of the scribes and Pharisees while pointing out that the common people gladly listened to the Savior.

Throughout Matthew's gospel, he draws our attention to the One who is the rightful King of Israel. Jesus is portrayed as being born a King, living and dying as a King, and coming again as the ultimate King of Kings. It is our sincere prayer that as you read this gospel and study this commentary, your mind will be illuminated, your heart warmed, and your life challenged to become His disciple and follow Him wherever He leads you.

Ed Hindson
James Borland
Liberty University
Lynchburg, Virginia

Background of Matthew

Matthew's gospel serves as the introduction to the entire New Testament. It presents Jesus Christ as the promised Messiah of the Old Testament. Thus it is saturated with 130 references to the Hebrew Scriptures, emphasizing that Jesus is the fulfillment of the prophecies and types of the Old Testament.[1]

Matthew himself was a customs officer (tax collector) in the territory of Herod Antipas. He was a man of some education who could read and write. He would have had to be conversant in Aramaic, Latin, and Greek in order to fulfill his obligations. With such linguistic abilities, he was the prefect person to write this gospel account of the King and His kingdom.

W. Graham Scroggie observes, "It was while he was sitting at the toll office, near Capernaum, on the Great West Road from Damascus to the Mediterranean, that Jesus called him."[2] Like many of the disciples, his name was changed after his dramatic encounter with the Savior. Originally known as Levi (Mark 2:14), he came to be known as Matthew. As Cephas became Peter, and Saul became Paul, so this backslidden Jewish collaborator became a herald of the good news of the kingdom of heaven.

Michael Wilkins notes, "The name Levi may be an indication that he was from the tribe of Levi and was therefore familiar with Levitical practices."[3] However, his occupation as a tax collector ("publican") made him despised by his Jewish countrymen who considered such people the worst of sinners. Wilkins adds, "Since tax collectors were fairly wealthy and were despised by the local populace . . . Matthew's calling and response were completely out of the ordinary and required nothing short of a miraculous turn-around in this tax collector's life."[4]

Like so many of Jesus' converts, Matthew's personal transformation was itself a testimony to the Savior's miraculous power. Thus his gospel emphasized

Christ's power over Satan, sin, sickness, death, and disease. From his opening chapter, the transformed disciple presents Jesus as the promised Messiah, the son of David, the son of Abraham, and the virgin-born Son of God. He is none other than Immanuel—"God with us" (Matt. 1:23; cf. 28:20).

Portrait of the King

The four gospels present a fourfold view of the life of Christ. With the exception of scant references by ancient secular writers, our entire knowledge of the life of Jesus comes from these gospel accounts.[5] Most likely, the early accounts were passed on verbally and then recorded in Greek manuscripts between A.D. 60 and A.D. 90. All four gospels build upon genuine historical tradition and preserve different aspects of it so that we might see the Savior in the fullness of His person.

The basic purpose of the Gospels is to present the gospel message, the good news of the Redeemer-Savior. They present Jesus as the Messiah of Israel, the Son of God, and the Savior of the world. The Gospels were written so that their readers would come to believe in Christ and receive eternal life (cf. John 20:31). They view Jesus as the Lord of glory who is presently alive and active in heaven. They are like four portraits of the same subject. "While there is only one person behind these portraits," writes Richard Burridge, "a full understanding of Jesus will be better gained by taking a stroll through the portrait gallery."[6]

The four gospels present four portraits of Jesus, each in its own characteristic manner. I. Howard Marshall comments, "The greatness of this person could not have been captured in one picture. So we have four portraits, each bringing out its own distinctive facets of the character of Jesus."[7] Matthew, the Hebrew tax collector, writes for the Hebrew mind. Mark, the travel companion of Paul and Peter, writes for the Roman mind. Luke, Paul's physician-missionary, writes with the Greek mentality in view. John's Gospel is different by nature from the other three. It is an interpretation of the facts of Jesus' life with an emphasis on His deity.

Four Portraits of Christ	
Matthew	Christ the King of the Jews
Mark	Christ the Servant of the Lord
Luke	Christ the Son of Man
John	Christ the Son of God

Oxford professor Robin Griffith-Jones pictures Jesus as "a rabbinical writer, a master of rich, allusive stories that draw on the ancient themes of Judaism and interpret them afresh."[8] He sees Jesus as a wise teacher, steeped in the Law (Torah) who offers his readers a "new book of the Law," in which Jesus is the fulfillment of the hopes and dreams of the Old Testament.

Matthew presents Jesus as the rightful "King of the Jews" and bookends his gospel with the statements of Gentiles who recognize this truth. In the opening narrative, the wise men come from the East seeking the baby who has been born "King of the Jews" (2:2). As Matthew closes his gospel, Pilate authorizes the inscription: "THIS IS JESUS THE KING OF THE JEWS" (27:37). In between, Matthew presents Him as exactly that, urging his Jewish readers to believe the truth that even Gentiles could clearly see.

Matthew offers an apologetic for the messiahship of Jesus of Nazareth. He quotes the fulfillment of Old Testament prophecies, makes the case for the genealogical rights of Jesus to the throne of David, and records the Savior's numerous references to the "kingdom of heaven," the preferred Jewish expression for the "kingdom of God." Further, Matthew assumes that his readers understand Jewish prophecies, festivals, and traditions, clearly indicating his intent to persuade Jewish readers that their Messiah had come. John MacArthur observes, "Matthew's writing offers an apologetic for the messiahship of Jesus Christ. The full identity and nature of the predicted King are initially presented and explained in the gospels. . . . Like a divine spotlight, they focus on Jesus and . . . show Him to be the only One who fulfills all the requirements of those prophecies."[9]

Promise of the Kingdom

Louis Barbieri raises the insightful question of why David's name appears before Abraham's in the opening genealogy.[10] The answer is clear. Matthew is presenting Jesus as a King. He does not need to convince his Jewish readers that Jesus is Jewish. They know that. What they are questioning is whether He is the rightful heir to David's throne.

But Jesus did not literally bring in the kingdom in the way most Jews had hoped. Therefore, Matthew develops his central thesis, which revolves around three key elements: (1) presentation of the King, (2) rejection of the King, and (3) postponement of the kingdom.

One cannot read Matthew's gospel without realizing that his doctrine of the kingdom is essential to his understanding of Jesus' relationship to the Old Testament prophecies of the coming King and the messianic kingdom. Stanley Toussaint comments, "Matthew explains God's kingdom program as it relates to Israel, . . . He shows first of all that the Jews rejected an earthly kingdom when they rejected their King (21:28–22:10; 11:16–24). He then goes on to show that because Israel rejected its King, its Kingdom is postponed."[11]

Matthew's Doctrine of the Kingdom

The kingdom would be ruled by the Son of David (Matt. 1:18–25).

The King of the Jews would be "the Christ" of Psalm 2 (Matt. 2:2–6).

The herald of the "kingdom of heaven" would be John the Baptist (Matt. 3:1–3; Isa. 40:3).

The "kingdom of heaven" was at hand because the King, the Son of God, was present (Matt. 3:1–17).

The "kingdom of heaven" would have a series of rules and laws administered by the King (Matt. 5–7).

Christ spoke of the kingdom in mysteries, in spiritual parables, because of the hardness of the hearts of the people of Israel (Matt. 13).

The "kingdom of heaven" would be removed from that present generation and given to a future generation (Matt. 21:43).

The "kingdom of heaven" will someday be established on earth by the King, the Son of Man (Matt. 24–25).

In regard to the postponement of the kingdom, it is important to note that God's promises to Israel were not canceled because they failed to recognize Him at His first coming. The question of the disciples in Acts 1:6 makes this clear. They asked, "Lord, is it at this time You are restoring the kingdom to Israel?" Jesus responded by reminding them that the timing of the kingdom was in the Father's authority, and they were to wait for God's timing in this matter.

Jesus then prepared to ascend back into heaven. If God had been finished with Israel or if the church was supposed to replace Israel, this would have been the perfect opportunity for Jesus to explain this to the disciples. But He did not even begin to suggest that the church was the new "Israel" of God. Not at all! He simply told the disciples to wait for the coming of the Spirit to fulfill the promise to build the church in the meantime.

The Old Testament clearly teaches that the Messiah will reign on earth from Jerusalem. Since Jesus did not fulfill these prophecies in His first coming, they will be fulfilled at His second coming. John F. Walvoord says of Matthew's gospel that "it was designed to explain to the Jews . . . why Christ suffered and died, and why there was the resulting postponement of His triumph until His second coming."[12]

Primacy of Matthew

From the earliest days of the church era, Matthew has always held the primary place among the four gospels. R. V. G. Tasker observes, "The Gospel of Matthew occupies first place in all extant witnesses to the text of the four gospels and in all early lists of the canonical books of the New Testament."[13] Matthew's emphasis on the Old Testament predictions in preparation for the gospel makes it an ideal bridge from the Old Testament to the New Testament.

The book itself is technically anonymous, especially if one compares it with the ascriptions to Pauline authorship in each of Paul's thirteen recognized epistles. But as D. A. Carson points out, "We have no evidence that these gospels ever circulated without an appropriate designation . . . (*kata Matthaion*, 'according to Matthew') or the like."[14] What this means is that no manuscript of the Gospels has even been found without a title at the beginning that ascribes authorship. Thus, even the earliest manuscript of Matthew states that Matthew wrote it. In fact, the very earliest traditions credit the first gospel to Matthew, the disciple of Jesus. Papias, the second-century bishop of Hierapolis; Irenaeus, the Bishop of Lyons; Origen in the third century; and Eusebius, who wrote his *Historia Ecclesiastica* in the fourth century, all agree that Matthew was the author of this gospel and that he originally wrote it in Hebrew, probably meaning Aramaic, the common spoken language of the early Christians. However, there is no trace of an Aramaic "original," and the earliest quotations (early second century) from Matthew are in Greek.[15]

It is difficult to determine at this time whether Matthew, as we know it today, is a Greek translation of his Aramaic original or was originally written in Greek.[16] Scholars, both conservative and liberal, are divided on this matter. Some have even suggested that Matthew may have written a separate Hebrew or Aramaic document of the "sayings of Jesus." However, an examination of the Greek gospel does not favor the idea that it is a translation, for it has none of the characteristics of a translated work. For example, Matthew's gospel includes quite a number of Aramaic terms and phrases. But none of the Aramaic phrases are translated.[17] The conclusion to be drawn, as John Walvoord points out, is "these would be intelligible to Jewish Christians, but if Matthew was translated from Aramaic into Greek for the benefit of Gentile Christians, these terms would require an explanation. The fact that the terms are not translated tends to prove that the Gospel of Matthew was originally written in Greek, even though intended for an audience that also understood Aramaic."[18]

Since Matthew was bilingual, it is possible that he wrote both an Aramaic "gospel" of the sayings of Jesus and the Greek gospel that now bears his name. Catholic scholars (Lagrange, Chapman, Butler) have tended to uphold the idea of an Aramaic original, while liberal Protestants (Allen, Albright) have favored the idea of a Greek original based on the priority of Mark as its major source. Conservative scholars (Kent, Lenski, Walvoord) have generally rejected the idea that Matthew was dependent upon Mark as a source document and hold to the view that Matthew himself wrote the Greek version of his gospel as an original apostolic witness to Christ.

Two major critical views have generally asserted that Matthew was dependent on previous sources. These two concepts deny the idea that Matthew's gospel was written first: (1) the *priority of Mark* as the basic source document of both Matthew and Luke and (2) the previous existence of a *common source document,* referred to as "Q" (German, *quelle,* "source") to all the Synoptics. The Q theory has fallen on rough ground among some form critics.[19] Neither view has substantially proven its case, even though many evangelicals hold to the priority of Mark. W. R. Farmer and L. Keck are among several modern scholars to return to Griesbach's theory on the priority of Matthew.[20] There does not seem to be compelling evidence to rule out the basic independence of Matthew, Mark, and Luke in their writing of the Synoptic Gospels. Matthew, of course, was an eyewitness to the events, and that knowledge would shape his presentation. Luke, the traveling companion of Paul, consulted eyewitnesses, as he says (Luke 1:1–4), whose testimonies would flavor his gospel. Mark is said to be the disciple of Peter, another eyewitness, which would shape his overall presentation as well.[21]

The literary debate over the primacy of Matthew may never be settled based on extant evidence. Those favoring Matthew point out that he was a personal disciple of Jesus. Therefore, who best should speak first on the Savior's behalf? They ask, as an apostle, why would he depend on Mark? Those favoring the primacy of Mark argue that the verses common to the Synoptic Gospels appear to depend on Mark as the original source. They also point out that 96 percent of the substance of Mark and 80 percent of its actual language is found in Matthew. Regardless, the early church chose Matthew's gospel as the primary account and always listed it first.

Personality of the Author

Several internal factors clearly support the fact that Matthew was the author of the gospel that bears his name. First, the gospel refers to Matthew by name

(Matt. 9:9), whereas, Mark (2:14) and Luke (5:27) refer to him as Levi. Guthrie points out that he is called Matthew in all the lists of the apostles and raises the question, "Could it be that for the author of this gospel the name Matthew came to have greater significance than the name Levi, from the time of his dramatic call to follow Jesus?"[22] Such a practice by the disciple would be similar to that of Paul referring to himself as Paul, not Saul, in his letter.

Second, the author shows unusual familiarity with money and coins, which one would expect from a former tax collector. In the dispute over paying taxes, Mark and Luke use the common term *dēnarion*. Matthew alone uses the more precise term *nomisma* (state coin). Matthew also uses three terms for money that occur nowhere else in the New Testament: "tribute" (*didrachmon*), "money" (*statēr*) and "talent" (*talanton*). He also uses "gold" (*chrusos*), "silver" (*arguros*) and "brass" (*chalkos*), which are used elsewhere in the New Testament, but do not appear in any other gospels. In addition, Matthew refers to the "penny" (*dēnarion*), "silver-piece" (*argurion*) and "tribute" (*kēnsos*), which also are used in the other gospels.[23]

Matthew alone records the two parables of the "talents" (large amounts of money of the highest value). He also includes references to "debt," "reckoning," and "moneychangers," which do not occur elsewhere in the Gospels but which would be very familiar to a tax collector (KJV, "publican"). Matthew also uses numbers and lists with clerical precision. Alfred Plummer was one of the first to observe that incidents and sayings in Matthew's gospel are frequently arranged in numerical groups of three, five, or seven.[24]

A unique statement within the book of Matthew provides further internal evidence to its authorship. The account of the call of Matthew (chap. 9) is followed by that of a meal taken by Jesus in the company of "publicans and sinners." One way to translate this passage is to say that the meal took place "at home," or literally "in the house" or "in his house" (9:10). The parallel account in Mark 2:15 makes it clear that this feast took place in Levi's (i.e., Matthew's) house. B. F. Atkinson points out, "The phrase 'at home' means 'in my (that is in the author's) house.' Here, therefore, is a phrase that betrays the identity of the author."[25]

Place and Date of Writing

There is no indication within the text of Matthew as to where it was written. Scholars are divided on whether it was penned in Jerusalem or Antioch of Syria. Those favoring Jerusalem point to the frequent references to Jerusalem throughout this gospel. Those favoring Antioch point to Jesus' prediction of the destruction of Jerusalem (chap. 24) and suppose that Matthew was writing to a Jewish-Christian audience in Antioch after the destruction of the temple. However, the latter view often presupposes this on the basis of their rejection of the predictive nature of Jesus' prophecy.

Scholars favoring the earlier date of Matthew's gospel point to several internal references to the "temple" (24:1–2), the "holy place" (24:15), impending trouble (24:16), and the "holy city" (27:53). All indicate that Jerusalem was still standing when Matthew wrote his gospel. Scroggie points to the phrase "to this day" (NASB; Matt 27:8; 28:15) to indicate that Jerusalem was still intact at the time of this writing.[26] Robert Gundry argues that the passage in 17:24–27 teaches Jewish Christians to refuse to pay the temple tax and thus not contribute to their fellow Jews rejection of the gospel.[27] This was only applicable if the temple was still standing when Matthew wrote this passage.

There are two tiny phrases in Matthew that hint at a time for Matthew's writing. Matthew 27:7–8 says that the Potter's Field "has been called the Field of Blood to this day." Matthew 28:15 says that the soldiers' lie about Jesus' body being stolen was still being spread among the Jews "to this very day" (NIV). This indicates that some time has elapsed between those events and the writing, but it does not call for a significant time lapse. If Matthew was written first, because historically the gospel went to the Jews first, then a date in the 50s would not be out of the question. This is especially so if one views Luke as having been written before the book of Acts, the latter of which records events only up to about the year A.D. 62.

Gundry also argues at length for Luke's dependence on Matthew.[28] Observing that Luke's gospel and Acts end with Paul still alive in prison, it is a fair assumption that they were written in A.D. 60–62, before Paul's execution in A.D. 63–64. This would date Matthew prior to Luke, meaning that his gospel would have been written sometime between A.D. 50 and A.D. 60. D. A. Carson concludes that any date between A.D. 40 and A.D. 100 fits the data but leans to A.D. 58–62 as the most likely date for Matthew's gospel.[29]

The early date for the composition of Matthew favors the idea that it was written in Jerusalem before the fall of the city in A.D. 70. Regardless, the first gospel assumes that the readers are well acquainted with the geographical details of Jerusalem. Several specific references appear throughout the gospel: the proximity of Jerusalem to Bethlehem (2:9–11), Bethphage (21:1), and the Mount of Olives (24:3); the Kidron Valley road (21:6–10); the moneychangers in the temple (21:12); the temple courts (21:23); the palace of the high priest (26:3); Gethsemane (26:36); the Potter's Field (27:7–10); the Praetorium (27:27); and Golgotha (27:33).

The gospel records reflect the reality of the details of Jesus' life. They were not written in an intellectual vacuum. They tell of real people in real places in real history. There really were Pharisees and Sadducees. Herod and Pilate were historical figures whose existence is dated and verified. The geographical places named in the gospel accounts actually existed, and their archaeological remains stand as testimony to their existence in the time of Christ.

Plan of the Gospel

Matthew's gospel is written with evangelistic fervor. He deliberately sets out to prove that Jesus is the promised Messiah—the King of the Jews. He also portrays Him as the Teacher of Righteousness who properly explains the Law of Moses and its application to everyday life. In His Sermon on the Mount, Jesus says, "you have heard . . . but I say to you" (5:21–22, 27–28, 31–34, 38–39, 43–44). In each case, the Savior speaks with divine authority. He tells His disciples that their acts of righteousness must come from the heart and should not be done merely to be "seen by men" (6:1–6).

In chapter 22, Jesus upstages every Jewish religious sect in one day. Pharisees, Sadducees, and Herodians are all silenced by His wisdom and insight. In chapter 23, He condemns the false religious leaders of Israel, and in chapter 24, He predicts the destruction of the temple. Throughout Matthew's gospel, the emphasis is on the teaching of Jesus. In all, Matthew records six lengthy sermons (or discourses) of Christ:

1. *Sermon on the Mount (Matt. 5–7)*

2. *Charge to the Twelve (Matt. 10)*

3. *Parables of the Kingdom (Matt. 13)*

4. *Teaching on True Greatness (Matt. 18)*

5. *Denunciation of the Pharisees (Matt. 23)*

6. *Olivet Discourse (Matt. 24–25)*

Three-fifths of the whole gospel (more than 600 verses out of 1,068) records the words of Jesus. Matthew alone tells of the coming of the magi, the flight into Egypt, Peter walking on the water, the "woes" against the Pharisees, Christ's betrayal for thirty pieces of silver, and Judas's suicide. He alone records the parables of the tares, the hidden treasure, the goodly pearl, the fish net, the unmerciful servant, the laborers in the vineyard, the two sons, the marriage of the king's son, the ten virgins, and the talents.

Matthew uses 115 words found nowhere else in the New Testament. The vast majority of these come from Jesus' sermons. It seems obvious that Matthew, a former tax collector, recorded specific details of Jesus' teaching and preserved them in his gospel. Whether these were originally recorded in the "sayings" (*logia*) in Aramaic, as Papias suggests, is now difficult to determine. The Greek gospel appears originally to have been written in Greek rather than translated from an Aramaic original. But it certainly contains the unique message of Jesus as He originally intended it.

The most unique term in Matthew's gospel is "the kingdom of heaven" (Greek, *he basileia tōn ouranōn*) which occurs 32 times. It appears only in Matthew and nowhere else in the New Testament. By contrast, "the kingdom of God" occurs 15 times in Mark, 33 times in Luke, and only 5 times in Matthew (6:33 [ESV]; 12:28; 14:28; 21:31, 43).

Several writers have attempted to demonstrate a theological distinction between the two terms, but it is obvious that they are used interchangeably. Hendriksen notes, "There is no essential difference between the two appellations."[30] He also observes that the plural usage of "heavens" (*ouranōn*) indicates the Hebrew mind of the author (cf. Gen. 1:1; Dan. 2:44; 7:13–14). It was typical of the Hebrew Bible to replace the name of God with "heaven" out of respect for the divine name. Thus Matthew indicates the Hebraic nature of his own thinking.

Lessons on Evangelism

Repentance, the changing of the mind, has to do with the rejection of sin and acceptance of Christ the Savior (Matt. 3:1–12).

Salvation does not come through one's pedigree or origin of birth, but through faith (Matt. 3:8).

Water baptism is an outward sign of repentance. It does not cause one to be saved (Matt. 3:11).

True salvation will be the baptismal work of the Holy Spirit (Matt. 3:11–12).

The results of salvation will be that one will follow Christ (Matt. 9:9).

The heart of salvation is to believe that Christ is the Son of the living God (Matt. 16:15–16).

Toussaint observes that the evangelistic and didactic character of Matthew's gospel is emphasized in his use of the verb "to disciple" (Greek, *mathēteuō*).[31]

It occurs three times in Matthew (13:52; 27:57; 28:19) and only once elsewhere (Acts 14:21). Matthew's name in Hebrew (*Mattithiah*) means "gift of Yahweh." But the Greek form *Maththios* sounds similar to the term "disciple," which Matthew uses almost exclusively.[32] Could it be that the tax collector turned disciple thought of discipleship as making "Matthews" of the lost as a reflection of his own experience?

The evangelistic nature of the gospel is evidenced by Matthew's frequent references to Gentiles: wise men from the east (2:1); the healing of the Roman centurion's servant (8:5–13); the faith of the Canaanite woman (15:21–28); "many shall come from east and west, and recline at the table with Abraham, and Isaac, and Jacob, in the kingdom of heaven" (8:11–12); "Go therefore and make disciples of all the nations" (28:19–20).

The Gospel of Matthew is a superb literary masterpiece. It introduces us to the message of the gospel and serves as the perfect bridge from the Old Testament to the New Testament. To the Jews, the evangelist speaks about the promised Messiah. To the Gentiles, he paints a portrait of a Savior for all people. But more than anything else, Matthew shows us a Teacher whose teachings surpass all others. It is no wonder he said of Him, "The multitudes were amazed at His teaching; for He was teaching them as one having authority" (Matt. 7:28–29). Undoubtedly, it was that same authoritative person who captured Matthew's own heart at the tax collector's booth in Galilee when He simply but profoundly said: "Follow Me!" (Matt. 9:9).

Outline

I. Coming of the Messiah (1:1–4:11)
   A. His Ancestry (1:1–17)
   B. His Advent (1:18–2:23)
   C. His Ambassador (3:1–12)
   D. His Approval (3:13–4:11)
      1. Baptism of Christ (3:13–17)
      2. Temptation of Christ (4:1–11)
II. Ministry of the Messiah (4:12–27:66)
   A. In Galilee (4:12–18:35)
      1. His message: Sermon on the Mount (5:1–7:29)
         a. The Beatitudes: Character described (5:3–20)
         b. Six illustrations: Character applied (5:21–48)
            (1) First illustration: Murder (5:21–26)

(2) Second illustration: Adultery contrasted with lust (5:27–30)

(3) Third illustration: Divorce contrasted with marriage (5:31–32)

(4) Fourth illustration: Oath taking as opposed to speaking the truth (5:33–37)

(5) Fifth illustration: Retaliation as opposed to forgiveness (5:38–42)

(6) Sixth illustration: "Love your neighbor" contrasted with "love thy enemy" (5:43–48)

c. True spiritual worship: Character expressed (6:1–7:12)

(1) First example: Almsgiving (6:1–4)

(2) Second example: Praying (6:5–15)

(3) Third example: Fasting (6:16–18)

(4) Fourth example: Giving (6:19–24)

(5) Fifth example: Worry or anxiety (6:25–34)

(6) Sixth example: Judging others (7:1–12)

d. The two alternatives: Character established (7:13–27)

2. His miracles: Signs of divine authority (8:1–9:34)

a. The cleansing of a leper (8:1–4)

b. The healing of the centurion's servant (8:5–13)

c. The healing of Peter's mother-in-law (8:14–17)

d. The calming of the storm (8:18–27)

e. The healings of the Gadarene demoniacs (8:28–34)

f. The healing of the paralytic and lessons on righteousness (9:1–17)

g. The healing of the woman with the issue and the raising of the ruler's daughter (9:18–26)

h. The healings of the blind and dumb men (9:27–34)

3. His missionaries: Sending of the Twelve (9:35–12:50)

a. Jesus' Sees Their Need and Calls Us to Compassion (9:35–38)

b. Excursus: John the Baptist and Christ (11:1–30)

c. Excursus: A dispute with the Pharisees (12:1–50)

4. His mystery: Secret form of the kingdom (13:1–58)

a. The parable of the sower (13:3b–23)

b. The parable of the tares (13:24–30; 36–43)

c. The parable of the mustard seed (13:31–31)

d. The parable of the leaven (13:33–35)

e. The parable of the hidden treasure (13:44)

f. The parable of the pearl of great price (13:45–46)

g. The parable of the dragnet (13:47–50)

h. Excursus: The use of parables (13:51–58)

5. His malediction: Seriousness of rejection (14:1–16:28)

   a. The death of John the Baptist (14:1–12)

   b. The feeding of the five thousand (14:13–21)

   c. The walking on the water (14:22–36)

   d. The conflict with the Pharisees over ritual (15:1–20)

   e. The healing of the Gadarene woman's daughter (15:21–28)

   f. The feeding of the four thousand (15:29–39)

   g. The Pharisees and Sadducees rebuked (16:1–12)

   h. Peter's confession (16:13–28)

6. His manifestation: Special transfiguration (17:1–27)

   a. Excursus: Paying the temple tax (17:24–27)

7. His mercy: Sanctification of forgiveness (18:1–35)

   a. Personal forgiveness (18:1–14)

   b. Church discipline (18:15–35)

B. In Judea (19:1–27:66)

1. His presentation as King (19:1–25:46)

   a. His journey to Jerusalem (19:1–20:34)

     (1) Jesus' teaching on divorce (19:1–12)

     (2) The rich young ruler (19:13–30)

     (3) The parable of the laborers (20:1–16)

     (4) The coming suffering of Christ and His disciples (20:17–28)

     (5) The healing of the two blind men (20:29–34)

   b. His joyful (triumphal) entry (21:1–46)

     (1) The messianic arrival at Jerusalem (21:1–11)

     (2) The cleansing of the temple (21:12–17)

     (3) The cursing of the barren fig tree (21:18–22)

     (4) The question of authority (21:23–46)

   c. His jealous critics (22:1–23:39)

     (1) The parable of the marriage supper (22:1–14)

     (2) The Herodians: Question of tribute (22:15–22)

     (3) The Sadducees: Question of the resurrection (22:23–34)

(4) The Pharisees: Question of the law (22:35–23:39)
d. His judgment: Olivet Discourse (24:1–25:46)
    (1) Signs of the present age (24:5–14)
    (2) Signs of the Great Tribulation (24:15–28)
    (3) Signs of the coming Son of Man (24:29–42)
    (4) The parable of the two servants (24:43–51)
    (5) The parable of the ten virgins (25:1–13)
    (6) The parable of the talents (25:14–30)
    (7) The judgment of the nations (25:31–46)
2. His rejection as King (26:1–27:26)
    a. His denial by His disciples (26:1–56)
    b. His denunciation by the Sanhedrin (26:57–75)
    c. Hid deliverance to Pilate (27:1–31)
    d. His death for humankind (27:32–66)
III. Triumph of the Messiah (28:1–20)
    A. His Resurrection (28:1–8)
    B. His Reappearance (28:9–15)
    C. His Recommission (28:16–20)

CHAPTER 1

The Birth of the King
Matthew 1:1-25

Preview:

Matthew begins by giving the genealogy and birth of the Messiah, Jesus Christ. The purpose of this is not only to demonstrate that Jesus was uniquely qualified to be the King of the Jews, but also that he was divinely conceived and born into this world. The mention of four Gentile women in the genealogy shows Matthew's and God's concern for those outside the boundaries of Judaism.

Christ's Ancestry

Matthew begins his gospel by connecting the New Testament reader to the Old Testament. He emphasizes that Jesus descended from Abraham and David. Thus He is the legitimate heir to the messianic promise to the Jewish people. If indeed Matthew is writing to Jewish readers, he has their attention. He then proceeds to trace Jesus' ancestry through the line of Joseph, His legal father. The genealogy of Christ opens with a statement similar to the various divisions of the book of Genesis showing the unity of the Scriptures. In Genesis, ten *tôwlêdôwths*, generations, or genealogies, are given beginning with Genesis 2:4 and proceeding to Genesis 37:2. For the Jewish reader, this similarity would be striking and unforgotten.

Matthew's gospel emphasizes the importance and significance of biblical prophecy. He quotes Old Testament prophetic passages to prove that Jesus is in fact the specific and direct fulfillment of those prophecies.

"Jesus Christ" is the title most often used of the Savior. Jesus (Greek, *Iēsous;* Hebrew, *Y*^{e}*hôwshua'*) is His earthly name, meaning "savior." *Christos* is the Greek translation for "messiah" or "anointed"—technically "Jesus the Christ." He is also the "Son of David." By tracing Jesus' ancestry back to King David, through the line of Davidic kings, Matthew connects Jesus with His royal heritage. Despite six centuries of vacancy on the royal throne, the Messiah must be of royal descent. The genealogy here is that of Joseph, Jesus' legal father, whereas the genealogy of Luke 3:23–38 is that of Mary, His actual parent, showing His bloodline back to David. Both authors' purpose is to show that the messianic promises made to David's line are fulfilled in Jesus. Jesus was also the "Son of Abraham." He is the fulfillment of the covenant promises to Abraham, the forefather of the Jews (cf. Gen. 12:3; 13:15; 22:18). Since Matthew is writing primarily to Jewish readers, he naturally begins by emphasizing Jesus' Jewish parentage.

Next, Matthew lists Jesus' connection to the tribe of Judah (vv. 3–8). Judah was the father of the tribe so named. The promise of Jacob was that the leadership of the twelve tribes would come through Judah (cf. Gen. 49:8–12). The Jews understood this to mean that the Messiah would come from the tribe of Judah. Genesis 49:10 says that the scepter, or the rulership among the twelve tribes, would not depart from Judah until Shiloh ("he whose right it is" to rule) came, the latter being a reference to Christ.

Four "questionable" women appear in this genealogy in addition to Mary, the mother of Jesus—Tamar, Rahab, Ruth, and the "wife of Uriah." It was not customary to list the names of women in a genealogy; therefore, the inclusion of these names must be deliberate on the part of the author. Tamar was the mother of two illegitimate sons (Perez and Zerah) by Judah. Rahab was the converted prostitute of Jericho and the mother of Boaz. Ruth, the wife of Boaz, was a godly foreigner (Moabitess). The wife of Uriah is none other than Bathsheba, whose adultery with David is infamous. Her husband, one of David's thirty mighty men, was a Hittite. However, after a hasty marriage, she became the legitimate wife of David and the mother of Solomon. The curious feature of mentioning these women in this genealogy indicates that the evangelist wished to disarm Jewish criticism about the unusual virgin birth of Jesus by showing that irregular unions were divinely blessed in the Messiah's legal ancestry. "The evangelist's argument is that Jesus, born of a virgin mother, was nonetheless of the true lineage of David because Joseph was in fact legally married to his mother, Mary."[1]

Asa (vv. 7–8) was a king of Israel. Some manuscripts have Asaph instead of Asa. In fact, the New American Standard Bible note says the Greek has Asaph. This is incorrect. Both Asa and Asaph are Greek words. Some textual critics claim that Matthew made a mistake in the original by putting Asaph into the text, rather than Asa.[2] However, there is no textual evidence of this. Asa is correct.

Uzziah (vv. 9–10) is referred to as both Uzziah (Isa. 6:1) and Azariah (2 Kgs. 14:21). Three generations are omitted at this point. Matthew omits the names of Ahaziah, Joash, and Amaziah and then omits Jehoiakim after the name of Josiah. Homer Kent points out, "The omissions are doubtless due to his arbitrary shortening of the list to give three groups of fourteen."[3] Being familiar with rabbinical thinking, Matthew uses symmetry of numbers. He has, accordingly, divided the generations from Abraham to Jesus into three groups of fourteen each: from Abraham to David (vv. 2–6), from David to the Babylonian exile (vv. 6–11), from the exile to the birth of Jesus (vv. 12–16). The significance of the number fourteen seems to come from the numerical values of the Hebrew consonants in the name David, which add up to that number. The system of rabbinic sacred arithmetic was often based on hidden calculations. To what degree Matthew is following such a system is uncertain.

Matthew then continues (vv. 10–15). Amon was a king of Judah, as was Asa above. Some faulty manuscripts have Amos instead of Amon, but this is a mistake similar to the Asa and Asaph problem of verses 7–8. Jeconiah is also called Jehoiachin (2 Kgs. 24:8) and Coniah (Jer. 22:24) and was cursed from having any descendant upon the throne of David according to Jeremiah 22:30. It therefore should be noted that Jesus is not a natural descendant of his. The Jews of the exile recognized Jeconiah as their last legitimate king. The deportation to Babylon refers to the seventy years' captivity of the Jews in Babylon during the days of Daniel the prophet. Jeremiah predicts precisely seventy years of captivity (Jer. 25:11; 29:10); Daniel was well aware of that prophecy (Dan. 9:2); and 2 Chronicles 36:21 refers to the same time period. Shealtiel is named as the son of Jeconiah. This does not contradict Jeremiah 22:28–30, for the predicted childlessness of Jeconiah refers to reigning children, that is, he would have no son who would rule Israel as king. The reference to Shealtiel as the son of Neri in Luke 3:27 is better understood as being a totally different person, rather than the result of levirate marriage. It is assumed that the rest of this family record comes from Joseph's family annals.

Joseph is designated the "husband of Mary" (v. 16). The wording carefully inspired by the Holy Spirit avoids giving the impression that Joseph was the natural father of Jesus. As the husband of Mary, he was Jesus' legal father and the one through whom He had a right to David's throne. It is not said that Jesus "was born to" Joseph, which is a deliberate change from the preceding genealogical expressions. Every emphasis of the text at this point reinforces the idea of the virginal conception of Christ. The marriage of Joseph and Mary took place after the conception but before the birth of Jesus. "Fourteen generations" (v. 17) is the literary grouping used by Matthew to emphasize the three major periods of Israel's national history: theocracy, monarchy, and hierarchy. The use of "Therefore" implies that this is an artificial arrangement. The translation indicates, "So this makes fourteen generations." The obvious intent of this genealogy is to emphasize the legitimate messianic line of Jesus as the rightful heir of King David.

Major Periods of Israel's National History
2000–1000 B.C. . . . .*Abraham the patriarch to King David*
1000–605 B.C. . . . .*King David to the deportation to Babylon*
605–5 B.C. . . . .*Deportation to Babylon to the time of Christ*

Christ's Advent (1:18–2:23)

Mary was already bound or engaged ("betrothed," v. 18) to Joseph, although they were not yet actually married. Among the Jews, marriage vows were said at the betrothal and required a legal divorce to end them. The custom of the day usually required an interval of one year of betrothal before the bride could actually take residence in her husband's house and consummate their union. It was during this interval that Mary was "found to be with child." Her pregnancy naturally would have been assumed to be the result of an illegitimate union of adultery, a circumstance usually punishable by death (Deut. 22:23). At this point, Mary had not yet explained her situation to Joseph. Indeed, she hardly could have expected Joseph to accept her story of the miraculous conception of the child by the Holy Spirit.

"With child by the Holy Spirit" is the biblical explanation for the miraculous conception of Christ. There are at least five good reasons for the virgin birth. (1) To fulfill the prophecy of Isaiah 7:14 that a virgin would be with child, while still being a virgin. (2) To avoid the curse on Jeconiah as mentioned above (Jer. 22:30). (3) Because Christ, the second person of the Godhead, was already a person. To have a normal sexual union would have created another person. Christ only needed a body for his preexisting personhood. (4) Christ already had a father—God the Father. (5) To avoid receiving a sin nature. Luke 1:35 proclaims that the power of the Holy Spirit would overshadow Mary, producing a holy offspring by a miraculous virginal conception.

Because Joseph was a "righteous man," he decided to divorce Mary privately (secretly) rather than have her put to death. But while he considered what should be done, "an angel of the Lord" spoke to him in a dream. Prior to His birth, Jesus Christ, the second person of the Trinity, often appeared to people in the form of a man. These appearances in the Old Testament are called theophanies or Christophanies, but frequently the wording is "the angel of the LORD."[4] Since the Scripture clearly states that "no man has seen God at any time" (John 1:18), these appearances evidently refer to Christ rather than to God the Father. It is interesting that the references to God refer to Him as Lord (cf. Gen. 18:2, 13, 17). After His birth as Jesus, there were no more temporary physical appearances of God to man. After His resurrection, Jesus appeared to people as Himself in a glorified body.

"Put her away" means literally to divorce her. The Jewish betrothal had to be legally broken. Joseph's merciful attitude gives an insight into his true nature as a man. "Joseph, son of David," is what the angel called Joseph. In spite of his humble circumstances, he was a legitimate heir to the vacant throne of David. The angel orders him to take Mary as his wife because the baby she has conceived is "of the Holy Spirit." This divinely born miracle Son is the fulfillment of God's prophetic promises to the Jewish nation, which began in the book of Genesis with God's covenant with Abraham.

The naming of the child Jesus (Hebrew, $Y^ehôwshua'$) means "Jehovah saves." This points to the very purpose of Christ's coming into the world to save sinners. Placed early in the New Testament, this statement becomes the foundational concept of the gospel. Jesus, by His very name and nature, is the Savior. His infant cries broke the four-hundred-year silence of God. There had been no word from heaven since the days of the prophets. Only God could have orchestrated such a scene—the divine silence was broken by an infant's wail. God had come to earth as a baby!

The phrase "might be fulfilled" (Greek, *plēroō*) indicates the inevitability of the fulfillment of the words of the prophet, as well as the fact that Matthew saw Isaiah's statement as predictively fulfilled in the birth of Christ. R. C. Lenski observes, "The verb pictures the promise or prophecy as an empty vessel which is at last filled when the event occurs."[5] Arndt and Gingrich list this use of the word as "the fulfillment of divine predictions or promises."[6] There can be no doubt that Matthew firmly believed this reference was definitely a prediction of an event that was fulfilled in the birth of Jesus. One wishing to deny the predictive element of Isaiah or its acceptance by the early church cannot adequately do so on a philological-grammatical basis or on the basis of historical precedent.

Mary, the mother of Jesus, is called "the virgin," connecting her to the prediction found in Isaiah 7:14. Matthew uses the Greek word *parthenos* to translate the Hebrew word *'almâh* as the rendering for "virgin." His contextual usage of "fulfill" is almost certainly indicative of his understanding the Isaiah passage to contain a definitely predictive element. He recognizes the prophecy as coming from God (the Greek preposition *hupo* introduces the direct agent with a passive verb, whereas *dia* introduces the mediate agent). The Lord is the source of the prophecy, and the prophet is his mouthpiece. Thus God is the cause and the prophet is the instrument He uses.

The Importance of the Virgin Birth	
Predicted by Isaiah	Isaiah 7:14
Proclaimed by Matthew and Luke	Matthew 1:23; Luke 1:26–35
Prescribed by John	John 1:14
Preached by Paul	Galatians 4:4; 1 Timothy 3:16

The quotation of Isaiah 7:14 follows the Septuagint (LXX) rendering where *parthenos* is also used to translate the Hebrew *'almâh*. Perhaps no prophetic prediction has created a greater controversy than Isaiah's prediction of a virgin-born Son, which Matthew clearly claims to have been fulfilled in the birth of Christ.[7] The liberal interpretation of this verse attempts to deny the validity of Matthew's use of Isaiah 7:14 as a prediction of the birth of Christ.[8] The liberal argument is generally based on the faulty assumption that Matthew erred in following the Septuagint rendering of *parthenos*, which in turn, erred in its translation of *'almâh*. The RSV thus reads, "young woman," rather than "virgin."

There can be no doubt that the Greek term *parthenos* is always to be translated "virgin."[9] The real question is whether the Septuagint is correct in its translation of the Hebrew *'almâh*. Since the weight of legitimate scholarship supports the translation of the Hebrew word *'almâh* as being the most accurate word possible for "virgin," one can only conclude that the Septuagint translators were correct in their interpretation. The Dead Sea Scroll copy of Isaiah indicates the same usage as does the pre-Christian use of *parthenos* to translate *'almâh* in the Qumran literature.[10]

The virgin birth of Christ is undoubtedly the most essential doctrine underlying His deity. The prediction in Isaiah 7:14 of a virgin-born son calls His name "IMMANUEL, which translated means, 'God with us.'" This is a title describing the deity of the person of the Son of God rather than a name actually used by Him.[11]

Consider the overwhelming evidence for the messianic interpretation of Isaiah 7:14. The earliest Jewish translation (the Septuagint) supports it. Qumran literature and pre-Christian rabbinic writings support it. Matthew, Jesus' own personal disciple, defends it. All the early church fathers believed it, as did the medieval theologians and all the Protestant reformers.

The literal (single) fulfillment view of Isaiah 7:14, as quoted in Matthew 1:23, was universally accepted by the Christian church until the rise of higher criticism and liberal theology in the nineteenth century. This, in turn, gave rise to the so-called dual fulfillment view (applying the prophecy of Isaiah first to a contemporary and secondarily to Jesus) first advocated by Albert Barnes in 1840. Not until the twentieth century did the dual fulfillment view gain acceptance in evangelical circles. Like all accommodations to unbelief, it weakens the case for the literal fulfillment of Isaiah's prediction and leaves the biblical interpreter on flimsy grounds for advocating the exact fulfillment of other Old Testament prophecies.

The New Testament clearly states that Jesus Himself taught the disciples which Old Testament prophecies were about Him (Luke 24:44–45). Therefore, to say that Matthew made a mistake in applying Isaiah 7:14 to Christ is to say that his gospel is not inspired truth, that the angel who made the announcement was wrong, and that Jesus Himself was mistaken. One is surely on more solid exegetical ground to take the word of the biblical writers over that of so-called scholars. Certainly the New Testament writers believed in the fact of the virgin birth as the means of the divine incarnation. John wrote: "The Word was made flesh" (John 1:14), and Paul added, "God was revealed in the flesh" (1 Tim. 3:16).

Study Questions

1. Who were the five women mentioned in Christ's genealogy?

2. Explain how the genealogy of Christ is structured in three parts. What time periods do they represent?

3. How do we know that Jesus was virgin born?

4. What did Joseph intend to do when he found out that Mary was with child?

5. How was Joseph's mind changed about Mary's pregnancy?

6. What prophet predicted the virgin conception, and where is this prophecy found?

7. What are the differences in meaning between the names Jesus and Immanuel?

8. How do we know that Mary was a virgin until Jesus was born, even though she lived with Joseph?

9. What is the significance of the four women mentioned in Christ's genealogy? What importance should be attached to it? What is God trying to say to us through their inclusion?

CHAPTER 2

Who Is the King of the Jews?
Matthew 2:1–23

Preview:

Though Jesus has the right to the throne of David as shown through his royal genealogy, a usurper, Herod the Great, occupies that seat. Wise men seek the young king, but Herod thinks only of protecting his own interests. God the Father, however, protects the infant Jesus from all threats. Satan is in fact the mastermind behind all attempts to disrupt God's plans, but he fails once again.

Matthew relates the story of Jesus' birth at Bethlehem and the account of the visit of the wise men, which is unique to his gospel. In this account, Gentiles arrive in Jerusalem asking for the King of the Jews. At the end of his gospel, Matthew describes Pilate's inscription: "Jesus of Nazareth, the King of the Jews" (Matt. 27:37). Thus, Matthew "bookends" his gospel with the statements of Gentiles who recognize what many of his Jewish readers are asking: Is Jesus the King of the Jews?

The birthplace of Christ is designated as "Bethlehem of Judea," which was also called Ephrath (2:1–2). The town is five miles south of Jerusalem. Its name in Hebrew means "house of bread." Bethlehem is first mentioned in the biblical text in relation to Rachel's death (Gen. 35:19). It was also the town where Ruth met and married Boaz (Ruth 1–4). In all of Scripture, David and Jesus, who begin and end the messianic line, are the only kings of Judah who were born in Bethlehem. All the others were born in Jerusalem. This Judean city was the ancestral home of King David. It was also the original city of Joseph's ancestors. According to Luke 2:1–7, Mary and he traveled there from Nazareth and Jesus was born in a stable soon after they arrived. Very ancient

Christian tradition quoted by Justin Martyr refers to Jesus' birth in a cave, which today is covered by the Church of the Nativity.

Herod was known as Herod the Great and was the son of Antipater, an Edomite. Antipater helped Julius Caesar conquer Egypt, and for his services he was appointed procurator of Judea, Samaria, and Galilee. Antipater appointed his sons to rule under him. Herod ruled over Galilee from the age of twenty-six. After his father's death, he went to Rome to seek appointment as king. He became king by Roman decree in 40 B.C., and was later named "King of the Jews" by Augustus Caesar in 30 B.C. Herod died in 4 B.C. in Jericho shortly after the visit of the wise men and the birth of Christ.

"Magi" were originally the priestly caste among the Persians and Babylonians. These magi, or wise men, from the east were experts in the study of the stars. Tradition claims there were three royal visitors who were also kings. However, there is no real historical evidence to verify this. The fact that there were three gifts probably gives rise to the idea of there being three magi. All we are told in the text is that wise men came from the east to Jerusalem looking for the baby who had been born "King of the Jews."

The wise men naturally came to Jerusalem, the royal capital of Israel, seeking one whom they thought was to be born a king based on their calculations of the stars. What exactly this meant to them, we are not sure. Perhaps, through the science of astronomy they observed a new star and for some reason correlated that with the birth of a king. Why they would associate this star with Israel is uncertain. Kent says, "It is entirely conceivable that these men had made contact with Jewish exiles, or with the prophecies and influence of Daniel, and thus were in possession of Old Testament prophecies regarding the Messiah."[1] Some suggest the prophecy about the star of Jacob in Numbers 24:17 may have been familiar to them from contact with the Hebrew Scriptures. It is unlikely that this star could only have been a natural phenomenon, since it led the wise men to Jerusalem and later to Bethlehem. It almost certainly was a divine manifestation used by God to indicate the fact and place of the Messiah's birth and the place of His reign. It must have looked like a star but much like an airplane in the night sky looks like a star until one notices that it is moving. This supernatural manifestation was able to guide the wise men to the very house in which the young child resided.

Naturally, talk of the birth of a new king would upset Herod, the current ruler. He quickly gathered his scribes and demanded an explanation from them. The scribes belonged mainly to the party of Pharisees and functioned as members of a highly honored profession. Charles Ryrie notes, "They were professional students and defenders of the law. . . . They were also referred to as lawyers because they were entrusted with the administration of law as judges in the Sanhedrin."[2] They asked "where the Christ was to be born." This demand is highly significant in that it implies that the Jews of that day were anticipating the coming of the Messiah. The answer is even more revealing of current Jewish beliefs about the Messiah in the first century A.D.

When the scribes replied that the Messiah would be born "in Bethlehem of Judea, for so it has been written by the prophet," they clearly anticipated a literal fulfillment of the Old Testament prophecies regarding the coming of the Messiah. The quotation is from Micah 5:2, where the prophet predicts that Bethlehem of the tribe of Judah will be the place where the governor or ruler of Israel shall originate. It is significant to note that Isaiah and Micah were contemporaries. Their prophecies of the coming of the Messiah interrelate to one another. Isaiah predicts the nature of His birth, and Micah predicts the place of His birth. The "Ruler" who will come from Bethlehem is none other than the child-ruler predicted in Isaiah 9:6, "For a child will be born to us, a son will be given to us; and the government will rest on His shoulders." The prophet goes on to proclaim that this ruler is the "Mighty God" and that the increase of His government shall never end. He will sit upon the throne of David forever. Therefore, only a divine King could fulfill such predictions.

Herod's fear of a rival ruler caused him to question "the time the star appeared" (v. 7). His subsequent slaughter of the children at Bethlehem from two years old and under was apparently calculated from the time given him by the wise men. Herod may also have added to the magi's calculation to make sure he achieved his goal of killing a possible rival. The fact that the child was found in a "house" (v. 11) and not the manger would indicate that Jesus was probably no longer a baby when the wise men found Him. In addition, if the wise men had presented their precious gifts prior to the public presentation of Jesus in the temple, Mary and Joseph no doubt would have offered the usual lamb, instead of just two turtledoves, the provision made for poor people (see Luke 2:22–24; cf. Lev. 12:8).

The wise men were guided to this place by the star, which "went on before them" (v. 9). This again indicates the supernatural nature of this star. "The Child" is designated in the Greek text as *paidion*, generally a "young child," irrespective of age. When the wise men arrived, they found the child with His mother in a "house." This would indicate that the family had now moved out of the stable into a rented home at Bethlehem. Whether the visit of the wise men occurred a few weeks or months after the birth of the child or one to two years afterward is uncertain. Since the wise men brought three gifts, that is, "gold and frankincense and myrrh," it has been assumed that they were three in number (some traditions have even given them names, but these are not necessarily established by fact).

Old Testament Quotations in Matthew

	Matthew	Old Testament
1	1:22–23	Isaiah 7:14
2	2:5–6	Micah 5:1–2
3	2:15	Hosea 11:1
4	2:17–18	Jeremiah 31:15
5	2:23	Isaiah 11:1; Jeremiah 23:5; 33:15; Zechariah 3:8; 6:12
6	3:3	Isaiah 40:3
7	4:4	Deuteronomy 8:3
8	4:6	Psalm 91:11–12
9	4:7	Deuteronomy 6:16
10	4:10	Deuteronomy 6:13
11	4:14–16	Isaiah 9:1–2
12	5:5	Psalm 37:11
13	5:21	Exodus 20:13; Deuteronomy 5:17
14	5:27	Exodus 20:14; Deuteronomy 5:18
15	5:31	Deuteronomy 24:1
16	5:33–37	Exodus 20:7; Numbers 30:2; Leviticus 19:12; Deuteronomy 5:11; 23:21; Isaiah 66:1; Psalm 48:2
17	5:38	Exodus 21:24; Leviticus 24:20; Deuteronomy 19:21
18	5:43a	Leviticus 19:18; Deuteronomy 23:6; 25:17
19	7:23	Psalm 6:8
20	8:17	Isaiah 53:4
21	9:13	Hosea 6:6
22	10:35	Micah 7:6
23	11:10	Malachi 3:1
24	12:7	Hosea 6:6
25	12:18–21	Isaiah 42:1–4

	Matthew	Old Testament
26	13:13–15	Isaiah 6:9–10
27	13:35	Psalm 78:2
28	15:4–6	Exodus 20:12; 21:17; Leviticus 20:9
29	15:7–9	Isaiah 29:13
30	18:16	Deuteronomy 19:15
31	19:4	Genesis 1:27; 5:2
32	19:5	Genesis 2:24
33	19:18	Exodus 20:13–16; 21:17; Deuteronomy 5:17–20
34	19:19a	Deuteronomy 5:16; Exodus 20:12
35	19:19b	Leviticus 19:18
36	21:4–5	Zechariah 9:9; Isaiah 62:2
37	21:9	Psalm 118:26
38	21:13a	Isaiah 56:7
39	21:13b	Jeremiah 7:11
40	21:16	Psalm 8:2
41	21:42	Psalm 118:22–23
42	22:31–32	Exodus 3:6, 15
43	22:37	Deuteronomy 6:5
44	22:39	Leviticus 19:18
45	22:44	Psalm 110:1
46	23:38–39	Psalm 118:26; Jeremiah 12:7; 22:5
47	26:31	Zechariah 13:7
48	27:9–10	Zechariah 13:13; Jeremiah 18:2; 19:2; 32:6
49	27:34, 48	Psalm 69:21
50	27:35	Psalm 22:18
51	27:39	Psalm 22:7; 109:25
52	27:43	Psalm 22:8; 71:11
53	27:46	Psalm 22:1–2

It has been suggested that the gifts were in recognition of Jesus as King, Son of God, and suffering Savior. The gold would stand for His deity, the frankincense for His high priestly ministry, and the myrrh for that used in his burial.[3] It is also significant that they "worshiped Him," indicating their recognition of the deity of the one whom they were worshiping. Again, Matthew has reasserted the importance of the deity of Christ. He is the virgin-born Son, "God with us," who deserves our worship as well.

Separate special divine revelations in the form of "warnings" were given both to the wise men and to Joseph by dreams (vv. 13–15). Thus instructed, the wise men did not return to Herod, and Joseph and Mary fled with the baby into Egypt.[4] It should be remembered that there was a large Jewish population in Egypt at that time, especially in and around the city of Alexandria. The holy family would have been inconspicuous during their stay and would have been welcomed by members of their own race.

The exact location of their exile is not specified. The death of Herod occurred in 4 B.C. It should be remembered that our present calendar is off in its calculation by about six years (this would place the birth of Christ at ca. 6–5 B.C.). Herod's death is recorded in detail by Josephus (*Antiquities* 17.6.5). Matthew relates the flight to Egypt by Jesus' family to the statement in Hosea 11:1 that refers historically to the deliverance of the Hebrews from Egypt. Matthew records that this was done that it might be "fulfilled." Since the Old Testament statement is not a direct reference to Christ, it is apparent that the writer saw this prophecy as a type of Christ.[5]

The bitter reaction of Herod when he "slew all the male children" at Bethlehem was unrecorded in the history of that period (vv. 16–18). This should not surprise us, because of the king's frequently outraged retaliation on people. He, in fact, murdered his wife and three sons. Josephus calls him a man "of great barbarity towards all men equally" (*Antiquities* 17.8.1.191). "Rachel weeping for her children" (v. 18) is a quotation of Jeremiah 31:15. The calamity of Israel's mourning at the time of the exile is correlated here to this renewed calamity brought on by Herod, whose very act of ruling is a direct result of that captivity, which had been caused by Israel's sin. "Rachel weeping" is a reference to Rachel, the mother of Benjamin, and thus the tribe of Benjamin. She stands as the symbol of the Benjamite mothers and their sorrow. Also, note that she died just outside of Bethlehem herself (Gen. 35:19). Therefore, Matthew's use of this reference is not inappropriate to Jewish eyes and ears.

"When Herod was dead" refers again to the death of the king in 4 B.C. He was succeeded by his son Archelaus, the son of his Samaritan wife, Malthace. Archelaus was as brutal as his father. Thus, Joseph, again warned in a dream, returned to Nazareth, avoiding any further residence in Judea. The phrase "He shall be called a Nazarene" is a reference to Christ's coming from the city of Nazareth. It should not be taken to mean that He was a Nazirite. A Nazirite was not to drink wine, touch anything unclean, or cut his hair. It was probably a misunderstanding that caused early Roman artists to depict Jesus with long hair. The proof that He was not a Nazirite is found in the fact that he did not keep the other two provisions of the vow. Many of the very people whom He came to minister to were considered "unclean" by the people of His day. Since no particular Old Testament passage is cited, it seems best to understand this verse as referring to a fulfillment of those prophecies that indicate that the Messiah would be of insignificant origin and despised by people (e.g., Isa. 53:3). With the usurper gone, Matthew now proceeds to tell the story of the true King of the Jews—Jesus of Nazareth.

Study Questions

1. Just who was Herod the king? Recount what you can of his life.

2. Who were the magi from the east, and why do some believe there were just three of them?

3. How might the magi have known of the significance of the star they followed?

4. Is it not strange that the chief priests and scribes knew where Jesus was to be born but never went to see him? Or was that part of God's providential way of saving Jesus' life?

5. Where is the Scripture found that predicts Messiah's birth in Bethlehem? Give the reference.

6. Explain why the "star" could not have been a conjunction of planets or some other astronomical wonder far out in space. See verse 9.

7. What then was the star like?

8. What might the three gifts from the magi represent? What practical value did they have for Mary and Joseph at the time?

9. How many times did an angel appear in dreams to various individuals in this chapter, and what was the message of each appearance?

10. Which two different Old Testament prophetic books are quoted to say, "Out of Egypt did I call My Son," and "Rachel weeping for her children"?

11. What was there about Archelaus that made Joseph afraid to return and live in Bethlehem?

CHAPTER 3

The Mission of the King
Matthew 3:1-17

Preview:

Matthew, as with the other two Synoptic Gospels, jumps ahead to the public presentation and baptism of Christ. A gospel is not a biography covering the entire life of the Messiah. Rather, it focuses on His important work. Jesus' initial introduction to Israel brings the reader face-to-face with this imposing figure. His baptism, with its accompanying signs, clearly indicates Christ's supernatural mission.

Christ's Ambassador

The forerunner of Christ was John the Baptist. He was the son of Zacharias and Elizabeth and was a cousin of the Lord (cf. Luke 1:5–80). The significance of his preparatory ministry cannot be overestimated. Even Josephus (*Antiquities* 18.5.2) refers to him by name. John was a child of promise whose birth had been announced by the angel Gabriel to his father who was a priest. His birth was accompanied by the promise: "For he will be great in the sight of the Lord . . . and he will be filled with the Holy Spirit" (Luke 1:15). Jesus said of him that there was none greater than John during the Old Testament dispensation (Matt. 11:11). This could imply that John the Baptist was the epitome of the message of the Old Testament itself. In a very real sense, he was the last of the Old Testament prophets.

Matthew's reference to John the Baptist assumes that his readers were familiar with him. There is no connection anywhere in Scripture to relate John to one of the Essene communities or to the Qumran sect (of the Dead Sea

Scrolls). The real significance of John seems to be his appearance in the "wilderness of Judea," the eastern part of the province lying east of the mountain ridge and west of the Dead Sea. This infertile area may rightly be called a "wilderness." The area receives less than two inches of rain each year, and vegetation is extremely space.

John's appearance, preaching a message of repentance, is in fulfillment of Isaiah 40:3, "Clear the way for the LORD." The words of the prophet originally formed the part of his message to the Babylonian exiles, who eventually returned to their own land. John, the last of the prophets of Israel, was now commissioned to prepare the way for the King. R. V. G. Tasker observes, "The reign of God was immediately to be made manifest in Israel in all its fullness in the Person and the work of none other than the Messiah Himself."[1] John is presented as the prophet sent in the spirit of Elijah "before the coming of the great and terrible day of the LORD" (Mal. 4:5). His appearance (wearing a rough coat of camel's hair and having a leather belt around his waist) and his dynamic and often scathing preaching, certainly depicts him in the lifestyle of Israel's ancient prophets. Jesus would later say of John the Baptist, "I say to you that Elijah already came" (Matt. 17:12).[2]

The Ministry of John the Baptist

The prophecy of his coming ministry to be a forerunner of Christ (Isa. 40:3).

His birth prophesied to Zacharias and Elizabeth (Luke 1:5–16).

His birth (Luke 1:57).

Beginning of his ministry (Matt. 3:1–12).

Herod Antipas has John arrested (Matt. 14:3–5).

Salome, the stepdaughter and niece of Herod Antipas, has John killed (Matt. 14:6–11).

To "repent" means to change one's mind, leading to a change in one's actions. So, repentance (Greek, *metanoia*) is basically "a change of mind" that results in a change of conduct. Repentance is not sorrow or remorse, though it may include these. It involves a complete change of attitude regarding God and sin and is often accompanied by a sense of sorrow and a corresponding change in conduct. Such repentance does not arise within a person of his or her own volition, but is the result of God's mercy in leading the person to it (cf. Acts 5:31; Rom. 2:4; 2 Tim. 2:25). Thus repentance involves the very process of conversion whereby people are born again. When people repent, in the biblical sense of the term, they have a change of mind about God, Christ, sin, and themselves. They no longer view themselves as no worse than anyone else, but as undone, completely lost and on the way to hell. Christ is no longer just a wonderful teacher, but is seen as God Himself, who gave Himself to die in the sinner's place.[3]

John's message of repentance was necessary in order to prepare people for the "kingdom of heaven" which was "at hand." The phrase "kingdom of heaven" is used only in the Gospel of Matthew and seems to be based on similar references in the book of Daniel. The phrase "kingdom of God" is used more frequently by Mark and Luke. The change is perhaps due to Matthew's Jewish background and outlook. Since the Jews regarded it as blasphemous to refer to God by name, it is possible that Matthew substituted the word *heaven* for that reason. None of the other three gospels use the phrase "kingdom of heaven," but Matthew on occasion uses "kingdom of God" (Matt. 6:33; 12:28). Though not identical in meaning, the two phrases apparently are sometimes used interchangeably in the gospels. Both phrases "indicate God's kingship, rule or sovereignty."[4] The kingdom of heaven is the rule of heaven over earth. The Jews of Jesus' day were looking forward to the coming of the Messiah who would reign in a Davidic kingdom on earth. It is this kingdom that Christ proclaimed as a literal earthly kingdom, based on spiritual principles. He demanded a right relationship with God for entrance into that kingdom. Therefore, John the Baptist's ministry is clearly seen as a time of preparation for the coming of Christ and proclamation of His kingdom.

"Referred to by Isaiah the prophet." All four Gospels relate this prophecy to a fulfillment in the life and ministry of John the Baptist (Mark 1:2; Luke 3:4; John 1:23, cf. Isa. 40:3). "Make his paths straight" refers to the straightening or preparing of one's life in a right relationship with God to prepare for the coming of the King. John's dress of "camel's hair, and a leather belt" was similar to Elijah's clothing (2 Kgs. 1:8) and was the usual dress of prophets (Zech. 13:4). "Locusts" were an allowable food (cf. Lev. 11:22) and were eaten by the very poorest of people. The reference in verse 5 to "Jerusalem . . . and all Judea" relates to the people of those places. John's ministry was received with great enthusiasm in its early stages. So great was his success that even many of the Pharisees and Sadducees came to this baptism (v. 7).

John rebuked the Pharisees, asking them to give evidence of "fruits of repentance" (v. 8). There can be no doubt that the New Testament concept of repentance grows out of its biblical usage in the Old Testament where the term (Hebrew, *shûwb*, "turn") means far more than an intellectual change of mind.

Genuine repentance proves itself by the fruits of a changed life. John the Baptist further rebuked them for their belief in nationalistic salvation. "We have Abraham for our father" means they were trusting their physical descent for salvation, rather than their spiritual relationship to the father of faith. "From these stones" may be a reference to Isaiah 5:2, but is probably to be taken in the natural setting of the shore along the Sea of Galilee. The axe about to chop the "root of the trees" is a reference to the impending judgment coming upon Israel (God's chosen tree, cf. Rom. 11) if they reject the Messiah-King. Again, fruitlessness is depicted as a lack of conversion and spiritual life. No fruit means no life in the soul.

Terms of Repentance

Old Testament (Hebrew)

Shûwb, "to turn around" or "turn back"

A na, "repentance" or "contrition"

Nâcham, "to relent" or "change one's mind"

The Septuagint (Greek translation of OT)

Epistrephō, used to translate *shûwb*, "to turn" or "return"

New Testament (Greek)

Metanoia (noun), "change of mind"

Metanoeō (verb), "to repent" or "to change one's mind"

"I baptize . . . in water" (vv. 11–12). There are three classes of water baptism in the New Testament—John's, Christ's, and Christian baptism. John's baptism in water was not Christian baptism. The death and resurrection of Christ had not yet occurred in order to be depicted by this baptism. John's baptism was similar to the Old Testament oblations (washings) that symbolized a cleansing of personal repentance on the part of a believer. Christian baptism began at Pentecost and carries the significance of picturing one's identification with Christ in His death, burial, and resurrection. Christ's own baptism was unique. Notice that Jesus submitted to this baptism to "fulfill all righteousness" (v. 15). Somehow, Christ identifies with the sinners He has come to save. It could even be a pledge of His own coming death, burial, and resurrection.

"He [Himself] will baptize you with the Holy Spirit" refers to the spiritual rebirth of the regenerate who shall receive the baptism of the Spirit (cf. 1 Cor. 12:13), which clearly indicates that all believers have received the baptism of the Spirit. This experience began at Pentecost (Acts 2) and was repeated upon every new group of converts: Samaritans, (Acts 8), Gentiles (Acts 10), and John's disciples (Acts 19), until it became normative for all Christian believers. The baptism with the Holy Spirit is mentioned just once in each of the four Gospels, here in Matthew and in Mark 1:8, Luke 3:16, and John 1:33. In Acts 1:5 Jesus repeats the promise of the upcoming baptism with the Holy Spirit. One would expect the phrase in Acts 2:4, but instead it reads that the believers "were all filled with the Holy Spirit." But Acts 10:44–47 is explained by Peter in Acts 11:15–16 as being the baptism of the Holy Spirit. Only 1 Corinthians 12:13 explains what is meant by that work of God. It places the believer into the spiritual body of Christ and makes him or her one with all other believers in receiving the full benefits of Christ's finished work on the cross.

The term "and fire" is better translated "or with fire." The immediate context certainly indicates that to be baptized with fire is the result of judgment (notice the reference to purging and burning in the next verse). Other than the visible tongues (billows) of fire that appeared over the disciples' heads at Pentecost, references to fire burning up unprofitable chaff refer to judgment rather than cleansing. The "winnowing fork" (v. 12) refers to a wooden shovel used for tossing grain into the wind to blow away the lighter chaff, leaving the good grain to settle in a pile. The chaff would then be swept up and burned. The unquenchable fire refers to the eternal punishment of hell or the lake of fire. Thus the Baptist warns that those who are not baptized with the Spirit will be burned in the fires of hell.

Christ Is Accepted

All four gospels relate this event (cf. John 1:31–33) with unquestioned historical verification. While this section of Matthew's gospel centers upon Galilee, Jesus now goes south to the Jordan River "to be baptized" (v. 13). The word *baptize* (Greek, *baptizō*) is an Anglicism. The Greek letters of the word are simply transposed into English, so it is a transliteration. John "tried to prevent" Jesus from being baptized (v. 14) for the obvious reason that Jesus needed no repentance of sin and John felt unworthy of this opportunity. The tense of the Greek verb emphasizes that John tried to hinder him. Thus this was no casual hesitation on the part of the Baptist who clearly recognized who Jesus really was.

"Permit it at this time" means 'Allow it to be" or "Let it happen." Jesus sought this outward identification with John's ministry "to fulfill all righteousness." By identifying Himself with those whom He came to redeem, Jesus inaugurated His public ministry as the Messiah. In regard to the Jewish religious observances, Jesus always met the duties of a faithful Jew: synagogue worship (Luke 4:16), attendance at feasts (John 5:1, cf. Deut. 16:16), and payment of the temple tax (Matt. 17:27). However, Jesus sometimes ignored Jewish man-made customs, such as the washing of hands (Mark 7:4–8).

In the process of His baptism, Jesus "went up immediately from the water." The descending of the Spirit of God fulfilled the predicted sign to John in order to indicate the true Messiah (cf. John 1:33; Isa. 11:2). Homer Kent writes, "As the Spirit came upon Old Testament prophets for special guidance at the start of their ministries, so now He came upon Jesus without measure."[5] The dove was a symbol of innocence and purity (cf. Matt. 10:16) and served as an ideal symbolic representation for the Holy Spirit since it is a totally defenseless animal. Jesus made it clear that the ministry of the Holy Spirit was to glorify Christ and not Himself (John 16:13–14).

The "voice out of the heavens" is that of God the Father (see also Matt. 17:5; John 12:28 where He speaks at the transfiguration and just prior to the crucifixion) giving His verbal approval to the ministry of His beloved Son. There can be no doubt that all three persons of the Trinity are actively involved here as distinct persons of the Godhead. The Father speaks, the Spirit descends, and the Son is baptized. The Father loves the Son, and the Trinity provides the opportunity for this to be exhibited as all three persons of the Godhead are active in this one event. Thus the baptism of Christ inaugurates the time when the triune God would act in history to bring about the salvation of humankind.

Study Questions

1. Where was the wilderness where John the Baptist preached?

2. What did John likely mean when he announced that the kingdom of heaven was "at hand"?

3. What famous passage in Isaiah did John use to describe his ministry as Christ's forerunner?

4. What was strange about John's attire and eating menu, and which Old Testament prophet did he most resemble? See also Luke 1:17 and Matthew 11:13–14.

5. How does the baptism John performed on others differ from the meaning of his baptism of Christ?

6. Why do you think Jesus wanted to be baptized by John?

7. How does verse 16 intimate the idea that God is a triune being?

8. Whose voice was heard from heaven, and could the crowd hear and understand the spoken message?

9. Compare Matthew 3:16–17 with Matthew 17:5 and John 12:28. How are these three events similar, and how do they differ?

CHAPTER 4

Temptation of Christ
Matthew 4:1–25

Preview:

It was God's purpose to demonstrate the sinless character of His Son, and the temptation was His means of doing so. Jesus was not so much confronted by Satan, but rather met Satan head on. This event helps the reader to understand more about the person of Christ. He is the perfect, virgin-born Son of God, qualified to be the Messiah by virtue of His lineage and His sinless character.

The Temptation of Christ (4:1–11)

Following His public baptism, Jesus was "led up by the Spirit into the wilderness" (4:1) referring to the elevation of the Judean wilderness. The historical setting of the temptation, which was directed against Jesus' human nature, indicates that this was a literal experience that He really conquered, not merely a mental victory over His own thoughts. The references to the work of the Holy Spirit make clear the interrelation of these two members of the Godhead. In His earthly work, Jesus depended on the ministry of the Holy Spirit to empower Him.

That Jesus was "tempted by the devil" is clearly presented as a fact. The three attacks against Christ were genuine temptations. Some liberal critics say that for Jesus to really understand humans and to be able to intercede for them, Christ must have experienced sin Himself. That logic is faulty. Only the one who has not been blown over in the hurricane knows the full force of the wind. The one who falls over with a 70 mph gust can never experience the true force of the 200 mph gale. The fact that Jesus never yielded to any temptation means that only He experienced the full force of what temptation really is.

The account of the temptation leads to the obvious question: Could Jesus have sinned? When theologian Francis Schaeffer was asked that question, he said, "Yes, but he did not." His position was that Jesus appeared as the second man, Adam. He had to face temptation even as Adam and Eve did. It was His probation. He could have sinned, just as Adam did, but He depended on God's provision for His strength and thus did not sin. This acknowledges the true human nature of Jesus. He was 100 percent man. He did not have a sin nature, but a sin nature is not part of true humanity. Sin is an intrusion into humanity. Jesus had the original sinless recipe of humanity, just as Adam and Eve did.

Others hold, however, that Jesus was no ordinary man. As the virgin-born God-man, His divine nature could not sin (cf. 1 Sam. 15:29) and thus held His human nature in check. Some have objected that the impeccability (i.e., He was not able to sin) of Christ denies the reality of Satan's temptation. Such an objection is meaningless when one remembers that Satan's rebellion against God has already been defeated in Christ's atonement, but his rebellion is nevertheless real, even though the outcome of God's victory is certain. The same is true of the temptation of Christ. One may attack a battleship with a canoe. The outcome of the attack is already certain, even though the attack is real. Even though gold may be subjected to a test and will always pass the test, the test is still valid. Jesus was tested, and He passed the tests victoriously. Whether one concludes that He could or could not have sinned, the outcome was still the same—He did not sin!

Jesus "fasted forty days and forty nights" (vv. 2–3), a remarkable feat of human endurance indicating the physical strength of the former carpenter. While the three major tests followed this period, other tests evidently had occurred throughout the forty days (Luke 4:2). His real physical hunger serves as the setting for the first temptation by "the tempter" (Satan). The incident is couched in the questioning aspersion "If You are the Son of God," indicating Matthew's purpose for including this record of Jesus' victory: it proves that He is, in fact, the Son of God! The urgency to turn the stones into bread appealed to Jesus' most basic human need in light of the extensive fast. The natural result of using His divine power in this regard would certainly have led to the desire to eat the bread. One mistake would have led to another. However, Jesus refused to use His divine prerogative to benefit Himself. In fact, He never did a miracle to benefit Himself. His heart was always reaching out to others. Jesus was led into the wilderness by the Holy Spirit. There was no food there. If His Father wanted Him to eat, He could provide for such. In the absence of such provision, however, Jesus would remain completely dependent on His Father.

The victory in each aspect of the temptation is related to Jesus' use of Scripture: "It is written" (v. 4). First, He quoted Deuteronomy 8:3, "Man does not live by bread alone, but man lives by everything that proceeds out of the mouth of the LORD." The source of bread is more important than the bread itself. Later, Jesus would say, "I have food to eat that you do not know about" (John 4:32). His source of strength was obedience to the Father's will, and He would not even work a miracle to avoid personal suffering when such suffering was a part of God's purpose for Him. What a Savior!

The second temptation took place in the "holy city" (Jerusalem) on the "pinnacle" of the temple, which towered above the Kidron Valley. Evidently, Jesus was transported there by Satan's power, and this time the devil quoted Scripture (out of context) in order to get Him to sin and to ultimately shake His faith in the Word. Satan used Psalm 91:11–12, urging Jesus to "throw Yourself down." Again, Jesus replied with Scripture (Deut. 6:16) that He was not to "put the LORD your God to the test" by such a presumptuous action. The very passage of Scripture quoted by Satan actually goes on to promise God's ultimate victory over him! Jesus' use of the Scripture again silences the tempter. Interestingly, Arno Gaebelein believes that Satan appeared physically to tempt Christ,[1] but none of the temptations require that Satan be seen by Jesus. One can search the Scriptures and never find a fallen angel appearing in physical form. Every case of an angel appearing to man is that of an unfallen angel sent on a mission by God and given a form in which to appear and present a message.

The third temptation takes place on a "very high mountain" (v. 8). The highest mountain in the entire near east is Mount Hermon, which rises to over nine thousand feet and is snow-capped all year. That the mountain is real seems clear in the text, though its exact location is unidentified. Despite the grandeur and almost miraculousness of this temptation, there is nothing in the passage itself to indicate that these temptations were only in the mind of Christ. Clearly they are depicted as being real experiences that actually occurred in the human life of the Messiah.

Satan showed Jesus "all the kingdoms of the world," which he promised to give Jesus if He would acknowledge and worship Satan as the prince of the world. Some hold that Satan could actually fulfill this promise, since Paul calls him "the god of this world" (2 Cor. 4:4). However, Daniel clearly told Nebuchadnezzar that "the Most High is ruler over the realm of mankind, and bestows it on whomever He wishes" (Dan. 4:25). The invalidity of the temptation is, therefore, almost laughable. Satan, though the god of this world, is never depicted in Scripture as actually controlling or possessing any real power over the kingdoms of the world. While Satan may influence a king or a group of kingdoms, God is always depicted as being on the throne, over the earth, which is His footstool. That Satan, the usurper, would attempt to give the kingdoms of the world to Jesus, the Messiah, the rightful King, is the height of absurdity! Like many of Satan's temptations, he offers something that in reality he cannot deliver.

The Temptation of Christ—Matthew 4:1-11

Temptation	Satan's Goal	Christ's Response	Lesson for Believers
Lack of dependence on God	Satisfying first a basic human need	Depend on God for more than the physical (Deut. 8:3)	Spiritual truth overrides physical needs
Testing God	Using God's power foolishly	Do not ask God to rescue one from acting foolishly (Ps. 91:11-12)	Do not tempt God by acting foolishly
To fail to worship and serve God	To cause Christ to worship Satan	Only God is to be worshiped (Deut. 6:13)	There is no one to worship and serve but the Lord God

For Christ to fall down and worship Satan would have been to acknowledge the devil's lordship over Him. In His direct rebuke, "Begone, Satan!" Jesus clearly asserts His lordship over the old serpent whose head He will soon crush. Matthew's statement that "then the devil left Him" shows that his order of the temptations is the chronological one (cf. Luke 4:1–13). In a demonstration of spirit and power, Jesus overcame the tempter, showing that He is the One who enables us to overcome temptation as well. "Resist the devil and he will flee from you" (James 4:7).

Beginning of Christ's Ministry in Galilee

Matthew designates four clear geographical areas in relation to the ministry of Christ: Galilee (4:12), Peraea, the area "beyond," or east of the Jordan (19:1), Judea (20:17 [on the way to Jerusalem]), and Jerusalem (21:1). The author, along with Mark and Luke, thus omits some of the early Judean ministry,[2] and begins with Jesus at Capernaum in Galilee where he had first met Christ himself (cf. 9:9). "John had been taken into custody" (v. 12). The circumstances of the arrest and eventual beheading of John the Baptist are recorded in chapter 14. It is very important to note that all of the material in John 1:1–3:24 took place before John was cast into prison.

Jesus already had a number of disciples. Andrew, Peter, James, John, Philip, and Nathanael were followers of Jesus in John 1. They had seen the miracle of the water turned into wine (John 2:1–12), and they had accompanied Jesus to Jerusalem where He cleansed the temple, had a forceful discussion with the Jews, and encountered Nicodemus. Thus, when Matthew introduces Christ to his readers in this chapter, Jesus is already quite familiar with His main disciples. According to typical Jewish culture of that time, young Jewish men would seek out a great rabbi and request to be his disciple. In the case of Jesus, He came seeking ordinary men to be His disciples.

It appears that a widespread persecution of the followers of John and Jesus took place at this time (vv. 13–16). Luke 4:16–31 explains the reason for Jesus leaving Nazareth was an attempt on His life after a synagogue service at Nazareth. From this point on, Capernaum became the headquarters of Jesus' ministry to the house of Israel. This city was a Roman settlement near the Sea of Galilee and was the center of the Roman government of the northern provinces of Israel. "This was to fulfill" (vv. 14–16) refers to the coming of Christ into Galilee in fulfillment of the prophecy of Isaiah 9:1–2, ". . . beyond the Jordan, Galilee of the Gentiles. The people who were sitting in darkness saw a great light." Jesus Himself was that great light that now would shine forth in His earthly ministry to the people of Galilee who had so long been despised by their Judean cousins in the south.

"Repent; for the kingdom of heaven is at hand" (v. 17). The message of John the Baptist is now clearly proclaimed by Jesus Christ. However, Jesus, as the Messiah, is not calling on His listeners to prepare for the coming of the kingdom but rather announces that the kingdom is here. In a very real sense, the first coming of the King is an honest, straightforward presentation of the kingdom promised by the Old Testament prophets to the people of Israel. Thus we find unusual miracles attending Jesus' presentation of this kingdom: incurable diseases and incomprehensible afflictions are cured by the power of His touch and His word. John Walvoord has correctly said, "The kingdom blessings promised in Isaiah 35:5–6, due for fulfillment in the future kingdom, here become the credentials of the King in His first coming."[3] The kingdom is "at hand" because the King is on the scene.

Calls to Repentance	
John the Baptist	Matthew 3:2–11; Luke 3:8
Jesus Christ	Matthew 4:17; Luke 13:3–5; 24:47; Revelation 2:16, 22; 3:3, 19
Apostle Peter	Acts 3:19; 5:31; 8:22; 11:18
Apostle Paul	Acts 20:21; 26:20; Romans 2:4; 2 Corinthians 12:21; 2 Timothy 2:25

"Simon who was called Peter, and Andrew" became the first two disciples called publicly by Jesus (vv. 18–20). Andrew had earlier introduced his brother to Jesus on another occasion (cf. John 1:40). The invitation "Follow me" called these earlier believers into a permanent ministry to be shared with Christ. Prior to this point, they had followed Jesus on a part-time, itinerate basis. Now the decision is to follow and serve Christ full-time. "I will make you fishers of men" clearly indicates the nature of this ministry. They would receive special training in bringing people into the kingdom. These former fishermen would literally become fishers of men! There can be no doubt that aggressive personal evangelism was and still is a major priority in the believer's life. Our obedience to the lordship of Christ is evidenced by our carrying forth the mission to which He has committed us. Having "left the nets," these disciples entered into a new relationship and would never again be able to fully return to the occupation they once held so dear. There can be no greater calling than to serve Christ full-time with every effort of our lives.

James and John were also brothers and fishing partners with Simon and Andrew (vv. 21–22). Matthew and Mark agree that they were "mending their nets," but Luke seems to differ. The two accounts can be simply harmonized. As two men were mending nets, the other two were fishing. Jesus then came upon them and called them all to follow Him. The statement in verse 22 that they immediately responded to His call gives us a perfect picture of true obedience to the lordship of Christ. To obey is to respond immediately in an attitude of faith.

The closing verses of the chapter summarize and survey the Galilean ministry of Jesus. This ministry concentrated on a presentation of the "gospel of the kingdom" to the Jews. Jesus as the Messiah (the Anointed One) had arrived to set up the long-awaited kingdom. Accompanying this announcement were miracles of healing. Going from city to city throughout Galilee caused His fame to spread quickly, so that "great multitudes" followed Him from Galilee, the Decapolis, Jerusalem, Judea, and beyond Jordan. Thus followers were gleaned from virtually every geographical area of the nation of Israel in the days of Christ. This is no insignificant feat when one realizes that no prophet had arisen in Israel for over four hundred years. The silence of the intertestamental period had been broken by the proclamation of the good news of the kingdom, first by John and then by Jesus!

Study Questions

1. What part did the Holy Spirit play in the temptation of Christ?

2. From where did Jesus obtain His responses to Satan's temptations?

3. Did Satan recognize Christ's deity, and did Satan have the power to "give" Jesus rulership over "all the kingdoms of the world"?

4. What city did Jesus make His headquarters after leaving Nazareth to begin His public ministry? Why would this have been a good decision?

5. Why does Matthew often use the phrase, "This was to fulfill what was spoken" by a certain prophet? What prophet does Matthew cite in this chapter, and can you locate the exact passage?

6. Compare the statements of John and Jesus found in Matthew 3:2 and 4:17. What significance do you draw from this comparison?

7. Compare Matthew 4:12 with John 3:24. Does this not suggest that Jesus knew Peter and Andrew and James and John before He called them in Matthew 4:19?

8. What purposes did the miracles Jesus performed have?

9. Jesus ministered to many others, but who ministered to Jesus in Matthew 4? What do you suppose the nature of this ministry was?

CHAPTER 5

Sermon on the Mount
Matthew 5:1-48

Preview:

After presenting Jesus' person, Matthew exhibits Jesus' principles. The Sermon on the Mount demonstrates the primary teaching of the Messiah, the King of the Jews. This is the first of six of Christ's full-length discourses recorded by Matthew. These discourses are of a spiritual nature yet are filled with practicality. Following His beatitudes, Jesus confronts some of the Jews' distorted teachings about the law.

A Message to the Heart and Mind of Man (5:1-3)

The nature of the kingdom that Jesus proclaimed has long been a controversial area of interpretation among Christian scholars. While these interpretations do not divide us between orthodoxy and heresy, they nevertheless formulate our fundamental understanding of the nature and message of the church today. Liberalism taught that the keeping of the Sermon on the Mount was to be regarded as the message of the gospel. Thus it predicated a system of salvation by good works. Some dispensationalists, at times, have tended to relegate everything related to the kingdom as being under the Old Testament dispensation, thus having no significant application to the church today. Still others recognize the truths within this kingdom message but hold that its precepts are impossible to attain, thus nullifying its significance for the Christian.

Nowhere in the presentation of the message of the kingdom does Jesus indicate that this message is significantly different from the proclamation of evangelism by the church. The difference, rather, seems to be in relation to those to whom the message is directed. During the early period of the Gospels, the message of the kingdom of heaven was directed to the nation of Israel and contained the potential fulfillment of the promised kingdom to the Jews. To the Gentile nations of the Church Age, the proclamation of the message is that God will gather a people for Himself from all nations into this great kingdom. The prerequisites for entrance into this kingdom included repentance (Matt. 4:17), righteousness (Matt. 5:20), and faith (Matt. 18:3); or, in summary, being born again (John 3). Because the people rejected these requirements, Christ taught that His earthly reign would not be centralized in the nation of Israel but in a gathering of a people from among the nations of the earth.

The opening verses of the Sermon on the Mount (5:1–2) indicate that this message deals with the inner state of mind and heart that is the indispensable absolute of true Christian discipleship. It delineates the outward manifestations of character and conduct of the true believer and genuine disciple. George Lawlor, a dispensationalist, writes, "We do not find basic, fundamental Law here, for law cannot produce the state of blessedness set forth herein."[1] Rather, the quality of life herein described is the necessary product of grace alone. As Jesus states the outward legal requirements of the law and then carries His listener beyond the letter of the law to the true spirit and intent of the law, He describes a lifestyle no human being could live in his or her own power. Thus the life of the believer described by Jesus in the Sermon on the Mount is a life of grace and glory that comes from God alone. To make this quality of life the product of human efforts (as does the liberal) is the height of overestimation of human ability and underestimation of human depravity. To relegate this entire message, Jesus' longest recorded sermon, to a Jewish-only lifestyle, as do hyper-dispensationalists, is to rob the church of its greatest statement of true Christian living!

The depth of spiritual truth proclaimed in this message of the kingdom, however, does not present the gospel of justification by faith in the death, burial, and resurrection of Christ. This sermon is an exposition of true spirituality, not the gospel of salvation. It tells us how to live as believers, not how to become believers. Arthur Pink says, "Its larger part was a most searching exposition of the spirituality of the law and the repudiation of the false teaching of the elders."[2] Jesus made it clear that the spirit of Christ goes beyond the outward demand of the law. The Christian, though not under the law, is to live above the law.

It has always been difficult to clearly draw the distinction between the relationship of law and grace. Martyn Lloyd-Jones has observed, "Some so emphasize the law as to turn the gospel of Jesus Christ with its glorious liberty into nothing but a collection of moral maxims. It is all law to them and there is no grace left. They so talk of the Christian that it becomes pure legalism and there is no grace in it. Let us remember also that it is equally possible so to overemphasize grace at the expense of the law as again, to have something which is not the gospel of the New Testament."[3] He goes on to note that the Sermon on the Mount and the message of the kingdom do have definite application to the Christian today. It was preached to people who were meant to practice it not only at that time but ever afterwards as well. The late James M. Boice keenly observes that that "world" of the Sermon on the Mount cannot be restricted to life in the future millennial kingdom, since it includes tax collectors, thieves, unjust officials, hypocrites, and false prophets.[4]

New Testament Parallels to the Beatitudes	
Blessed are the poor in spirit (v. 3).	Having a meek and quiet spirit (1 Pet. 3:4).
Blessed are those who mourn (v. 4).	Mourn and weep, the Lord will exalt you (James 4:9–10).
Blessed are the gentle (v. 5).	Do not brawl but be gentle (Titus 3:2).
Blessed are those who hunger and thirst for righteousness (v. 6).	We are to live to righteousness (1 Pet. 2:24).
Blessed are the merciful (v. 7).	Show mercy with cheerfulness (Rom. 12:8).
Blessed are the pure in heart (v. 8).	Keep yourself pure (1 Tim. 5:22).
Blessed are the peacemakers (v. 9).	Wisdom from above is peaceable (James 3:17).
Blessed are the persecuted (v. 11).	Persecuted for the cross (Gal. 6:12).
Blessed are the reproached (v. 11).	For Christ we suffer reproach (1 Tim. 4:10).
Your reward is in heaven (v. 12).	Inheritance reserved in heaven (1 Pet. 1:4).

Embodied in the Sermon on the Mount is a summation of Jesus' basic ethical teaching of the life of a born-again person. While the Sermon on the Mount is not a way of salvation, neither is it only a message to those under the law, for it obviously goes beyond the law. It is a presentation of Christian discipleship that can be wrought in the soul of an individual only by the power of God. This message does not tell one what to believe in order to be saved; it tells one what it is like to be saved. It explains the quality of the life changed by the saving grace of God. Its basic truths are reiterated everywhere throughout the New Testament epistles. There is no fundamental contrast between this message and the message of Paul. Both are in agreement that "the just shall live by faith!"[5]

In the Sermon on the Mount, Jesus states the spiritual character and quality of the kingdom He wished to establish. The basic qualities of this kingdom are fulfilled in the church He would establish. Virtually every section of this message is repeated in substance elsewhere throughout the New Testament. There is nothing here to indicate that this message is to be limited in its application only to the people of Israel. Notice in the opening verse that his disciples came to Him and He began to teach them the following message.

The Beatitudes: Character Described (5:3–20)

"Blessed" (Greek, *makarioi*) means "happy" (v. 3). This is a basic description of the believers' inner condition as a result of the work of God. Homer Kent says that it is virtually equivalent to being "saved."[6] These Beatitudes, like Psalm 1, do not show a person how to be saved, but rather describe the characteristics of one who has been saved. The "poor in spirit" are the opposite of the proud or haughty in spirit. These are those who have been humbled by the grace of God and have acknowledged their sin and therefore their dependence on God to save them. They are the ones who will inherit the "kingdom of heaven." It is obvious in this usage that the kingdom of heaven is a general designation of the dwelling place of the saved.

Those that "mourn . . . shall be comforted" (v. 4). The depth of the promise of these statements is almost inexhaustible. Those who mourn for sin will be comforted in confession. Those who mourn for the human anguish of the lost will be comforted by the compassion of God. Being poor in spirit is properly followed by mourning for sin and its consequences. It is practically the same as repenting for one's helpless, hopeless, lost condition.

"The gentle . . . shall inherit the earth" (v. 5) refers again to those who have been humbled before God and will inherit, not only the blessedness of heaven, but will ultimately share in the kingdom of God on earth. Here, in the opening statements of the Sermon on the Mount, is the balance between the physical and spiritual promise of the kingdom. The kingdom of which Jesus preached is both "in you" (lit., "in the midst of you") and is "yet to come." The Christian is the spiritual citizen of the kingdom of heaven now. Jesus exhibited this trait as seen in his conduct before the bitter accusers at His trial and crucifixion. Philip interpreted Isaiah 53:7, "As a lamb before its shearer is silent, so He does not open His mouth" as applying to Christ (Acts 8:32). This ethic of gentleness and meekness is the exact opposite of the world's view of the way to get ahead. Jesus taught that humility comes before honor. James, the Lord's brother, knew what Jesus taught, and he said, "Humble yourselves in the presence of the Lord, and He will exalt you" (James 4:10).

These future possessors of the earth are its presently installed rightful heirs, and even now they "hunger and thirst for righteousness" (v. 6). They experience a deep desire for personal righteousness, which is, in itself, a proof of their spiritual rebirth. Those who are poor and empty in their own spiritual poverty recognize the depth of their need and hunger and thirst for that which only God can give them. To hunger means to be needy. It is joined with to thirst; the born-again person has a God-given hunger and thirst (inner passion) for righteousness. This hungering and thirsting continues throughout the life of the believer. He or she continues to hunger and to be filled and to hunger and to be filled. God supplies the believer's every spiritual need daily. This act of hungering and thirsting after righteousness is the by-product of a regenerated life.

Lawlor rightly says that this is the description of a person who has already been saved.[7] Nowhere does the Bible command unbelievers to hunger after righteousness in order to be saved. Rather, Paul clearly states "there is none who understands, there is none who seeks for God" (Rom. 3:11). The biblical writers make it clear that while man must come to Christ for salvation, it is not within man's normal ability and desire to want to come to God. Therefore, God is depicted throughout the New Testament as the seeking Savior going after the lost. "They shall be filled" (Greek, *chortazō*) refers to a complete filling and satisfaction. The psalmist proclaimed: "For He has satisfied the thirsty soul, and the hungry soul He has filled with what is good" (107:9). This filling comes from God, who is the total source of satisfaction of His people. It comes now and it will continue to come throughout eternity to those who hunger and thirst for it now.

Those who are "merciful . . . shall receive mercy" (v. 7) has reference to those who have been born again by the mercy of God. Because divine love has been extended to them, they have the work of the Holy Spirit in them producing a mercy that defies explanation by unregenerate people. Jesus Himself became the ultimate example of this when He cried from the cross, "Father, forgive them; for they do not know what they are doing" (Luke 23:34). The form of proverbial teaching should not confuse the order of these statements. For example, believers do not show mercy in order to obtain mercy; they show mercy because they have obtained mercy. In so continuing to show the evidence of the grace of God in their lives, they continue to receive that grace. In other words, they are not saved simply because they show mercy and are kind to people. He shows mercy and is kind because they are saved.

Those who are truly saved shall "see God." These are the "pure in heart" (Greek, *katharoi*, v. 8). Their lives have been transformed by the grace of God.

They are not yet sinless, but their position before God has been changed. They have the new birth, saving faith, and holiness. The process of sanctification is ever conforming them to the image of Christ (Rom. 8:29), which image consists in "righteousness and holiness of the truth" (Eph. 4:24). Purity of heart is both the end of our election and the goal of our redemption. We read in Ephesians 1:4, "He chose us in Him . . . that we should be holy," and in Titus 2:14, "[Christ] gave Himself for us, that He might redeem us from every lawless deed and purify for Himself a people for His own possession." To this we add Hebrews 12:14, "Pursue peace with all men, and the sanctification without which no one will see the Lord."

The next description deals with the "peacemakers" (v. 9). They are the ones who are themselves at peace with God and live in peace with all men (cf. Rom. 5:1). They are called "the" peacemakers, for these are not social reformers, but rather the ones reformed by the regenerating power of the gospel. They are peacemakers because they themselves are at peace with God. They have entered into the peace of Christ and thus are able ambassadors of God's message of peace to a troubled world. Hence they shall be called "sons of God." These only shall be called the sons of God! Throughout the Beatitudes, Jesus clearly underscores that only those who have the life-changing qualities herein described are citizens of His kingdom.

As Jesus develops His message, He makes it clear that such a life causes His people to be in direct contrast to the world in which they live. Therefore He reminds, "Blessed are those who have been persecuted for the sake of righteousness" (v. 10). The plural use of "you" in verse 11 indicates that Jesus foresaw this persecution as touching all His followers. Notice 2 Timothy 3:12, "And indeed, all who desire to live godly in Christ Jesus will be persecuted (Greek, *diōkō*)." The nature of this persecution implies a driving or chasing away, a withstanding or keeping one from his goal. This does not mean that every Christian will necessarily suffer physical abuse as evidence of true salvation. While many Christians have sealed their faith with their blood, many more have had to withstand the social temptations and pressures of the world in order to live effectively for Christ.

Again, Jesus warns that people shall "cast insults at you, and persecute you" (v. 11). This became true during His ministry, in the lives of the apostles, and throughout the history of the church. But in Tertullian's words, "The blood of the martyrs became the seed of the church." The persecution spoken of here is twofold. First, it involves a physical pursuing of the persecuted, and second, a personal attack of slander against them.

"Rejoice" (v. 12) is the command that grows out of the blessedness of the believer. The phrase "Rejoice, and be glad" means rejoice, but even more, exalt! The believer who is the blessed one may not only rejoice in tribulation but may rejoice exceedingly to the point of exaltation. Therefore, he or she glories in tribulation even as the apostle Paul (cf. 2 Cor. 1:3-7; 12:7-10). "Your reward in heaven is great" focuses attention on the eternal, spiritual destiny of all things. If God is as real as He claims, if the Bible is true, if heaven is to be gained, then there is no temporary earthly trouble or persecution that can thwart the child of God from the eternal glory that lies ahead. In Romans 8:18, Paul proclaims, "For I consider that the sufferings of this present time are not worthy to be compared with the glory that is to be revealed to us."

The Beatitudes are followed by a summary statement of the basic character of the Christian's life as salt and light (vv. 13-16). "You are the salt [Greek, *halas*] of the earth;" again the phrase "you are" indicates that only the genuinely born-again person is salt and can help meet the needs of the world. The salt adds flavoring, acts as a preservative, gives thirst, melts coldness, and heals wounds. Thus it is a very appropriate description of believers in their relationship to the world in which they live. The term "has become tasteless" refers to its essential saltiness. Jesus was actually saying that if the salt loses its saltiness, it is worthless. The implication of this statement is that if a Christian loses his effectiveness, his testimony will be trampled under the feet of men.

"You are the light of the world" describes the essential mission of the Christian to the world. The word "light" in Greek is *phōs*, from which we get the word "photo" in English. We are God's photos to display Him to the world. He is the condition (salt) to meet the world's needs, and he has a mission (light) to the world. His light is to clearly shine forth into the darkness of human depravity. He is to set it up on a lampstand, not hide it "under the peck-measure," or bushel basket in modern terms. Inconsistent living and unconfessed sin in the life of the believer will become a basketlike covering that hides the light of God. God provides the light, and it continues to shine, but as believers we must keep our lives clean before the Lord in order not to cover up the light He has placed within us. Darkness is the absence of light, and darkness alone cannot dispel the light, but the smallest light can dispel the greatest darkness. Therefore, let your light shine through a clean life before the Lord and before the world in which you live.

Having laid the foundation of the message in the summary statements of the Beatitudes, Jesus now proceeds to show the superiority of His message to that of the Law of Moses. He makes it clear that He did not come to abolish the Law (v. 17). That is, the New Testament gospel is neither contrary nor contradictory to the Old Testament Law; rather, it is the ultimate fulfillment of the spiritual intention of the Law. Whereas the Pharisees had corrupted the Law with legalism, Jesus now took the law beyond mere outward observance to the inner spiritual intention of God. For He had come to fulfill the Law and its fullest implications. In his earthly life, Jesus accomplished this by meeting its strictest demands and going beyond its mere outward requirements. As our Savior, Jesus not only bore our sins, but He has also established a perfect righteousness that is given to us as a gift of God. Our sin was thus imputed to Him, and His righteousness was imputed to us.[8]

"Truly I say" is a unique form used by Jesus throughout His preaching to draw attention to the authority of His message. "Truly," the Greek word *amēn*, means "certainly, verily, a solemn assent." It is used as a designation of authoritative teaching. "The smallest letter or stroke" refers to the minutest marks and letters of the Hebrew alphabet. A jot is the smallest letter of the Hebrew alphabet, called *yodh* (׳). It functions as a Y does in English and looks similar to an apostrophe. The stroke, or tittle, is a small projection on the edge of certain Hebrew letters to distinguish them from one another. For example, the Hebrew *daleth* (ד) differs from the *resh* (ר) only by the use of this diminutive stroke in the upper right area of the *daleth*. Jesus was teaching that even the smallest statement in the Law must be fulfilled. It is not to be taken as some promise regarding the copying of the text. First Samuel 13:1, for example, has suffered from copyist errors. Jesus indicated rather that no part of the text that God gave us would ever go unfulfilled.

Because of the seriousness of the Law, Jesus emphasized the importance of keeping even its smallest details. However, in the ultimate plan of God, the Law was not meant to become an extra burden on human souls. Rather than directly pointing the way to salvation, the Law convinced people of the need of the Savior. Therefore, whoever so teaches others but does not live what he teaches, "shall be called least in the kingdom of heaven" (v. 19). It is interesting that a person may be saved and a member of the kingdom of heaven yet be hypocritical in his or her attitude toward the Law. "But whoever keeps and teaches" the principles and precepts of the Law shall be "called great in the kingdom of heaven." This simply means that God will reward the faithfulness and effectiveness of our lives and there will be varying degrees of blessing and reward in the kingdom.

Because of the necessity of righteousness as a requirement to enter heaven, Jesus then declared that except His hearers' "righteousness surpasses that of the scribes and Pharisees" they will not enter heaven (v. 20). The significance of this is seen in the fact that the Jews of Jesus' day considered these people to be the most religious in all Israel. However, for many of them, their religion was merely an outward show of self-righteousness. What the Savior demands is a kind of righteousness that is so godly that it cannot be the product of human effort but must be the gift of God. This righteousness Christ would establish in His life and death would be made available as God's free gift. This is the righteousness that would exceed that of the scribes and Pharisees.

Six Illustrations: Character Applied (5:21–48)

In communicating the depth of His message, Jesus used a series of contrasts (listed below in two categories) between the outward demand of the law and the inner attitude of heart desired by God. In this series of contrasts, we see the depth and dynamic of the teaching of Jesus Christ, the great Master Teacher. Here we discover the practical application of genuine Christian character to true spiritual living. Here we see the gospel in action. Here is piety on the pavement of life. Christians may live above the demands of the law and the temptations of the world because they have an inner depth of character that is the product of God's divine nature within him.

The Law	The Spirit
Law came by Moses (John 1:17).	Grace and truth came by Christ (John 1:17).
The Law brings death (Rom. 7:5).	The Spirit gives life (Rom. 7:6).
The Law curses us (Gal. 3:13).	Christ redeems from the curse (Gal. 3:13).
The works of the Law does not save (Gal. 3:2).	The receiving of the Spirit saves (Gal. 3:2–3).
No one is justified by the Law (Gal. 2:16).	The saved are justified by faith through the Spirit (Gal. 2:16; 3:1–5).
Believers are not under the Law (Gal. 5:18).	Believers are led by the Spirit (Gal. 5:18).
Believers are not subject to the Law (Gal. 5:1-3).	Believers live through the Spirit (Gal. 5:5).

First Illustration: Murder Versus Anger (5:21–26)

Jesus introduces the illustrations that follow with a literary formula. He notes, "You have heard that the ancients were told" (v. 21), or "You have heard that it was said" (v. 27), or simply "It was said" (v. 32). Christ's own answer in each case is introduced by a phrase such as, "But I say unto you" (vv. 22, 28, 32, 34, 39, and 44). Jesus puts Himself forward as the authority, something the religious teachers of that day rarely did. Christ begins this series of contrasts by quoting the statement of the law, "You shall not commit murder" (Ex. 20:13). The reference is clearly understood in its context in both the Old Testament and New Testament as referring to an act of murder, not just killing in general. It must be remembered that the God who commanded the children of Israel not to murder one another also commanded them at times to kill an enemy in order to defend their nation. Jesus goes beyond this outward demand of the law by stating that "every one who is angry with his brother" is in just as great danger of judgment as a murderer, for anger is the emotion and inner intention that leads to murder.

The term *raka* (meaning "vain fellow" or "empty head") was a Hebrew or Aramaic expression of contempt (cf. 2 Sam. 6:20). "The supreme court" is a reference to the Jewish religious council called the Sanhedrin. "You fool," (Greek, *mōros*) means "stupid." We have developed the English word *moron* from this term. Those using such a malicious expression would be in danger of "fiery hell." This statement has often caused concern and confusion in the mind of many commentators. What does it really mean? The idea clearly seems to be that if one makes light of his fellow man, he will be in danger of committing slander. But if one makes bitter, damning statements with reference to hell toward his fellow man, he will actually be in danger of hell himself. The concept is that one making such statements is not likely to be a born-again person. The Greek term for hell, *geenna*, was the Hellenized form of the name of the Valley of Hinnom at Jerusalem in which fires were constantly burning to consume the refuse of the city. This valley provided a powerful and graphic picture of the ultimate destruction of hell and the lake of fire (cf. Jer. 7:31; 2 Chr. 28:3; 2 Kgs. 23:10). Christ locates the root of murder in the heart of the angry man and states that God's judgment will be just as swift on anger as it will be upon murder.

Having made a comparison between the command not to murder and the inner motive and heart intention of hatred, Jesus then illustrated the seriousness of this matter by referring to one who would attempt to buy off his conscience by giving something to God without clearing his conscience with his offended brother (vv. 23–24). He reminded them that if "you are presenting your offering at the altar" without reconciling with the offended party, God will not receive the intended gift. Bringing a gift to the altar refers to bringing it to the temple so that it might be consecrated. Therefore if conflict exists between any two people, it is God's desire that they reconcile the conflict before attempting to give a gift to or do an act of service for the Lord. Many people undoubtedly try to suppress the guilt of their sin by an outward act that they hope will please God in some way. Therefore, Jesus commands that we leave our gift before the altar and "first be reconciled" to our brother before we make our offering. To be reconciled means to be brought back into fellowship or favor with our fellow man. Having resolved the personal conflict, we have then but to return and perform the act of service unto the Lord. The performance of our duty to others does not free us from the obligation of direct service to God.

The Savior then went on to remind that even if "your opponent at law" disagrees with you, it is to your advantage to reconcile with him so that he will not "deliver you to the judge" (vv. 25–26). Many people make the foolish mistake of assuming that just because they think they are right in a given situation, God will necessarily vindicate them. Jesus' exhortation here is to urge us to go out of our way to avoid legal conflicts before human judges (cf. v. 40). The payment of debt and the prison referred to here simply mean the normal legal process that one would encounter in a civil suit. The term prison (Greek, *phulakē*) does not refer to purgatory, as suggested by some Roman Catholic interpreters, but to the full measure of punitive justice.

Second Illustration: Adultery Contrasted with Lust (5:27–30)

"You shall not commit adultery" was the demand of the Law (Ex. 20:14). Jesus went beyond this outward command to reveal that its act is the result of an inner attitude of lust. "Every one who looks" characterizes the man whose glance is not checked by holy restraint and results in an impure lusting after women. It has often been argued that there is a difference between an appreciation of beauty and a lustful, lurid look. The lustful look is the expression of the heart attitude that says in essence, "I would if I could." The act would follow if the opportunity were to occur. By taking his listener beyond the outward statement of the Law to its real intention, Jesus was trying to get his attention off the physical and onto the spiritual.

Most men could claim that they had not committed the sin of adultery, but very few could honestly say that they had not committed the sin of lusting, which could easily turn into adultery. Thus, the statement of cutting off one's hand or plucking out one's eye definitely is not to be taken literally. It is a hyperbole, the use of an exaggeration for effect. This is a common literary device, a figure of speech. What Jesus implied is that if "your right eye makes you stumble" then the logical thing to do would be to "tear it out." His point is not that one should literally pluck out his eye but that one should recognize that the source of lust comes from within the mind and heart of man, not from the physical organ itself. The right eye is not the source of sin; the heart of man is that source. Someone who had plucked out his right eye in an attempt to deal with lust would simply become a left-eye luster! The real source of the sin of adultery comes from within man's heart, not his eyes.

The seriousness of the sin of lusting is thus illustrated by this graphic comparison. Ultimately, it would be better for a person to be physically maimed than to enter into hell forever. However, doing physical damage to oneself does not in any way guarantee entrance into heaven. What Jesus simply taught was that man must bring the passions of his heart under control of the Spirit of God.

Third Illustration: Divorce as Contrasted with Marriage (5:31–32)

"And it was said" (v. 31) is again a reference to the Old Testament commandment of the Mosaic regulation (cf. Deut. 24:1). The normal custom of the ancient Near East was for a man to verbally divorce his wife. The Arab custom was to say "I divorce you" three times, and the divorce was finalized without any legal protection of any kind to the wife. In contrast, the ancient Law of Israel insisted on a "certificate of dismissal" or certificate of divorce. This written statement gave legal protection to both the wife and the husband. Jesus explained elsewhere (cf. Matt. 19:8) that Moses' concession was not intended as a license. In ancient rabbinic Judaism, Moses' statement had been variously interpreted from meaning adultery (Shammai) to the trivial matters of personal preference (Hillel). The only legitimate exception for divorce allowed by Christ is possibly for "the cause of fornication" (Greek, *porneia*), meaning sexual unfaithfulness. Charles Ryrie notes that fornication may mean adultery prior to or after marriage, as well as unfaithfulness during the period of betrothal.[9]

These statements make it clear that adultery or fornication is legitimate grounds for divorce. However, the legitimacy of the divorce does not necessarily establish the legitimacy of remarriage. That one *must* divorce an unfaithful wife or husband is nowhere commanded in Scripture. To the contrary, there are many examples of extending forgiveness to the adulterous offender (cf. Gen. 38:26; Hos. 3:1; John 8:1–11). Nor does the discovery of premarital fornication on the part of the wife necessarily demand a divorce, as is indicated by Atkinson.[10] Sexual involvement alone does not necessarily constitute a marriage in the sight of God (cf. the example of Judah and Tamar, who were both widowed at the time of their illicit sexual involvement). Though this temporary union produced twin sons, it resulted in no permanent marriage.

Great care needs to be exercised when interpreting the New Testament passages regarding divorce and marriage.[11] It should be remembered that Jesus made His statements about divorce to people who were already married so that they might take seriously the marriage relationship. These statements were not necessarily made to add an extra burden to the already divorced person.

The responsibility of divorce is clearly laid upon the one seeking the divorce. "Everyone who divorces his wife" without biblical basis "makes her commit adultery." Lenski translates this latter phrase as "brings about that she is stigmatized as adulterous,"[12] and regards the sin of the one who does the divorcing as bringing about an unjust suspicion upon the divorcee.

Fourth Illustration: Oath Taking as Opposed to Speaking the Truth (5:33–37)

The basis of Old Testament swearing, or oath taking, is found in Exodus 20:7; Leviticus 19:12; and Deuteronomy 23:21. To "make false vows" (v. 33) means to swear falsely, to forswear, or to perjure oneself. Oaths taken in the name of the Lord were looked upon as binding, and perjury of such oaths was strongly condemned by the Law. Such phrases like "as the Lord liveth" or "by the name of the Lord" emphasize the sanctity of such oaths. Ryrie states: "Every oath contained an affirmation of promise of an appeal to God as the omniscient punisher of falsehoods, which made an oath binding."[13] By the time of Christ, the Jews had developed an elaborate system of oath taking, which often formed the basis of actual lying. For example, one might swear that he had told the truth according to the dome of the temple, while another might swear by the gold on the dome of the temple! In other words, there were stages of truth and thus also of falsehood within the system of taking oaths. In our time this custom is found in phrases such as, "I swear by God," "Cross my heart and hope to die," or "I swear on my mother's grave."

All such oath taking, Jesus announced, was unnecessary if one were normally in the habit of telling the truth. Thus His command was "make no oath at all." This does not have reference to cursing, as such, but to oath taking. Christians are not to take oaths by heaven, earth, or the city of Jerusalem. They are not to swear on the basis of their own head or any other physical feature. They are simply to speak the truth in such a way that their "yes" means yes and their "no" means no.

"Let your statement be 'Yes, yes' or 'No, no.'" When you say yes, make sure that that is what you mean. When you say no, make sure that also is what you mean. Mean what you say; say what you mean. Anything that is more than a simple affirmation of the truth "is of evil." When we add an oath to our regular affirmation of the truth, we either admit that our normal conversation cannot be trusted, or that we are lowering ourselves to the level of a culture that normally does not tell the truth. This does not necessarily mean that it is wrong to "swear to tell the truth" in a court of law. The point is that it should be unnecessary in a genuine Christian society to have to swear to tell the truth at all!

LAW	SPIRIT
Murder	No anger
Adultery	No lust
Divorce	Commitment
Oath taking	Speak the truth
Retaliation	Forgiveness
Hate your enemy	Love your enemy

Fifth Illustration: Retaliation as Opposed to Forgiveness (5:38–42)

The principle of retaliation, *lex talionis*, is common in both Jewish and other ancient Near Eastern law codes (cf. the Code of Hammurabi). The judicial penalty of "An eye for an eye, and a tooth for a tooth" is stated in Exodus 21:24 as a means of ending feuds. However, Jesus is clearly saying this method is not a license for vengeance. Many times an offended person will overreact to the offense and retaliate in such a way as to return a greater injury than he received. An example would be, "You put out my eye so I'm going to kill you." The idea here is that to the Jews of Jesus' day, it was common to attempt to retaliate upon the offender through the arm of the law, especially in a nation dominated by a foreign power.

The Savior's point is that we should "not resist him who is evil" (v. 39). Evil is seen here, not as a state, but rather as the action of the evil ones or the malicious ones. It represents the evil and sinful element in people that provokes them to acts of evil. Jesus shows how believers should respond to personal injury. He is not discussing the government's obligation to maintain law and order. The question of nonretaliation or nonviolence is often discussed in relation to these verses. These passages alone do not mean that a man should not defend his family or his country, but rather, that he should not attempt personal vengeance, even through the means of the law, to compensate for a personal injury.

Why should Jesus make such a statement? Certainly these words were spoken to remind those who would be His disciples not to expect divine justice from an unregenerate society. All justice ultimately is in the hand and heart of God. As long as human governments prevail, justice will be limited by humankind's finite abilities. The disciples of the kingdom are to look to the King Himself for ultimate vindication. The practical application of this truth is that believers should not attempt to justify themselves or inflict vengeance even through legal means. They are to place their total confidence in the ultimate sovereignty of God over the affairs of their lives. (See Rom. 12:19, "Leave room for the wrath of God.")

Jesus gives five examples of how believers should react to unfair or unreasonable treatment. First, in retaliation to physical violence, they are to "turn to him the other [cheek] also." Man's normal impulse is to strike back, but the disciple is not to be a normal man. He is to "overcome evil with good" (Rom. 12:21). This is probably one of the most feared statements in the entire Bible. People have gone to great lengths in an attempt to explain it away. Nevertheless, it remains the most pungent statement of Jesus' ethic. The lives of believers are to be lived with such a quality of spiritual verity and justice that they need no physical retaliation to defend or justify their position. There is no greater example of this ethical truth than the life and death of Jesus Himself!

Second, whether robbed by personal assault or compulsory litigation, the believer is to respond with confidence in that which is eternal, rather than that which is temporal. If the believer is sued in order that the accuser may "take [his] shirt," he is to also let him have his coat (v. 40). The shirt (Greek, *chitōn*) is the undergarment or tunic. The coat (Greek, *himation*) is the more expensive outer garment worn over the tunic. Jesus taught us to have confidence in an almighty God who is completely aware of the injustices done to us and totally capable of evoking ultimate eternal justice. He must be trusted even when legal litigation goes against the believer. In our society, we would phrase Jesus' teaching, "If someone takes your suit coat, give him your overcoat as well."

Third, in ancient times government agents were in a position to compel forced service upon a subjugated people. A Roman soldier, for example, could compel a Jewish native to carry his armor or materials for one mile, in order to relieve the soldier. Jesus now says that if someone compels you to walk a mile, "go with him two" (v. 41). The believer is to be willing to "go the extra mile." Doing double our duty, if with the right attitude, not only proves the loyalty and faithfulness of our cooperation to human authority, but likewise also proves the spiritual intention of our hearts. It also provides an opportunity to witness effectively out of our life message. It would have been foolish for the believer of Jesus' day to reluctantly go only a mile with a Roman official and then attempt to share the gospel with him. By going the second mile, he proved the innermost intention of his heart.

The fourth example is that of lending to "him who wants to borrow from you" (v. 42). Jesus made it clear that a loan should be looked upon as a potential gift. When we lend something to someone, we should not expect to receive in return. Is that not impractical? Yes it is! But that which is spiritual is not always that which is practical. There are many statements in Proverbs against borrowing, lending, and surety (cf. Prov. 6:1; 11:15; 22:7; 27:13). While we are warned of the dangers of borrowing and lending, Jesus made it clear that the believer ought to be willing to lend to those in need.

Finally, even the beggar is to be ministered to through the provision of giving to "him who asks of you." This statement certainly forms the basis of all Christian charity and provides the proper social application of the message of the gospel to the physical needs of man as well as to his spiritual needs. However, when we receive charity letters seeking donations, God expects us to use common sense, to evaluate the merits of the need, the needs of our family, and our ability to give. The balance has to be that "if any one does not provide for his own, and especially for those of his household, he has denied the faith, and is worse than an unbeliever" (1 Tim. 5:8). Paul also commanded, "If anyone will not work, neither let him eat" (2 Thess. 3:10).

Sixth Illustration: Loving Your Neighbor Contrasted with Loving Your Enemy (5:43–48)

The law of love, sometimes called "law of Christ," summarizes the ethical principle of the Sermon on the Mount (vv. 43–48). "Love your neighbor" summarizes the entire second table of the law (cf. Lev. 19:18–36). But the unscriptural addition "hate your enemy" was a popular concept in Jesus' day.[14] The admonition "love your enemies" is one of the greatest statements Jesus ever made. The love enjoined in this passage is that which originates from God Himself! We are not commanded to attempt to love our enemies on the basis of mere human affection, but on the basis of a love that comes from God. This kind of love holds a unique place in the New Testament, for it is the gift of God and the fruit of the Spirit to believers only. It is not something that people can muster within themselves. Rather, it must come from God Himself into the lives of believers (cf. Gal. 5:22; 1 Tim. 1:5).

How do we love our enemies? Notice that the passage makes it clear that we do not have to attempt to work up an artificial feeling of love. The quality of love commanded here is expressed by giving. We are to pray for those that persecute us. Loving an enemy involves doing good things toward that enemy in order to win him or her over to the cause you represent. The message of the kingdom, therefore, is that we will win over those who oppose us more readily with love than with hatred. It is not in the divisiveness of contention that we win our greatest converts, but in the application of the heart of the gospel and the love of Christ.

Principles of Christian Love

Believers love because Christ first loved us (1 John 4:19).

To love God is to love the brother also (1 John 4:21).

To love God is to keep His commandments (1 John 5:3).

A believer cannot love God and hate his brother (1 John 4:20).

The one who loves Christ keeps His words (John 14:24).

Love is more important than exercising spiritual gifts (1 Cor. 13).

The greatest love is to lay down one's life for a friend (John 15:13).

In summarizing the importance of love, Jesus emphasized that love was a necessary proof of salvation: "that you may be sons of your Father who is in heaven." An initial reading of this text out of its context might seem to imply that loving one's neighbor automatically makes one a child of God. However, the New Testament is clear that love is an evidence of the one who is already saved by the grace of God (cf. 1 John 3:14). Humans have a natural tendency to love those who love them; therefore, Jesus reminds us that we are to love our enemies as our brothers, for "even the tax gatherers" love those who love them. Matthew himself was one of these public officials of Jewish nationality who worked for the Roman government as a tax collector. The people generally despised them. The idea here is that even the most hated people of the day loved their own friends. Therefore, the true child of the kingdom is to have a quality of love that goes beyond that of the world.

This section of the Sermon on the Mount is summarized with the statement "Therefore you are to be perfect" (v. 48). Since the New Testament makes it clear that even the believer is capable of sin, the term "perfect" here (Greek, *teleios*) is not to be taken as absolute sinless perfection. Rather, it is used in relation to the matter of love in this context. Homer Kent says, "As God's love is complete, not omitting any group, so must the child of God strive for maturity in this regard."[15] Those of us who would live as citizens of heaven must learn to behave like children of God on earth.

Study Questions

1. Besides the Beatitudes in Matthew, there are several others in the New Testament. Can you find these by using a concordance?

2. How do the Beatitudes resemble the gospel message?

3. What is the meaning of Jesus' method of saying, "You have heard . . . but I say unto you?" What is the contrast He intends to show?

4. Explain the contrast and difference in meaning between verses 27 and 28. Is it that one is the more external prohibition, while the other makes sin a matter of the heart?

5. How are the injunctions of verses 29–30 hyperboles, rather than literal commands?

6. Where is the quotation in verse 38 from? What is the *lex talionis*?

7. What is Jesus' point in saying, "turn . . . the other [cheek]," "let him have your coat also," and "go with him two [miles]"?

8. How did the Jews think they could get by with hating their enemies?

9. What is the meaning of Jesus' injunction in verse 48, "you are to be perfect"?

CHAPTER 6

Living by Faith
Matthew 6:1–34

Preview:

In contrast to the moral issues presented in chapter 5, Jesus now examines certain issues that require faith in the life of a believer. Jesus assumes that his disciples will live righteously and in doing so will meet the needs of the poor, pray, and fast. It takes faith to give away money and pray to a God that you cannot see. It also takes faith to lay up treasures in heaven rather than on earth and to depend on God for all your daily needs.

True Spiritual Worship (6:1–7:12)

The nature of the true spiritual person previously described is now illustrated in acts of true spiritual worship as contrasted with traditional hypocritical worship. Again, Jesus goes beyond mere outward conformity to the law to the inward conviction of the spirit. The following examples are given to illustrate this point: giving, praying, fasting, and serving.

First Example: Almsgiving (6:1–4)

Jesus warns, "Beware of practicing your righteousness before men" (6:1) just to gain human recognition. That practical righteousness is in view is obvious. The one who does righteousness (or gives of his possessions, or even praying or fasting) "before men" merely "to be noticed by them" has "no reward" from the Father in heaven. True worship is to result from the desire to serve

God, not people, since pleasing God is far more important than pleasing people. Loss of reward is incurred by gaining the reward of human recognition as an end in itself. This does not mean that all human recognition is necessarily wrong. The implication of the text is simply that we are to serve the Lord because we love Him, not just because we desire something from Him.

Therefore, in all of our giving we are not to "sound a trumpet" (v. 2) before us in a hypocritical manner of drawing attention to ourselves. This metaphorical phrase means that we are not to "publicize" our righteousness, for such performers are "hypocrites" (from the Greek, "play actor"). Thus, Jesus warns against "acting like the hypocrites, whose aim is to win human praise . . . whose parade and pretense are spiritually futile."[1] Those who parade their righteousness through the streets receive the honor of people, and "they have their reward," meaning that God will add nothing extra to that reward. They have received all they are going to get, right here and now on this earth. There will be no future reward in heaven. But those who are willing to serve Him "in secret" (v. 4), God will reward openly.

The phrase "Do not let your left hand know what your right hand is doing" (v. 3) means that our giving of finances to the work of the Lord, while balanced to the needs of our family, also should be done so freely that our right hands cannot keep up with our left. We literally empty our pockets as fast as we can! At times giving is to be spontaneous. Notice that this passage does not state that it is wrong to give systematically, use church envelopes, or receive tax-deductible receipts. One thing it does teach is that one should not give by those means only. There are ample examples of systematic giving in Scripture to build or repair the temple and to provide for the needs of the underprivileged, for example. Planned giving is certainly biblical and encouraged, but all of our giving should not be limited to our predetermined plan or system. In addition, we are not to congratulate ourselves on how much we give, whether in relation to others, or just in our own mind. It is possible to give liberally but to be smug and satisfied that we have done our part or given so much. That is ruled out by Christ's admonition.

The real key to success of this kind of giving is found in the phrase "your Father who sees in secret will repay you" (v. 4). Giving by faith, out of a cheerful heart, depends on our total confidence in the fact that God does indeed see us and know our needs. God sees in secret that which no person may observe and rewards His own. The woman who gave her two mites gave not to be seen by people, but simply by God. The reason why she could give 100 percent of her income was because she had learned that God was able to supply 100 percent of her needs (Luke 21:1–4; cf. Mark 12:41–44). It took faith on her part to give while trusting God wholly. Christians likewise, are to give, not to receive rewards, but so that our love might be expressed to God who shall reward us. Our giving to the work of Christ spreads the message of the gospel throughout the world. Notice again that these verses certainly do not condemn public giving, but rather, speak against giving out of the wrong attitude and for the wrong motive.

Second Example: Praying (6:5–15)

Praying, like giving, is to be done unto the Lord, not unto people. Many professing Christians, if they were honest, would have to admit that they pray to be heard of men. Jesus said that the hypocrites of His day "love to stand and pray in the synagogues" (v. 5). Both a time and place for prayer were customary in the ancient Jewish synagogue (cf. Mark 11:25). Therefore, Jesus is not condemning the practice of public prayer, but the misuse of it! Because of the statement "go into your inner room," some have suggested that all public prayer is wrong. This would be contrary to the rest of the New Testament statements about prayer, commandments and restrictions regarding prayer, and examples of prayer meetings (cf. Acts 12:12; 1 Tim. 2:8). The idea of an inner room or "prayer closet" helps to remove distractions that would hinder the prayer life and allows the complete pouring out of one's heart to God.[2]

The principle here is also that believers should not make a show of prayer nor of the answers to prayer they receive in such a way as to call unnecessary attention to themselves. Again, it is the God who sees in secret who rewards us openly. Here the intimate father-child relationship between God and believers is clearly emphasized. It is the experience of private devotional prayer that ultimately prepares one to pray effectively in public. Most people who say they cannot pray in public do not pray effectively in private either!

Having a Quiet Time with the Lord

The believer should delight in God's law day and night (Ps. 1).

The soul should quietly wait to hear from the Lord (Ps. 62).

Daniel had a practice of regular prayer alone with the Lord (Dan. 6:10).

Christ urged His disciples to have time for private prayer (Matt. 6:6).

Christ spent time alone in prayer (Mark 6:46).

Jesus warned that we "do not use meaningless repetition" (the Greek *battalogeō* denotes babbling or speaking without thinking). Such praying was characteristic of the heathen. A good example of this is found in the ecstatic babblings of the false prophets in the Old Testament and in the prophets of Baal who confronted Elijah on Mount Carmel (cf. 1 Kgs. 18:26–29). Some religions spin a "prayer wheel" to make the prayers go around in a repetitive fashion. Jesus condemns the use of empty repetition as an attempt to overcome the will of God by wearing Him out. It is not the length of prayer, but the strength of prayer that prevails with God. Jesus Himself prayed all night prior to His crucifixion but on most other occasions prayed very briefly. He is not condemning lengthy prayers, although there may not be anything particularly spiritual about them. He is merely emphasizing that prayer must be a sincere expression of the heart, not mere accumulation of verbiage. God is not impressed with words, but with the genuine outcry of a needy heart.

Many have questioned the meaning of the statement "your Father knows what you need, before you ask Him" (v. 8). "Then why should we pray?" they ask. Prayer is not a human's attempt to change the will of God. God's method of changing our will is to bring it into conformity with His will. More than changing *things*, prayer changes *people*. Prayer is not conquering God's reluctance to answer, but laying hold of His willingness to help! Prayer, in the life of the true believer, is an act of total confidence and assurance in the plan and purpose of God. It is not an expression of panic and desperation.

The following sample prayer is given to the disciples as an example of a suitable prayer. It is neither lengthy nor irreverent. It contains a depth of piety and a pinnacle of power. This prayer, often called the "Lord's Prayer," is in reality a disciple's prayer, for Jesus gave it to His disciples as a sample of the true principle of spiritual prayer. In no way does the prayer itself embody all of His teaching about prayer. And certainly, having just warned against vain repetition, He did not intend for this particular prayer to be meaninglessness recited. This does not mean, however, that this prayer may not be recited as an act of public worship. Some Christians feel such recitation is too liturgical, while others feel that the omission of ever repeating this prayer is a failure to grasp its true significance. Certainly if we are to follow its example properly, we may benefit from repeating it as it was given by the Lord Himself. To place this prayer under law and eliminate it from Christian usage is to deny the great essence of what the prayer is all about.

The very beginning phrase, "Our Father," is uncommon to the prayers of the Old Testament. Martyn Lloyd-Jones has commented, "So when our Lord says, 'Our Father,' He is obviously thinking of Christian people, and that is why I say that this is a Christian prayer."[3] By contrast, see the ultra-dispensational approach of Arno Gaebelein, who refers to the Lord's Prayer as one of the rags of popery Luther brought with him from the Roman Catholic Church. He evaluates the church's use of the Lord's Prayer as "decidedly unchristian, nor can it be proven from the New Testament that it is intended for the church."[4]

The two major elements of the prayer are adoration and petition. "Hallowed be Thy name" addresses the attention of the prayer toward God and reverence for His name and His person. "Hallowed" (Greek, *hagiazō*) means to be held in reverence and awe of holiness. God's name was so sacred to the Old Testament Jew that human lips never pronounced it. Thus His name is the expression of His very essence. The biblical usage of the concept of a name is a characteristic description of the basic character of the person to whom the name is applied. To hallow God's name is to recognize the manifest excellence of His character. Since the prayer is directed to our spiritual Father, only a child of God who has been born again can rightly pray this prayer.

The phrase "Thy kingdom come" (v. 10) refers to the eschatological nature of this prayer. Notice that the kingdom is to be prayed for, implying that it has not already arrived. The kingdom represents the full and effective reign of God through the mediatorial office of the Messiah. The disciples were not to think of their own convenience as their foremost expression in prayer, but the full and quick realization of the effective rule of God on earth in the hearts of people. That rule is realized through the regenerating process of the new birth in the lives of individuals. It will reach its pinnacle when the last enemy (sin and death, 1 Cor. 15:24–28) has been destroyed at the Lord's return. The recognition of "Thy will be done" emphasizes the idea that prayer is to bring about the conformity of the will of the believer to the will of God. Prayer is an act of spiritual expression that brings us into conformity to the very nature and purpose of God.

The section of petitions begins with the request to "give us this day our daily bread." Bread (Greek, *artos*) may be applied to the provision of food in general (v. 11). The term "daily" (Greek, *epiousios*) denotes "indispensable."[5] The concept of daily provision of bread fits perfectly with the Old Testament example of the daily provision of manna to the Israelites while they were wandering in the wilderness (Ex. 16:14–15). In a similar sense, while the Christian pilgrim takes his journey through a strange land that he does not yet literally possess, but which has been promised to him, it only stands to reason that God would make a similar provision to this New Testament, gospel-age wanderer. We must also remember that the manna could only be used on the day it was given. Nothing remained for the next day. We cannot rely on yesterday's supply to meet today's needs, but we must spiritually meet with God every day to feast on a fresh provision.

The phrase "God forgive us our debts" (v. 12) refers to sins, which are our moral and spiritual debts to God's righteousness. The believer makes this request for forgiveness of sin. To be saved, one need not necessarily name all of his or her sins, but must confess that he or she is a sinner. For continued spiritual growth and cleansing, the believer acknowledges his or her sins in particular. Notice that we seek forgiveness "as we also have forgiven," not *because* we have forgiven. Our expression of forgiveness does not gain salvation for us. We are to seek forgiveness in the same manner as we forgive others. Forgiveness is the evidence of a regenerate heart.

"Do not lead us into temptation" (v. 13) is a plea for the providential help of God in our daily confrontation with the temptation of sin. James 1:13–14 makes it clear that God does not tempt us to do evil, but rather that we are tempted of our own lusts. However, God does test us in order to give us the opportunity to prove our faithfulness to Him. In both Hebrew and in Greek, the word for tempt is also the word for test. Abraham, for example, was asked by God to offer up his son, Isaac (Gen. 22:1; cf. KJV's "tempt" with NASB's "test"). From God's point of view, this was a test, to allow Abraham to obey and to be strengthened in the process. From Satan's viewpoint, it was a temptation to cause Abraham to fail. It is never God's desire to lead us unto evil itself. Therefore, if we resist the devil, we are promised that he will flee from us (James 4:7).

The prayer closes with a doxology of praise—"For thine is the kingdom [Greek, *basileia*] and the power [Greek, *dunamis*] and the glory [Greek, *doxa*], forever. Amen"—which may be a liturgical interpolation from 1 Chronicles 29:11. Though omitted in some manuscripts, these words constitute a fitting climactic affirmation of faith.

In the first three petitions of this prayer to the Lord, our soul rises directly to God; in the three following, we face the hindrances of these aspirations; and in the last petition, we discover the solution to all these difficulties. Rudolph Stier draws a unique parallel between the two tables of the Decalogue and the two sections of the Lord's Prayer.[6] In the first petition, the believer's soul is awed with the character of God; in the second petition, with His grand purpose; and in the third petition, with His moral condition. In the second part of the prayer, the children of God humble themselves in dependence upon divine mercy in the fourth petition. They seek forgiveness in the fifth petition; gracious guidance in the sixth petition; and deliverance from the power of evil in the seventh petition. Thus this arrangement may be readily suggested by dividing the prayer into two parts:

	*Hallowed be **Thy** Name*
Relationship to God:	***Thy** Kingdom come;*
	***Thy** will be done;*

Relationship to people:	*Give **us** this day our daily bread;*
	*Forgive **us** our debts;*
	*Lead **us** not into temptation;*
	*Deliver **us** from evil.*

Finally, the rich doxology expresses the certain hope that our prayers will be heard and that God, in view of His great character, will bring to pass the highest good in our lives. Thus prayer is the expression of the believer's confidence in the ultimate plan and purpose of God. J. P. Lange has suggested the following comparison between the statements of the Beatitudes and the petitions of the Lord's Prayer:[7]

Beatitudes	**Lord's Prayer**
Blessed are the poor in spirit: for theirs is the kingdom of heaven.	*Hallowed be thy name* (the name of God which opens to us the kingdom of heaven).
Blessed are those who mourn: for they shall be comforted.	*Thy kingdom come* (heavenly comfort into our hearts).
Blessed are the gentle, for they shall inherit the earth.	*Thy will be done on earth as it is in heaven.* (this meekness, the characteristic of heaven, shall possess the new earth).
Blessed are those who hunger and thirst for righteousness, for they shall be satisfied.	*Give us this day our daily bread.*
Blessed are the merciful, for they shall receive mercy.	*Forgive us our debts as we forgive our debtors.*
Blessed are the pure in heart, for they shall see God.	*And lead us not into temptation.*
Blessed are the peacemakers.	*But deliver us from evil.*

The comparison between these two pinnacles of piety is striking indeed. The inexhaustible expression of devotion and simplicity of language in both the Beatitudes and the Sermon on the Mount give them depth of expression that goes beyond the temporal and touches the eternal.

Jesus next turns our attention to the importance of forgiveness. "If you forgive men. . . . But if you do not forgive men" (vv. 14–15). These two verses have caused consternation among some of God's people. Is Jesus saying that an unforgiving person cannot be saved? Yes, basically He is! If someone cannot forgive others, Jesus says, it proves that he has never really experienced the true forgiveness of God in his own life. Likewise, if one is really saved, he knows God's forgiveness and cleansing in such a personal way that he cannot refuse to forgive others for their faults.

Third Example: Fasting (6:16–18)

"Whenever you fast" (v. 16) is a reference both to fasting prescribed under the Mosaic Law in connection with the Day of Atonement (Lev. 16:29–30) and the voluntary fast of Jesus' day. Jesus assumed that His disciples would fast. But the Pharisees added two fast days, on Monday and Thursday of each week, as a case of public display and piety. The true purpose of fasting was intended, however, for deep contrition and spiritual communion. Fasting was especially emphasized as an effective means of dealing with temptation (cf. Isa. 58:6). The Pharisees regarded the practice of fasting as meritorious (cf. *Taanith* 8:3) and appeared in the synagogues negligently attired. Their sad disfigurement of face and the wearing of mourning garb gave them an opportunity to exhibit their superior ascetic sanctity before the people. The phrase "put on a gloomy face" (Greek, *aphanizō*) literally denotes covering their faces and is a figurative expression for mournful gestures and neglected appearance of those wanting to call attention to the fact they are enduring. This was often done with dust and ashes (cf. Isa. 61:3) and is similar to the modern Roman Catholic concept of Ash Wednesday. In the original, there is a play upon two cognate words meaning, "they make their faces unappearable," that they may "appear unto men."

This passage is not to be taken as a command against fasting but rather against the misuse of the spiritual exercise of fasting. Kent observes: "Fasting that requires spectators is mere acting."[8] Though Jesus Himself instituted no fast for His disciples, voluntary fasting does appear in the early churches (cf. Acts 13:2). The injunction to "anoint your head" relates to the ancient custom of anointing one's head when going to a feast. In other words, Jesus was saying that when we fast we are to do so secretly unto the Lord, while outwardly maintaining the appearance of joy and triumph which is the end result of true fasting.

Just as we have observed some interesting parallels within this sermon, so again we discover the contrast between outward acts of worship and inward attitudes of devotion. Outward worship stresses giving while inward worship stresses surrender. Outward worship manifests praying; inward worship manifests trust. Outward worship is characterized by fasting; inward worship is characterized by judging oneself.

Outward Worship	Inward Worship
Focused in Jerusalem (Acts 8:27).	Focused on the Father's desire that people worship Him (John 4:23).
Often done on festive occasions (John 12:20).	True worship is in spirit and in truth (John 4:24).
Often brings people to fall on their knees (Mark 15:19).	True worship is making melody in the heart (Eph. 5:19).
Believers share in worship by speaking psalms and hymns to one another (Eph. 5:19).	True believers worship by means of the Spirit of God (Phil. 3:3).

The obvious contrasts are that a proper attitude toward giving will arise from the proper inward attitude toward one's possessions. Praying will resolve all worrying. Fasting, in judging oneself, is to be preferred over judging others.

Fourth Example: Giving (6:19–24)

The common error of Judaism was to regard material wealth as always indicating the blessing of God. While it is true that the book of Proverbs promises material blessings to those who honor God's financial principles, it does not imply that all wealth is a necessary sign of blessing. The Proverbs themselves indicate that many become temporarily wealthy because of ill-gotten gain. The contrast between these two sections of examples, both inward and outward, is directed specifically at the false spirituality of the Pharisees that arose from worldly-mindedness.

Because the false spirituality of people causes them to lay up treasures for themselves in a worldly sense, they "have their reward." Thus their desire to be seen by others and to lay up treasures through the outward attention of others, as if some self-meritorious work could make them more acceptable to God and others, is provoked by their wrong attitude toward material possessions in the first place. Therefore, "treasures upon earth" are temporary and of short duration. These earthly possessions are at the mercy of "moth and rust . . . and . . . thieves" (v. 19). Even if temporal possessions escape the clutches of the marauder, they are still likely to become moth-eaten and rusty. In other words, they do not last. Our materialistic technological society in the twenty-first century all too often has overlooked the simplicity of this truth. Our attention to wealth, possessions, social status, and retirement benefits too easily causes us to trust that which humans can provide rather than that which God has already provided. Simple appreciation of the natural provisions of God is frequently neglected in favor of the plastic provisions of our contemporary technology.

"Lay up for yourselves" (vv. 20–21) is an injunction to prioritize our "treasures." There is nothing wrong with laying up treasures for yourself. Jesus specifically advises one to do so in verse 20. The location of the treasure, however, is of the utmost importance. The attention of the believer is directed toward "treasures in heaven." Laying up "treasures" implies the addition or accumulation of things. The two kinds of treasures are conditioned by their place (either on earth or in heaven). The concept of laying up treasure in heaven is not pictured as one of meritorious benefits but rather of rewards for faithful service, as is illustrated elsewhere in the teaching of Jesus. The ultimate destiny of our lives is either earthly or heavenly, and the concentration of our efforts will reveal where our real treasure is. In contrast to the legalistic attempt of Judaism to establish a spiritual treasure on earth, Jesus calls the attention of His disciples to that true and eternal treasure that is heavenly. The only way humans will ever overcome their natural inclination toward materialism and wealth is to place the priority of their possessions in heaven. If one were as concerned about spiritual benefits of his life as about material possessions, his motivations would be pure indeed.

One of the most important things a pastor can encourage his people to do is to give of their means to God's work. The reason for this is that wherever your treasure is (either here on earth, or in heaven) "there will your heart be also" (v. 21). Heavenly minded people are so because they have assets there. If our treasure remains in our wallets or bank accounts, houses, cars or stocks and bonds, then that is exactly where our hearts will be also.

The "lamp of the body" is associated with the eye (v. 23). The concept here is based on the ancient idea that the eyes are the windows through which light enters the body. If the eyes are in good condition the body can receive such light. R. V. G. Tasker notes that Jesus, using this language metaphorically, affirms that if man's sight is healthy and his affections directed toward heavenly treasure, his whole personality would be without blemish.[9] The phrase "if . . . your eye is clear" indicates devotion to one purpose. The "single eye" refers to a single, fixed vision or goal. This reminds us of James's warning, "Let not that man [who doubts] expect that he will receive anything from the Lord, being a double-minded man, unstable in all his ways" (James 1:8). The phrase "if your eye is bad" refers to either disease or deception of vision.

Though many commentators suggest the idea of disease, the context seems to imply deception. The bad or "evil" eye (KJV) is not necessarily something mysterious or devilish, but rather a deceptive vision that causes the viewer to mistake the identity of an object. The mistake in this context is the darkening of the mind, and thus "how great is the darkness!"

Spiritual double vision causes one to believe that he can "serve two masters" (v. 24). Total loyalty to God cannot be divided between Him and loyalty to one's material possessions. A master (Greek, *kurios*) is a lord or an owner. That God claims total lordship over His own is obvious in this passage. The concept of the lordship of Christ has often been greatly mistaken. Even in the face of immediate denial on the part of His disciples, Jesus said to them: "You call Me Teacher and Lord; and you are right; for so I am" (John 13:13). There is no passage or command anywhere in the New Testament asking the believer to make Christ "Lord of his life" after salvation. The very experience of receiving Christ as Savior is looked upon throughout the Scriptures as an acknowledgment of lordship and ownership. If perfect obedience were required to make Christ our Lord, He would be the Lord of no one! It is the fact that He is already Lord that makes our disobedience so serious. As Lord and Master, He has the right to demand complete obedience. My disobedience as a believer is an act of sin against His lordship. The sin of a believer does not negate the lordship of Christ any more than it does His saviorhood.

Therefore, Jesus rightly proclaimed, "You cannot serve God and mammon." "Mammon" is derived from the Aramaic term for possessions or wealth. Jesus is not condemning money or possessions in and of themselves, but the improper attitude of enslavement toward wealth. His point here cannot be overemphasized in light of the affluent society of our day. Outside the boundaries of North America, the average Christian knows much more of the reality of poverty than we do. Within the depth of this message and its application, we may certainly see afresh that it is the "gospel of the poor."

Double-mindedness is an attempt to sit on the fence in relation to spiritual matters. There is no halfhearted service for God; we give all or nothing. Jesus gives the believer no option between loving God and loving the world. The regenerated heart is one that so longs for righteousness and desires the things of heaven that it lives above the temporal things of the earth. Why did God command Moses that any future king of Israel was not to "multiply wives for himself . . . nor shall he greatly increase silver and gold for himself"? (Deut. 17:17). The answer in that text is "lest his heart turn away." Jesus was warning about the same issue.

Fifth Example: Worry or Anxiety (6:25-34)

Adding doubt to the danger of possessions, Jesus now deals with the equally dangerous tendency of those who have no possessions: worry! The Greek word (*merimnaō*) means simply "do not be anxious" (v. 25). Three times Jesus gives a command to refrain from unhealthy anxiety (vv. 25, 31, 34). Floyd Filson notes that this word means to be so disturbed about material needs that we distrust God and are distracted from faithfully doing His will.[10] The implication of the text is that worrying about material and temporal things is the source of all anxiety. Such anxiety causes one to avoid the responsibility of work, which is in cooperation with God's way of making provision for us.

Anxious care is an inordinate or solicitous concern of grief about things beyond our immediate needs. It is the direct opposite of carefulness, cautiousness, and faith. Therefore, even the poor are not to worry needlessly about what they should eat, drink, or wear. The question, "Is not life more than food, and the body than clothing?" Indicates that inner mental stability must come from the spirit of a person and not from outward physical provisions. To set one's heart on material possessions or to worry about the lack of them is to live in perpetual insecurity and to deprive oneself of the spiritual blessings of God.

Jesus illustrated His point by referring to objects in nature that were immediately at hand: the birds of the air and the flowers of the field. Though the birds that fly through the skies appear not to labor, "your heavenly Father feeds them" (v. 26). How does God accomplish this? He does it through the normal process of nature. The question of adding a cubit to your life's span has been taken in several ways. Worry and anxiety are related to the length of one's life in this phrase. A cubit is a measurement of about eighteen inches. However, this reference is probably not to one's actual height, but to the length of one's life. The term "stature" (Greek, *helikia*) may in this place mean "age." Thus the idea seems to be that a man cannot add the smallest measure to the span of his life by worrying. In fact, modern medicine would tell us that worry actually shortens one's life. The New American Standard Bible note says, "Or, *height*." Most modern translations render the entire phrase idiomatically as referring to length of life. Thus we find, "a single hour to his life" (NIV), "a single day to your life" (REB), and "a single hour to his span of life" (ESV). The King James Version, New King James Version, New Jerusalem Bible, and New American Standard Bible note keep the literality of "cubit" and "stature." There the idea would be that God adds several cubits to the length of a newborn baby, but no one would think that by anxious care he could add that much to his normal height.

Jesus urges us to "observe how the lilies of the field grow" (v. 28); they appear to do nothing for themselves, yet God, through the processes of nature, which He controls, "arrays the grass of the field" (v. 30). Even Solomon, the great and wealthy king of Israel, was not arrayed in any greater beauty than the flowers of the field that God has made.

The key point of this passage is found in the phrases "Are you not worth much more than they?" (v. 26) and "Will He not much more do so for you . . . ?" (v. 30). The Bible makes it clear that God is the creator and sustainer of nature. He is not divorced from the world He has made. Indeed, "this is my Father's world"! This state of anxiety is related to having "little faith" (v. 30). Faith is total confidence in the provision of God. Faith in salvation is a total trusting of the complete work of Christ on the cross on our behalf. Scripture reminds: "Whatever is not from faith is sin" (Rom. 14:23). Therefore, a lack of faith will lead to a life of psychological anxiety. Since this lack of faith is identified with sin, Jay Adams is correct in asserting that most of humankind's emotional problems stem from their sin.[11] In the Sermon on the Mount, we have then, not only a directive for spiritual well being, but a manual for mental health as well.

Jesus assures us that our "heavenly Father knows" exactly what we need. The fact that God knows our needs should bring us comfort. But this does not relieve us of the responsibility of asking Him to provide our daily bread or of thanking Him when it comes. Matthew Henry once said that no matter who brings it, it is God who sends it.

This portion of the Sermon on the Mount is summarized by the statement "seek first His kingdom" (v. 33). The disciples who have pledged their allegiance to the King must continue seeking the kingdom and its righteousness. The present imperative form of the verb (Greek, *zēteō*) indicates a continual or constant seeking. The word first indicates one's first and ever dominant concern. The contrast between the spiritual and the material is again emphasized. The believer is to seek first the righteousness that is characteristic of God's kingdom and then "all these things" (i.e., material things) shall be added unto him.

Seeking the kingdom of God involves a continued hunger and thirst after righteousness. We are not only to seek the kingdom of God in the sense that we set our affections on things above, but we must also positively seek holiness in righteousness. The continual seeking here is similar to that of seeking the face of God. A true believer is never content with what he or she has in Christ, but is continually seeking to know Him better. Thus, we could say, "Keep seeking the kingdom of God," and as you do He will continually provide your needs. When our priority is spiritual, God will take care of the material, for where God guides, He provides. We need not even worry about tomorrow, for "each day has enough trouble of its own" (v. 34). This means that each day has its own troubles and challenges to be responsibly handled, without worrying about the hypothetical problems that could arise tomorrow. God is ever pictured in Scripture as the God of the present. "Now is 'the acceptable time,' behold, now is 'the day of salvation' " (2 Cor. 6:2). Walking with God is a moment-by-moment and day-by-day experience as we grow in grace and Christian maturity.

Study Questions

1. In verses 2, 5, and 16, Jesus assumes that His disciples will do what three things?

2. What are the possible meanings for "sound a trumpet" when someone is in the process of giving to God?

3. Does Jesus say anything about the proper posture for prayer in verse 5, or was standing just the custom of the day?

4. Why is secret prayer more important than prayer that is seen and heard by others?

5. Is the Lord's Prayer something that one should try to pray or recite every day, or is it a pattern for the types of things we should be concerned about in our prayers? Explain.

6. Verse 14 sounds very strict. What do you believe is the essence of Jesus' teaching in this verse? What is Jesus saying about someone's ability to forgive another?

7. Is fasting for today? For what reasons might one fast? Should you tell anyone else that you are fasting, or should it be between you and God?

8. What is the difference between earthly treasures and heavenly treasures? Describe what kinds of things would be in each category.

9. Could verse 21 be paraphrased, "If your treasure is on earth, your heart will be there too; and if your treasure is in heaven, that is where your heart will be also"? Explain.

10. Explain how worry is forbidden in verses 25–34. Have you memorized Matthew 6:33? If not, do so now.

CHAPTER 7

Two Choices
Matthew 7:1-29

Preview:
In this final portion of the Sermon on the Mount, Jesus contrasts the two lifestyles, ways, and even destinies of which He is speaking. There is a difference between a judgmental attitude and a prayerful manner. There is a narrow way and a broad way, ending up in two very different places. There is good fruit and bad fruit, a wise builder and a foolish builder. Jesus wants His hearers to see that a decision must be made as to which choice they will make.

Donald Carson notes that Jesus gives three warnings before he drives home the alternatives people must chose in light of His teaching. He notes, "The first two are cast in negative terms—we are not to be judgmental (7:1–5) and yet we are not to be undiscriminating (7:6). The third is formulated positively: We must persist in our pursuit of God (7:7–11).[1]

Sixth Example: Judging Others (7:1–12)

"Do not judge" refers to an unfavorable and condemnatory judgment. It is the final kind of judgment that only a well-qualified judge can give. This does not mean that a Christian should never render judgment of any kind under any circumstances. The New Testament Scriptures are filled with exhortations to "keep your eye on those who cause dissensions and hindrances contrary to the teaching which you learned" (Rom. 16:17); and "do not receive him into your house" (2John 1:10) if he denies Christ. Judging ourselves and those who have failed in their spiritual responsibility is a necessity of church discipline (cf. 1 Cor. 5). In fact, this very passage commands us not to "give what is holy to dogs" (v. 6), and to "beware of the false prophets, who come to you in sheep's clothing" (v. 15).

We must exercise discernment but not be judgmental. The point being made here is that we are not to judge the inner motives of another. We are not to render a verdict based upon prejudiced information. Nor are we to use ourselves as the standard of judgment, for "in the way you judge," you shall be judged. If we were judged in eternity merely on the basis of the verbal judgments we have rendered to others, we would all be condemned! "Lest you be judged yourselves" seems to refer to the ultimate judgment of God rather than our own judgment. The terms "speck" (Greek, *karphos*) and "log" (Greek, *dokos*) are used metaphorically for a small fault and a great fault. The mote was literally a small speck of sawdust, whereas the beam was literally a rafter used in building. Thus the idea of the text is that one cannot remove the speck from his brother's eye until he has removed the rafter from his own eye!

"You hypocrite" (v. 5) is the only statement that can be made for this play actor who pretends to be a physician when he himself is sick. Floyd Filson comments, "His concern to criticize and reform others is marred by uncritical moral complacency as to his own life."[2] The "dogs" and "swine" refer to those who have deliberately rejected the message of truth. These particular animals were especially repulsive to Jesus' audience. The connotation in verse 6 is not that we should not present our message to those who are the outcasts of society, for Jesus Himself went to the poor sinners among His people. Rather, the idea is that it is futile to continue to present truth to those who have refused what they have already heard. People cannot appreciate new truth until they have responded to the truth they have already received. Since the context deals with the matter of discernment and judgment, it may rightly be assumed that there is a proper place for such activity in the Christian's life. The main difference between judgment and discernment is that a judge merely pronounces a verdict, while discernment seeks a solution.

Earlier a paralleling contrast was drawn between the outward acts of worship (giving, praying, fasting) and the inward attitudes of devotion (possessing, praying, judging). It seems fitting that Jesus here makes a lengthy statement on the importance of prayer. This statement is not out of place as some have assumed; rather, it is the Christian alternative to judging. If we would sincerely pray for those whom we are prone to criticize, we would ultimately do them much more good. The three imperatives "Ask, seek, knock" are in the present tense in the original, suggesting both perseverance and frequent prayer. In the English language the first letter of each word forms the acronym ASK. Fervent and continual prayer is to be made on behalf of those for whom we are concerned.

Judgment	Discernment
Judgment is passing sentence on someone's actions	Discernment is making a decision on what may be right or wrong.
One must be careful in passing judgment (Matt. 7:2)	To be mature is to discern between good and evil (Heb. 5:14).
One who judges may also become condemned (Rom. 2:1)	To lack discernment is to be weak in faith (James 1:6).
There is a proper time for judgment (1 Cor. 4:5)	Discernment is needed to decide on doubtful things (Rom. 14:23).

God promises to answer all genuine prayer (v. 8). Everything that we need for spiritual success has been promised to us. God leaves us no excuse for failure. "Ask, and it shall be given to you; seek, and you shall find; knock, and it shall be opened to you," for everyone that does such will receive an answer. You are not cut off in any way from the blessings and provisions of God, for these are available to every one of His children.

Jesus illustrated His point by comparing the willingness of a human father to give his child a gift with our heavenly Father's eagerness to give us what we need. The term "evil" (v. 11) is used here of humankind's sinful nature. Even sinful men are kind to their children; therefore, "how much more" shall your heavenly Father delight to answer your prayers. Hence, rather than judging others, we are to treat them as we would like to be treated.

The statement in verse 12, "Therefore, however you want people to treat you, so treat them," is the biblical injunction that has often been called the Golden Rule. Similar statements are found in both Jewish and Gentile sources, but usually in the negative form, such as "Don't do to others what you would not want to be done to you." Following this negative injunction would result in people "not doing anything." Jesus' positive rule results in people being proactive and taking the first step in showing others kindness, helpfulness, and good deeds.

The phrase "this is the Law and the Prophets" indicates that the statement made here by Jesus is not intended to be unique, but rather a summarization of the second table of the Law. Verse 12 is not intended to be a total summary of Jesus' teaching and in no way exhausts or explains the gospel itself. An atheist could readily accept this statement by itself, but it would not get him to heaven. However, it is when we see this statement in the context of everything that Jesus taught that we understand its true significance. Rather than judge others, we ought to pray for them. If we would rather have people pray for us than criticize us, then we ought to be willing to do the same for them.

The Two Alternatives: Character Established (7:13–27)

The closing section of the Sermon on the Mount presents two choices to the listener. These are presented in a series of contrasts: two ways (vv. 13–14), two trees (vv. 15–20), two professions (vv. 21–23), and two foundations (vv. 24–29). This was a common method of teaching in both Jewish and Greco-Roman thought. Donald Carson comments, "The discipleship which Jesus requires is absolute; radical in the sense that it gets to the root of human conduct and to the root of relationships between God and man."[3]

"Enter by the narrow gate" (v. 13) means that one must come through the restricted passage of the narrow gate in order to reach the path that leads to eternal life. The order of the gate first and then the way suggests the gate is the entrance by faith in Christ unto the way of the Christian life. It is interesting to recall that Christians were first called those of "the Way" (cf. Acts 9:2; 19:9; 22:4; 24:14). Though the many are on the broad way, it only "leads to destruction" (eternal death). The gate that leads to life is so narrow that "few are those who find it." Christ Himself is both the gate and the way (cf. John 14:6), and God enables people to find that gate (cf. John 6:44). In the immediate context of Jesus' day, it could be assumed that His way was presented as that which is narrow and the way of the Pharisees as that which is broad. The contrast here is between the way of grace and the way of works. There are many on the broad road of life who are seeking to arrive in heaven by means of their own works, but only a few have received the grace of God that guarantees them heaven. We are reminded of Jesus' statement, "Many are called, but few are chosen" (22:14).

The warning "Beware of the false prophets" (v. 15) fits appropriately with the concept of the two ways. Since many are being led in the wrong way, it is obvious that wrong prophets are leading them. False prophets were prevalent in the Old Testament, whereas God's true prophets were often in the minority (as in Elijah's confrontation with the prophets of Baal). These false prophets appear in "sheep's clothing" but are in reality "ravenous wolves." This is a perfect description of those preachers who have denied or distorted the truth of the gospel. They look like lambs but they act like wolves. Their description is similar to that of the great false prophet in Revelation 13:11.

A true test of a prophet was the conformity of his doctrine to that of the Scripture (cf. 1 Cor. 14:37; Deut. 13:1–5). "Their fruits" not only refer to actions of their lives, but to the doctrines they proclaim. Having warned us against falsely judging others, Jesus now must remind us to beware and know such people. We are to be discerning enough not to be taken in by their cleverness.

The two trees are contrasted in relation to the fruit they produce. The searching question, "Grapes are not gathered from thorn bushes . . . are they?" reminds us of the origin of spiritual life that produces spiritual fruit. People cannot produce such fruit out of their own unregenerate nature. Because they are sinners by nature, they are sinners by choice. Not only must his choice be changed, but so also must his nature in order for him to make the right choice. "Every good tree bears good fruit" consistently, while a "rotten tree bears bad fruit" continually. Therefore, the normal and consistent production of fruit, whether good or evil, in a person's life will bear evidence whether or not that life is of God. Verse 19 makes it clear that the unfruitful life is a picture of the unregenerate that is "thrown into the fire." The term "fire" is used as an apparent picture of eternal punishment in hell. Those who reject the idea of literal fire in hell might think about this: the universe is mostly empty space, punctuated by great balls of fire.

The "rotten" (Greek, *sapros*) trees are quite useless. While the production of fruit in the life of a Christian may vary, some thirtyfold, some one hundredfold, no true Christian has the option of producing no fruit at all. No fruit means no life. The absence of life is the absence of the regenerating power of the Holy Spirit. Thus, the fruitless life is the proof of an unregenerate heart that can only be cast into hell. Always in the New Testament the changed life is the proof of one's profession of conversion (cf. 2 Cor. 5:17).

Not everyone professing Christ is genuinely saved. Even the outward verbal acknowledgment of His lordship is not enough in itself to save an unbeliever apart from true repentance and faith. A genuinely saved person is "he who does the will of My Father," the Greek present tense meaning that he is continually living in obedience to the will of God as the normal course of his life. He may fail at times, but his general course of consistency is to obey the will of the Father.[4] It is tragic to note that many will proclaim in that day, "Lord, Lord," and yet will be lost. On what do they base their profession? Their performance of "many miracles" causes them to think that they have attained salvation, yet the response of Christ, pictured here as the Judge, will be "I never knew you, depart from me, you who practice lawlessness." Those who are continually living in sin, as the normal course of their lives, have no assurance of salvation whatever. This does not mean that one must experience basic and initial changes in one's life to validate his claim to conversion. The phrase "practice lawlessness" is also progressive in Greek (i.e., they continue to work their iniquity).

In drawing His concluding illustration of the two foundations, Jesus begins with the word "Therefore" (v. 24). On the basis of all that He has taught and illustrated, He concludes that all who both hear and do His sayings will be saved. He is not adding works to faith, but, as James reminds us, He is showing faith by its works (James 2:17–18). Faith is the root of salvation, and works are its fruit. The works of man do not produce his own salvation. In fact, to the contrary, this entire message shows that human efforts alone are futile in gaining salvation. Having made His point, Jesus also clearly stated that while salvation is by faith, it is by a faith that shows itself in a changed life. This is a repentant faith, a life-changing faith, and a faith that works!

Building a Life on a Good Foundation

Christ's words are like a rock-solid foundation (Luke 6:48–49).

Christ is the only foundation for the Christian (1 Cor. 3:11).

The believer's good works are a treasure on a good foundation (1 Tim. 6:19).

Believers rest on God's firm foundation (2 Tim. 2:19).

The church is built on the foundation of the apostles (Eph. 2:20).

The contrast here is threefold: the wise man is the one who hears Jesus' sayings and practices them by building upon a foundation of rock; the foolish man does not practice these sayings and thus is building upon a foundation of sand. As a great master counselor, Jesus reminded His listeners that hearing this message alone would not change their lives. They must both hear and do what Jesus has said. The elements of the closing illustration are drawn from the simplicity of nature itself, the rock, the rain, and the winds. The rain (Greek, *brochē*) pictured here is that of a natural storm. However, it is implied as relating to the troubles and persecutions of life. The man whose house collapsed was at fault, not because he failed to labor, but because he did not lay the proper foundation. How lively must this imagery have been to an audience accustomed to the fierceness of an eastern tempest and the suddenness and completeness with which it sweeps everything unsteady before it! The sand represents human opinion and doctrines as opposed to "these words" (v. 28).

The entire Sermon on the Mount is addressed to believers and presupposes faith in Jesus as Messiah. The works that are done by believers are not based on themselves but on the rock (v. 24), which is Christ Himself (1 Cor. 10:4). He is the personal embodiment of all of His teachings. Thus, when He had finished the discourse, "the multitudes were amazed." R. C. H. Lenski notes that as Jesus spoke, crowds were in rapt attention, but when He ceased, attention relaxed and shocking amazement engulfed them.[5]

The outstanding feature of Jesus' teaching was His "authority" (Greek, *exousian*), meaning the divine approval and authoritative constraint with which He delivered His message. Such straightforward preaching, based on the depth of one's own life, was in direct contrast to that of the scribes. The scribes were the copyists of the law and the theologians of their day. The scribes had to rely on tradition for their authority, whereas Christ was His own authority. This undoubtedly disturbed the Pharisees, for He had no approval as an official teacher in their system. The Pharisees and Sadducees had to content themselves with quoting the opinions of tradition, as in Matthew 19, where they alluded to the opinions of Hillel and Shammai. Jesus, however, spoke as if He personally knew what He was talking about, because He did!

The note of authority in the Sermon on the Mount warns the readers of Matthew's gospel that they cannot ignore or reject Jesus' teaching without ruinous consequences. Why should we practice this sermon? Because of the beauty of its diction, its impressive pictures, its striking illustrations? No, we practice it because, beyond its moral, ethical, and spiritual teaching is the person of the Preacher Himself! In the closing verses of this chapter, we see that, without an ostentatious parade, our Lord calls attention to Himself as the focal point of the entire message. This is no mere restatement of the law but is the highest expression of the quality of Christian living that Christ alone can produce. The gospel is the message of the person and work of Jesus Christ. Its amazing "good news" is that He can do for us what we cannot do for ourselves. He can change a sinner into a saint!

Study Questions

1   How do we square Jesus' "do not judge" in verse 1 with the commands in verses 6 and 15 that require quite a bit of judgment? What distinctions are implied here?

2.   How is verse 7 to be seen as the ASK verse of the Bible?

3.   What do verses 13–14 tell us about how many people in this world are really saved?

4. How is one able to discern between true and false prophets?

5. Have you noticed that the key to knowing Jesus in verse 21 is not "saying," but rather "doing"?

6. According to verses 22–23, is it possible that some will prophesy, cast out demons, and perform miracles in Jesus' name, yet still end up in hell? How can this be?

7. Outwardly, in verses 24–27 the difference between the wise and foolish builders was their choice of foundations, but what did Jesus say was the real difference? Compare the two and try to think of what the differences are in terms of belief and actions.

8. What was the difference between Jesus' teaching "as one having authority," and that of the "scribes"?

CHAPTER 8

Power of the King
Matthew 8:1-34

Preview:

Matthew groups many of Jesus' miracles in the following three chapters. Certainly readers would be impressed with the five remarkable stories of healings and power over nature in this chapter. In rapid succession, Jesus heals a leprous man, a Roman centurion's servant, and Peter's mother in law, then stills the wind and the sea before casting some wicked demons out of a desperate man.

The Cleansing of a Leper (8:1-4)

The first miracle Matthew records is that of the healing of a leper who insisted, "You can make me clean" (v. 1). According to the Law of Moses, ceremonial uncleanness was attributed to leprosy (see Lev. 13:45-46). "He . . . touched him," which, instead of bringing uncleanness to Jesus, caused the total cleansing of the leper! The purpose of Jesus in giving the command "See that you tell no one," was to call attention away from the miracle itself and to appeal to the spiritual need in man. It is clear in the gospel accounts that the crowds were often attracted by Jesus' miracles but not always by His message. In addition, if he were to broadcast the means by which he had been made whole, there might be a prejudice against him when he reached the priest, the one who was to examine him and pronounce him clean. Jesus' command "Show yourself to the priest" was in obedience to the Mosaic Law regarding cleansing. He told the cleansed leper to "present the offering that Moses prescribed." These gifts are found in Leviticus 14:2-32, where they are typical of Christ's atonement and the cleansing it provided. By "for a testimony to them," Jesus meant that the offering would be evidence to the priest that the leper had indeed been cleansed. This would be a startling witness to the miraculous nature of Christ's appearing, because the average leper did not grow better with time, but only worse. The disease was practically incurable.[1] Therefore, the miracle was even more dramatic.

The Healing of the Centurion's Servant (8:5–13)

The story of the Roman centurion focuses on a Gentile who was impressed with Jesus' power and authority. Such recognition by a Gentile would have been rare in those days. A "centurion" (v. 5) was a rank between that of an officer and a noncommissioned officer (somewhat equivalent to that of a modern sergeant-major). It was a position of great responsibility in the Roman occupation force. The centurion's "servant" (Greek, *pais*), may mean either child or servant. In any case, he was dear to him, and his devotion was the kind of concern a father would show for a son. To be "paralyzed" was what we call palsy, but it included much pain and discomfort. "Servant" in verse 9 means "slave" (Greek, *doulos*). The centurion was impressed with Jesus, whom he likened to himself as one "under authority." He recognized that in dealing with the realm of sickness and death, Jesus had all the power of God behind Him. Jesus was not only *an* authority, He was *the* authority, able to simply speak and have His will carried out.

Jesus had come across a man with powerful faith—a Gentile! His declaration that He had "not found such great faith with anyone" in Israel (v. 10) must have been both depressing and encouraging at the same time. Israel was spiritually cold, but here was a Gentile who exhibited the kind of faith Christ desired. The words "from east and west," are taken from Psalm 107 (with allusions also to Isa. 49:12; 59:19; Mal. 1:11). Here Christ is referring to the gathering in of the Gentiles through the preaching of the gospel, culminating in their final gathering at the time of His second coming.

To "Sit down," means to recline (Greek, *anaklinō*) to eat. It was customary in those days to recline at meals, resting on one's left elbow. There are also references to this ancient custom in the great banquet parables of the wedding feast of our Lord (see 22:1–14). "The sons of the kingdom" are those to whom the kingdom really belongs. The natural claim to that kingdom had been given to the Jews. Their reception of Christ as Messiah could potentially have brought in the kingdom that had been promised by the Old Testament prophets. However, their eventual rejection of the Messiah caused the postponement of a literal kingdom on earth.

"Outer darkness" refers to the condemnation of the second death. "There shall be weeping and gnashing of teeth" refers to the severity of eternal punishment. "There" is used emphatically to draw attention to the fact that such severe punishment is in fact a reality. Even though he was a Gentile, the servant was healed because of the centurion's faith. The healing was instantaneous and complete. The contrast to this incident drawn by Jesus emphasized the foolishness of Israel's rejection of Him as Messiah.

The Healing of Peter's Mother-in-Law (8:14–17)

The reference to Peter's mother-in-law indicates that he was married, not celibate as Roman Catholics claim. She was "lying" (Greek, *ballō*, lit., "to be laid out or sick in bed") in Peter's house. Mark indicates that Andrew, James, and John were also present. In those days a bed was generally a mattress placed on the floor. "The fever left her; and she arose" indicates two miracles: (1) the fever was gone, and (2) her strength had returned. A fever always leaves one exhausted and worn out. Instead, she "waited on Him." She was apparently thankful to Jesus and wanted to return something for His generosity and mercy.

Jesus is then described as casting out "the spirits" (i.e., evil spirits, meaning demons or devils). Demons are not the departed spirits of human beings, but fallen angels. Revelation 12:4 speaks of Satan's fall from heaven, and the symbolism indicates that he took a large portion of the heavenly host with him. Matthew refers to these evil fallen beings as "the devil and his angels," as bound for "eternal fire" (Matt. 25:41). The gospel accounts are filled with incidents of demon activity and even resistance to the ministry of Christ. His power over their influence further vindicates His divine messiahship. After word spread of Christ's healing of Peter's mother-in-law, crowds gathered bearing other sick people. Jesus "healed all who were ill." Jesus' miraculous word and touch were for all. None was refused. None returned as he or she had been. All who met Him personally were transformed.

"Spoken through Isaiah" (v. 17) points to the following statement from Isaiah 53:4. Isaiah, like other prophets, spoke by means of the Holy Spirit (see Acts 1:16; 28:25; 2 Pet. 1:21). He said, "He himself took our infirmities, and carried away our diseases." Physical healing is not part of the gospel, and those who obtain salvation are not automatically healed of their diseases. Homer Kent notes that this indicates that these healings were only a partial fulfillment of what would be accomplished by Christ on the cross, when He would deal with the cause of physical sicknesses—sin itself.[2]

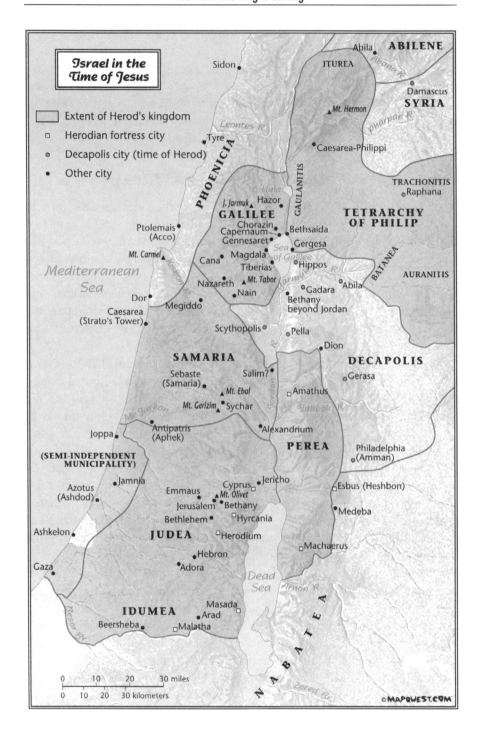

Israel in the Time of Jesus

☐ Extent of Herod's kingdom
☐ Herodian fortress city
☉ Decapolis city (time of Herod)
• Other city

The Calming of the Storm (8:18–27)

To get away from the crowds and be alone with His disciples, Jesus gave the order for them to set sail across the Sea of Galilee (v. 18). This lake is about eight miles wide and twelve miles long, and it sits seven hundred feet below sea level and is surrounded by mountains that reach to over three thousand feet in elevation. Cold air from the mountains often rushes down onto the warm sea, creating a sudden storm. To this day, storms may arise without warning on this otherwise tranquil setting.

The reference to a "certain scribe" (v. 19) is unusual, since scribes were usually spoken of in the plural. "Teacher, I will follow You," he said. These words indicated that he was willing to follow Christ both spiritually and publicly. He had apparently considered Jesus' teachings (the Greek word *didaskalos* here means "Teacher"), and wanted to become a disciple. Instead of making it easy to follow Him, Christ insisted that the scribe count the cost of such commitment to discipleship, for Jesus owned less than even the foxes and birds. They had homes, but Christ wandered about and had to depend on the hospitality of others everywhere He went. Becoming His disciple and following Him was no easy task.

The "Son of Man" is the title by which our Lord most frequently referred to Himself. No one else in the New Testament ever used this phrase to refer to Christ, but Jesus used it some sixty-five times in three different contexts—serving on earth, suffering and dying, and coming again in apocalyptic glory.[3] Jesus did not reject the title of Messiah, as seen in John 4:26–27, but because the Jews had different expectations about Messiah's coming, He chose to use the Son of Man phrase. This title originally came from Daniel 7:13 and had messianic significance. Our Lord deliberately used this title of Himself in order to emphasize that He was, in fact, the Messiah. See the connection between the two terms in Matthew 26:63–65 and how Jesus' use of Son of Man was considered a claim to deity.

The reference to "another of the disciples" must refer to a professed disciple who was unwilling to follow Him unconditionally. The request to "bury my father" probably meant he wanted to stay at home until his father had died. Jesus' strong reply, "allow the dead to bury their own dead," was not intended to be harsh, but rather to emphasize that the time to be about the heavenly Father's business was now. Even if this man's father had just passed away, to wait several days would have been delayed obedience. Jesus was testing the would-be disciple's willingness to submit totally to Him and His call to discipleship.

The Cost of Discipleship
To suffer with the Savior (Rom. 8:17)
To often live life with a death sentence (Matt. 10:21)
To be misunderstood and maligned (Luke 5:30)
To be persecuted when the Word is taught (Matt. 13:21)
To be persecuted for the sake of the gospel (Acts 8:1; 1 Thess. 2:2)
To suffer often like a common criminal (1 Pet. 4:15–16)

The cost of discipleship is emphasized by the account of the storm that challenged the disciples' faith. The "great storm" (v. 24) refers to a violent storm (Greek, *seismos*). "He Himself was asleep" shows that Jesus was human and could get so exhausted that not even the tossing waves and water sloshing in the boat could awake Him. These boats were about thirty to forty feet long and could accommodate a number of rowers. Jesus rebuked their "little faith" in light of the fact that He had commanded the trip across the Sea of Galilee. They were in the center of God's will. We should learn that we can and will face trials even when we are obeying God perfectly. In one of His most awesome miracles, Jesus simply "rebuked the winds and the sea," resulting in an instantaneous miracle of total calm!

The disciples were so stunned by this miracle that they asked: "What kind of man is this?" (v. 27). Their piercing question still speaks to us today. There has never been anyone like Him. His morality, character, wisdom, and power stand supreme. He and He alone is God. All others pale into insignificance next to Him.

The Healings of the Gadarene Demoniacs (8:28–34)

The "country of the Gadarenes" was an area on the eastern slope of the Sea of Galilee. It included the district of Gadara, one of the cities of the Decapolis. Both of these were included in the larger administrative district of Gerasa, whose center was the town of Gerasa in Gilead. "Two men who were demon-possessed" met Jesus. The description of two demoniacs is peculiar to Matthew; the parallel passages of the other Synoptic writings mention only one. Instead of this being a contradiction, Mark and Luke emphasize the more predominant convert of the two, whereas Matthew records the account of both men with whom Jesus dealt. It is an interesting fact that Matthew and Luke give much briefer accounts of this miracle (seven and twelve verses respectively), than does Mark (twenty verses). If there really was a Markan priority, one would expect a much larger section in both Matthew and in Luke.

"What do we have to do with You, Son of God?" the demons asked (v. 29). They reacted with resentment at Jesus' intrusion into their realm, asking a question that meant "What is there in common between us?" Their reference to Him as the Son of God indicates that the demons were fully aware of who Jesus was, and their question about being tormented "before the time" also indicates that they were aware of why He had come to earth. While the demons seemed to understand that they will ultimately come under the judgment of God, here their concern seems to be that of a premature suffering (Greek, *basanizō*). There is a distinct possibility that Jesus could cast some demons into hell fire before the final judgment.

The reference to a "herd of many swine," which Mark 5:13 says numbered about two thousand, draws attention to the fact that they were being kept illegally by Jews who were living in this Gentile region. Swine were considered unclean by the ordinances of the Mosaic Law (Lev. 11:7–8). "The whole herd . . . perished." This is Jesus' only recorded miracle that was destructive in nature. The demons asked Jesus to send them into the swine. Jesus simply said, "Begone!"[4] One need not imply that Jesus gave them some necessary permission. The fact to remember is that He evicted the demons because of His concern for the man. The spiritual principle in this incident is that those who are deliberately disobedient (as were the pig breeders) deprive themselves of divine protection and place themselves at the mercy of the forces of evil. Certainly, losing the herd of pigs, which were being kept unlawfully in the first place, was insignificant when compared to the man's gaining his spiritual health.

Instead of rejoicing in this miracle of deliverance, the local people "entreated him to depart from their region." Unfortunately, this incident ends in tragedy, as the people prefer their own business to the presence of the Savior whose power they now feared. Jesus never returned to preach in this area. Fortunately, however, as Mark records (5:20), at least one of the healed men "went away and began to proclaim in Decapolis what great things Jesus had done for him; and everyone marveled." Having been set free, the demoniac proclaimed the message of deliverance to others.

By the time we finish reading the eighth chapter of Matthew, we are struck with the awesome power of Jesus. This is no ordinary man. He never wrote a book, yet more books have been written about Him than anyone who has ever lived. He never traveled more than one hundred miles in any direction, yet people have traveled to the far reaches of the globe to proclaim His name. Why? Because there was never anyone like Him!

Jesus knew no social barriers. He ministered to publicans, sinners, harlots, fishermen, priests, and Roman soldiers. Even his enemies had to admit there was no rational explanation for His miracles. The blind could see. The lame could walk. The diseased were healed. And the possessed were delivered. No one else could do what He could do, because He alone is God in the flesh. In all of human history, Jesus stands supreme. There is no one greater. In fact, no one even comes close.

Study Questions

1. Did Jesus have to touch the leper to make him clean? If not, why do you think Jesus touched him?

2. What do you believe Jesus' purpose was in telling the cleansed leper to "tell no one," but to go to the priest to make the proper offering and be pronounced clean?

3. Explain the meaning of "centurion" using verse 9 as a backdrop. What point did the centurion make about Jesus that flowed out of his own experience?

4. Does verse 11 imply a bodily resurrection? How?

5. How many miracles did Jesus perform in chapter 8? Were two miracles involved in healing Peter's mother-in-law? Once a fever leaves, one usually still feels drained, but she arose and served.

6. What does the enigmatic phrase of verse 22, "allow the dead to bury their own dead" mean?

7. Explain how such a great storm could arise so quickly on the Sea of Galilee at night. What climatic and geographical conditions make such an event possible?

8. Compare Matthew 8:28–34 with Mark 5:1–20. What are some of the differences you notice?

9. How do you explain Matthew's version of two men and Mark's version of one man in this story? Does the phrase "If there were two men, then there was at least one" make sense?

10. Did the herd of swine become the first case of "deviled ham"?

CHAPTER 9

The Case for Christ
Matthew 9:1-38

Preview:
Matthew's story of Jesus has shown His kingly lineage, the significance of His baptism and temptation, the wonderful principles of His kingdom, and His power over disease, demons, and even nature. Who is this person? Now Matthew goes even further, showing that Jesus has the divine prerogative to forgive sin, heal the worst cases of sickness, and even raise the dead. Matthew's readers must begin to sense that this is no ordinary man.

The Healing of the Paralytic and Lessons on Righteousness (9:1-17)

Matthew continues his portrait of Jesus as the Messiah. So compelling is the evidence that Matthew himself answers the call to follow Christ and become one of His disciples!

"Getting into a boat, He crossed over" (9:1). Jesus never stayed where he was not wanted; thus He returned to "His own city," that is, Capernaum (cf. 4:13). This is the incident where the paralyzed man was lowered through the roof by his four friends because of their inability to penetrate the density of the crowd (see also Mark 2:1–12; Luke 5:17–26). Jesus' statement "Your sins are forgiven" shocked the Jewish observers. In reality, Jesus attended to the man's spiritual needs before He dealt with his physical problem. "This fellow blasphemes," accused some of the scribes. Because Jesus claimed to forgive sins, the religious leaders who were in attendance labeled him a blasphemer. They rightly understood that forgiving sins is a prerogative of God alone.

However, what they failed to comprehend was that Jesus was God incarnate. There He was, right in front of them, and they missed the whole significance of the moment.

Jesus instinctively knew the nature of their wicked attitude and asked them a pointed question: "Which is easier, to say, 'Your sins are forgiven,' or to say, 'Rise, and walk'?" Actually, it would have been far easier and safer for Him to say, "I forgive your sins," because no one could really tell if the sins were gone. But to announce a healing was something that could be immediately tested. Does the man get up and walk, or not? Jesus wanted them to understand that He not only had the power to deal with the symptom, but also with the cause of the sickness, which was sin. The audience was stunned again when Jesus healed the man of his paralysis; and "they were filled with awe" (lit., "they were afraid"; v. 9). His power over physical sickness was now clearly connected to His power over spiritual sickness as well. The One who could make him walk could also forgive his sins.

Matthew follows the story of the forgiven man with the account of his own call to follow Jesus. A Savior who could forgive sins and make the lame walk could indeed call a sinner like a tax collector to follow Him. "The tax office" refers to the toll booth in the street where tax collectors sat to receive various taxes. Matthew must have seen Jesus pass by often with His disciples, since He had made Capernaum His home. Jesus' call of Matthew shows that the apostles were just ordinary men who got up and left their secular employment to serve Christ full-time. Jesus did not choose doctors, lawyers, teachers, and rabbis, but rather common tradesmen to be His disciples. During this period of time, it was common for the best and brightest young Jewish men to seek a rabbi or teacher to instruct them. Only the smartest and most devoted were selected by the best teachers. The fact that Jesus' disciples were already adults with various occupations indicates that they were not qualified to be disciples of such teachers. Thus the account of the call of the disciples clearly indicates that Jesus chose ordinary men to follow Him. They did not even seek to be His disciples. Rather, He sought them and called them to follow Him.

Tax collecting was a lucrative business in the Roman Empire. Michael Wilkins quotes Josephus indicating that Herod Antipas received annual revenue of two hundred talents (approximately five million dollars) from the regions of Galilee and Perea.[1] For Matthew to walk away from such a financially secure position meant he was absolutely convinced that Jesus was the Messiah. We cannot read the biblical accounts of Jesus calling His disciples without being impressed by their immediate response. Fishermen had already dropped their nets to follow Him. Now a wealthy tax collector left his entire business enterprise to follow the Savior. His given name was Levi, a term generally applied to the family of priests, who held a place of prominence among the Jews. Matthew, however, apparently had fallen from grace among his Jewish relatives and had sunk about as low as a backslidden Jew could go. Levi had become a tax collector (publican) and a collaborator with pagan Rome. But Jesus was in the business of saving sinners, reclaiming backsliders and transforming lives. No one, not even Matthew, was beyond the touch of His grace.

"In the house" (v. 10) means "at home." Every detail of this passage indicates that the new disciple invited Jesus to his home for dinner to introduce Him to others who needed Him as well. We know from the other Synoptic writers that this house was Matthew's (see Mark 2:15; Luke 5:29, where the expression is phrased as "in his house"). The usage of the phrase meaning "at home" in this passage indicates that Matthew was both the owner of the home and the author of this writing. This statement serves as strong internal evidence for Matthew's authorship of this gospel.

"Those who are healthy" does not refer to physical stamina, but in the context, rather to one's spiritual condition. The Pharisees thought they were healthy, when in fact they were very "ill." Still, they criticized Jesus for ministering to those who knew they were unhealthy (spiritually), those referred to as "tax-gatherers and sinners." The entire incident emphasizes the importance of reaching the lost.

"The righteous" (v. 13) is used here in an ironic sense, meaning "self-righteous." Ultimately, as the Scripture tells us, "there is none righteous, not even one" (Rom. 3:10). John's disciples, as well as the Pharisees fasted, but Jesus' disciples did not. "Why?" they asked. The principle taught by our Lord here is that fasting is not an end in itself. It is to be practiced only under appropriate circumstances. The Pharisees' fasting was part of the righteousness of men, which the Lord condemned. "The attendants of the bridegroom" refers to the wedding guests. They cannot mourn "as long as the bridegroom is with them," that is, while the wedding festivities last, which might be for some days. "When the bridegroom is taken away from them" is an allusion to Jesus' coming death and ascension. Jesus' comments indicate three important factors: His current ministry is temporary, He will eventually leave, and His departure will inaugurate a new phase of His ministry.

"A patch of unshrunk cloth," if placed on a well-worn garment, would loosen and eventually tear off. "Wineskins" were frequently used in the ancient East as liquid containers. The strength of fermentation of the new wine would be too much for the partly worn, old, inelastic skins and would cause them to break. The principle expressed here is that Jesus Christ has come to bring in a new dispensation altogether, which cannot be fitted into the forms of the old Jewish economy. The principle taught here by illustration is that the rule of the law must be replaced by that of grace, which will now have free reign in the hearts of all believers. Jesus brought in the new covenant because the old one was obsolete and needed to be replaced. Likewise, Jesus did not come to merely patch up our lives, but to make them brand-new.[2]

Rule of Law	Rule of Grace
Because of sin the Law kills (Rom. 7:9–11).	Believers are saved by grace (Rom. 3:24).
The Law is holy but we are unrighteous (Rom. 7:12).	Believers are now servants of the new covenant (2 Cor. 3:6).
The Law is like a yoke of slavery (Gal. 5:1).	Believers are to serve in the "newness" of the Spirit (Rom. 7:6).
Believers are no longer to serve in the "oldness" of the letter of the Law (Rom. 7:6).	Believers who are justified by Christ are to walk by grace (Gal. 5:4–6).
Law brings the knowledge of sin but does not save (Rom. 3:20).	Believers live not under the law but under grace (Gal. 5:18).

The Healing of the Woman with the Issue and the Raising of the Ruler's Daughter (9:18–26)

Matthew now introduces a unique double miracle. While Jesus is en route to raise a girl from the dead, He heals a woman who is hemorrhaging.

"A synagogue official" refers to a magistrate. The other Gospels indicate that his name was Jairus (cf. Mark 5:22–43; Luke 8:41–56). "He bowed down" before Jesus. The New American Standard Bible note says, "Or, *worshiped.*" This suggests that Jairus recognized Jesus' deity and authority. In the parallel passages, we are told that Jairus's daughter was dying when the father first came and that she died while he was en route. Matthew combines these two phrases into one, saying, "has just died."

As Jesus proceeded to Jairus's house, the crowd thronged around Him. Among them was a woman who had been bleeding constantly for twelve years. The very nature of her condition made her "unclean" by Jewish standards. Keep in mind that people were crowding around Jesus. Arms, legs, elbows, and knees were bumping against Him. The woman probably had to struggle to reach Him. When she finally got close enough, she reached out by faith and touched "the fringe [tassel] of His cloak" (v. 20). In Luke's account

(Luke 8:45–47), Jesus stops and asks, "Who is the one who touched Me?" When the disciples insisted that several people were touching Him, Jesus responds that only one touched Him in faith, because "I was aware that power had gone out of Me." The woman seemed startled that He recognized what she had done. But He was pleased with her act of faith.

She explained that she believed Jesus was her only hope. I shall get well (lit., "be saved"), she thought. It was customary for a rabbi to address a young girl as "daughter." Jesus' exhortation to "take courage" means to cheer up. The further statement, "your faith has made you well," indicates that God's blessing on our behalf is usually in proportion to our willingness to trust Him.

The scene described here is typical of a Middle Eastern home where someone lay dead. Mourners were actually hired to make noise, thus "the crowd in noisy disorder." Jesus' statement that "the girl has not died, but is asleep" meant that her death, though real, was ultimately going to be a temporary "sleep" in light of the fact that He would quickly raise her back to life again. On the same principle, the "dead in Christ" (1 Thess. 4:16) are said to be asleep only in view of the certainty of their resurrection.[3] It should also be observed that those whom Jesus brought back to life during His earthly ministry later died a natural death, whereas those who are resurrected at the last day shall never die again.

Asleep in Jesus

Stephen "fell asleep" when he was killed (Acts 7:60).

Many who saw the resurrected Christ had "fallen asleep" (1 Cor. 15:6).

Christ is the "first fruits" of those who are asleep (1 Cor. 15:20).

All believers will not face death, or fall asleep (1 Cor. 15:51).

Those who are asleep in Jesus will be resurrected (1 Thess. 4:13–14).

Those who are asleep in Jesus will go before those who are raptured (1 Thess. 4:15).

The Healing of the Blind and Dumb Men (9:27–34)

The incident recorded in Matthew 9:27–28 is also peculiar to Matthew's gospel (cf. Luke 11:14–26). Two blind men called out, "Son of David," which was a messianic designation. The implication of their address seemed to indicate that they had put their faith in Jesus as the Messiah. "Into the house" probably refers to Matthew's house as in verse 10. Jesus asked the blind man, "Do you believe?" Notice the emphasis on faith again as the catalyst to this miracle as well as the previous one. "Let no one know about this!" Jesus warned them after giving them sight. Jesus did not want to be mobbed or to be known primarily as a miracle worker. (See also note on 8:4.) Their disobedience need not be viewed as a serious violation, but rather, as an overt exuberance from the effect of the miracle itself. B. B. Warfield observed, "When our Lord came down to earth, He drew heaven with Him. The signs which accompanied His ministry were but the trailing clouds of glory which He brought from heaven."[4]

Jesus' Sees Their Need and Calls Us to Compassion (9:35–38)

The connection between spiritual evil and physical illness is clearly illustrated in this incident. The "ruler of the demons" is Satan himself. The Pharisees were accusing Jesus of being in league with Satan. The people "were distressed and downcast." William Hendriksen gives the reason. "One thing is clear: few, if any have found the peace that passes all understanding. . . . Their leaders are always burdening them with legalistic niceties about Sabbaths, fasts, phylacteries, and tassels . . . [they] are oppressed by the burdens which the Pharisees place upon them."[5] The observation that they were "like sheep without a shepherd" is taken from Numbers 27:17. The quote is taken mainly from the Septuagint, but with altered construction. "He felt compassion for them" is actually a passive verb. Jesus was moved by compassion. Too often, perhaps, we see the need, just as Jesus did, but we do not allow the need to move us to compassion.

Praying for Missions

Paul and Barnabas were prayed for as they began their mission work (Acts 13:3).

New elders in mission churches were prayed for (Acts 14:23).

The Roman Christians prayed for Paul's mission work (Rom. 15:30).

The Corinthians helped Paul with their prayers (2 Cor. 1:11).

The Colossian church prayed for an open door for the gospel (Col. 4:3).

Verses 37–38 constitute one of the great missionary passages of the New Testament. Jesus pictures the world as a great spiritual harvest in need of laborers to gather it into the barn. He urges the disciples to pray that the Lord of the harvest will send forth the workers to gather it. Since Christ commanded us to pray this prayer, it should be on our lips and in our hearts daily. Homer Kent observes, "As so often occurs those who prayed were themselves sent."[6] John MacArthur adds, "It is possible to pray regularly for the salvation of a loved one, a neighbor, a friend, or a fellow employee and let our concern stop with our prayer. But when we earnestly pray for the Lord to send someone to those unsaved people, we cannot help becoming open to being that someone ourselves."[7]

Study Questions

1. When Matthew says that Jesus "came to His own city," (9:1), what city was that?

2. Why was it thought to be blasphemy for Jesus to announce that someone's sins were forgiven (vv. 2–3)?

3. Which is easier to say, "Your sins are forgiven" or "Take up your bed and walk"? Why?

4. Do you think Jesus proved His power to forgive sins by exercising His power to heal?

5. Is it not true that no one could tell if the sins were forgiven, but that everyone would know if He announced a healing that never took place?

6. When Jesus quotes from Hosea 6:6 in verse 13, is God saying to do away with the sacrificial system? Why or why not?

7. When the woman who was hemorrhaging touched Jesus' garment, was it her touching that healed her, or was it Jesus' power that healed her when she exercised faith in Christ?

8. When Jesus announced that the little girl was not dead, but rather asleep (before He raised her), was He speaking literally or figuratively?

9. If Jesus were casting out demons by the "ruler of the demons" (v. 34), would it not mean that He was in league with the devil?

10. Do you see Matthew 9:38 as one of the major prayer requests of Christ? Why?

CHAPTER 10

All the King's Men
Matthew 10:1–42

Preview:

The second of six major discourses is found in this chapter. The twelve disciples are selected and sent forth to minister. One should note that their commission is only to Israel. This is far different than the Great Commission, which sent them into the entire world, to every creature, with the gospel. Their message is also different here. It is a kingdom message.

Sending of the Twelve

John MacArthur observes, "The greatness of God's grace is seen in His choosing the undeserving to be His people and the unqualified to do His work."[1] This was certainly the case with the twelve ordinary men He chose to be His disciples.

The twelve disciples had been formed as a group some time previously. Now, after a time of instruction and training, they were sent on their first mission. This would be no ordinary preaching mission, since they were also given authority over demons and disease. Their miracle-working ministry was to attest to the legitimate claim of Jesus to be the Messiah.

The twelve apostles (Greek, *apostolos*) is the technical term that later came to be applied to the twelve disciples. The literal meaning of the term is a "sent one." In this passage their twelve names are arranged in six pairs, which probably corresponded to the arrangement in which they were sent out on the mission. Simon is Peter, who heads all four lists of the Twelve (cf. Mark 3:16; Luke 6:14; Acts 1:13). Since he appears to be the most prominent disciple in the early stages of Jesus' ministry, as well as in the early period of the church, it may well be that he exercised a natural leadership over the others. It does not follow from this, however, that his leadership was necessarily passed on to his successors.

The disciples are always listed in their same groupings of four. Andrew was actually the very first disciple, according to John 1:40–41. James and John were brothers and became part of the inner circle of three. Bartholomew was generally considered to be identical with the Nathanael of John 1:45–51. Luke gives the name of Thaddaeus as Judas (Luke 6:16). Simon the Canaanite (KJV) is most likely an Aramaic identification (*qan'ân*) that he had been a member of the nationalist party known as the Zealots, who resisted Herod the Great by force (cf., Acts 1:13).

Iscariot has been variously interpreted as meaning that Judas was a member of the tribe of Issachar, or an inhabitant of Kerioth in Judea (Josh. 15:25; Amos 2:2), or the one with the purse (lit., an apron worn by tanners, with a "purse" sewn in to hold money), or the one who was strangled (as a description of the manner of his death). The second view is the most probable, thus it has been generally recognized that he was the only disciple who was not a Galilean. It is interesting to think that Simon was probably coupled with Judas for three years yet never knew the false profession of Judas. Likewise, it is possible to know a professing Christian and never question the reality of his or her salvation.

The disciples were simple men, mostly Galilean fishermen. The only educated and prosperous disciple was Matthew, the converted tax collector, who gained his wealth by serving the Herodian and Roman officials. Each of them was called specifically and publicly by Jesus to follow Him. This was contrary to typical first-century Judaism, in which the *talmid* (disciple candidate) would generally apply to become the disciple of a famous rabbi by demonstrating his knowledge and skill in the Hebrew Scriptures. Instead of the disciples coming to Jesus, He went seeking them and called them to follow Him.

"The way of the Gentiles" refers to several Greek cities in Galilee that existed separately from the Jewish lifestyle. The apostles were instructed to avoid these towns and to confine themselves to the Jewish cities only. Stanley Toussaint points out the dispensational interpretation of this emphasis, noting the exclusiveness of their ministry to the house of Israel only.[2] The word "Gentiles" can be taken as an objective genitive, indicating that they were not to enter into a road even leading to the Gentiles, nor were they to enter into a city of the Samaritans. Thus, it is proper to conclude that the rightful King of Israel was still making the legitimate offer of the kingdom to Israel. Had Israel accepted their King, they would have had their long-awaited kingdom. Therefore, it was proper for the apostles to announce that the "kingdom of heaven is at hand." Various commentators have written much on the nature of the proximity of the "kingdom of heaven" in this passage. Some wrongly attempt to separate this from the "kingdom of God" when the two terms are used interchangeably in the Synoptic Gospels. Others wrongly apply the promise of the kingdom to the church and suggest that the church has now replaced Israel in God's eschatological plan. What is clear in this passage is that the King is sending out His emissaries to offer the kingdom exclusively to the people of Israel. This does not mean that He has no concern for the Gentiles, because that concern will be clearly demonstrated in His later ministry (e.g., Matt. 16:13–19; 28:18–20).

The Church Has Not Replaced Israel

The term **Israel** refers to the Jewish people and the twelve tribes.

Christ is yet to come to reign over Israel (Acts 3:18–21).

The repentance of the Jews will be part of Israel's future restoration (Acts 3:18–21).

Israel will be restored when Christ comes from heaven (Acts 3:20–21).

The church is now made up of Jews and Gentiles, and is a new body, a new building (Eph. 2–3).

The church will be removed from the earth before the Tribulation (1 Thess. 4–5).

Christ will come as Israel's king to reign on His throne in Jerusalem (Matt. 24–25).

The apostles were to acquire nothing in the way of money in their money belts. The fold of the robe, or the girdle, served the same function as our pockets. The bag refers to a wallet, actually a small bag for holding various articles. Tunics were the outer robes that corresponded to the Roman toga. Her singular staff, agreeing with Luke 9:3, has caused some to suggest that the meaning of Mark 6:8 is that they were to have one walking stick between a pair. The worker is "worthy of his support" means they were to rely on the gifts and hospitality of those to whom they preached. This same concept is quoted in 1 Timothy 5:18, taken directly from Luke 10:7, with the identical word order and spelling. The idea here is that the preacher of the gospel is to be supported by the freewill contributions of those to whom he ministers. Thus, the ministry of preaching is always viewed in the New Testament as a faith venture.

Hospitality was a normal part of Oriental life, and many offers of accommodation were probably received; however, the disciples were restricted to accepting hospitality only from those who received their message. "Shake off the dust of your feet" is a symbolic act of rejection and condemnation, the idea being that not even the dust of a wicked city was worthy of them. "Truly" (Greek, *amēn*) is a transliteration from the Hebrew that which gives emphasis to the statement that follows. It means "most certainly" or "assuredly." "More tolerable . . . in the day of judgment" teaches that there will be degrees of punishment. Just as there will be various degrees of rewards for believers, so there will be various degrees of punishment for unbelievers. Some will receive more retribution, and some less, dependent on the amount of light that was seen and rejected. Sodom and Gomorrah are referred to as an example of the divine judgment against those cities that reject God (see 11:23–24 for an application of this statement to Capernaum as well). "Shrewd as serpents" makes one think of the serpent who deceived Eve in the Garden of Eden (cf. Gen. 3:13). In the ancient East the serpent was commonly regarded as the wisest of beasts. The disciples needed a cautious wisdom to deal with the fierce opposition that they would face.

"Do not become anxious" means not to worry. We are to leave the concern entirely with God (see also Mark 13:9–13; Luke 12:11–12; 21:12–19). "It shall be given you" promises that the inner prompting of the Holy Spirit would tell them what to say in each situation they would face. "Children will rise up against parents" is a summary statement of Micah 7:6 (cf. Mark 13:12). It is a demonstration of how ruthless and fierce the battle for the minds of people can be. "On account of My name"—that is, because they belonged to Jesus—they would endure great persecution. It is the one who has endured to the end who will be saved is a promise of perseverance, not a teaching that salvation may be lost. Rather, it indicates that those who are truly saved will indeed endure to the end. The same is true, for example, of Revelation 3:5. It is a positive promise to the overcomer, not a threat about losing one's salvation.

Premillennialists view this passage as referring to the time of the Great Tribulation and the Second Advent, which are in the distant future. Thus, the reference to the coming of the Son of Man in verse 23 is to be viewed as eschatological. To imply that at this point Jesus merely viewed Himself as a forerunner to the yet-coming Messiah is ludicrous in light of all the statements made earlier in the Gospel of Matthew. Therefore, He must have His own second coming in view.

By His use of the relationship of disciple to teacher and slave to master in verses 24–25, Jesus was telling His disciples not to expect better treatment than He was going to receive from those who rejected Him. See also John 15:18–25 for an elaboration of this theme the night before the crucifixion.

> ## Premillennial View of the Second Advent
>
> Great cosmic events close the worldwide tribulation (Matt. 24:29);
>
> **Then** comes the Messiah, the Son of Man, to earth to reign (Matt. 24:30).
>
> The nations will be gathered against Jerusalem (Zech. 14:2).
>
> The feet of the Messiah will touch the Mount of Olives (Zech. 14:4).
>
> The elect saints will be gathered from around the world (Matt. 24:31).
>
> The Messiah will establish His throne and judge the nations (Matt. 25:31–46).
>
> The millennial kingdom will last one thousand years (Rev. 20:4–6).

Beelzebul refers to Satan himself, the ultimate evil demon.[3] The disciples are told not to fear him. Their enemies can only take their physical life, which cannot prevent their blessed resurrection to life everlasting. To God alone belongs the power of the second death. In other words, Jesus reminded them that it was more important to fear Him who had authority over the soul as well as over the body and who can bring both to eternal condemnation in hell (*Geenna*). It should be noted that God is the One who has authority to cast people into hell, and not Satan, who will himself be ultimately cast into everlasting fire.

The word "destroy" (Greek, *apollumi*) means to render unfit for the purpose for which something was made. In verse 28 it means to lose utterly. A. T. Robertson correctly notes that " 'destroy' here is not annihilation, but eternal punishment in Gehenna (the real hell)."[4] William Hendriksen likewise asserts, "The word 'destroy' is used here in the sense not of annihilation but of the infliction of everlasting punishment upon a person."[5] Conversely, Jesus reminded His disciples of the Father's loving care, even for the sparrows (common birds in Israel). A cent (Greek, *assarion*) was a copper coin worth about one-sixteenth of a denarius. Luke even says one could get five sparrows for two cents (Luke 12:6), apparently an extra one being given if four were purchased. "Apart from your Father," simply means without His being concerned. Here we are reminded of God's gracious providential care over His saints. We are worth far more than sparrows and, therefore, we can trust our Father's providential care over our lives.

Jesus calls us to "confess Me"—that is, acknowledge that you belong to Him. In reality, secret discipleship is a practical impossibility. Jesus constantly called for an open confession of Himself by His followers. We must be willing to acknowledge Jesus as Lord and Savior, with all that those terms imply. That we are to confess Jesus before others clearly indicates that a public confession of true Christian faith is a virtual necessity. The warning, "But whoever shall deny Me . . ." is in the aorist tense, referring not to one moment of denial (such as Peter's), but to a firm resistance to Christ that shall never cease. Therefore, it is not a single act of denial that makes one unworthy of being a disciple, but a refusal to confess Christ at all that eliminates one from being a true follower of Him.

The Savior also calls each of us to take up our cross (v. 38). This is the first mention of the cross in the New Testament.[6] It was the custom for a condemned man to carry his cross on the way to his own execution. There is plenty of evidence that our Lord anticipated the mode of His own death. These words come as the climax of His warning to the apostles that their mission would involve arrest and persecution, potentially culminating in their death. These important words also have a deep spiritual significance for every believer and constitute the basis of Paul's teaching about the identification of the believer with the cross of Christ (see Gal. 2:20). "Found his life" means to gain something out of life for oneself. Here the word means the self-life, or natural life, as opposed to the spiritual life. "Shall find it" refers to a life emptied of self and poured out in the service of Christ in this world, and which will find full enjoyment and blessing in the world to come.

Jesus Predicts His Own Death

Jesus' predicted His own death (Matt. 26:61; John 2:19–22).

He will lay His life down as a good shepherd (John 10:18).

The Shepherd will be stricken (Matt. 26:31).

He will "suffer" and be killed (Matt. 16:21; Luke 22:15).

His blood poured out will initiate the new covenant (Luke 22:20–22).

"In the name of a prophet" means "as a prophet." Those who are not prophets themselves may share in the labor and reward of the prophets by willingly supporting their ministries. "One of these little ones" is a reference to the fact that even the smallest service done to the least significant of Christ's servants shall be rewarded by the Lord Himself.

In many ways, this is the key chapter in Matthew's gospel. Having given the account of his own conversion in chapter 9, Matthew now explains the significance of the call to discipleship. Being a disciple is more than giving intellectual assent to the gospel. It involves a commitment of faith that results in a surrender of one's life to the lordship of Christ. John MacArthur writes, "Confess means to affirm and agree with. It is not simply to recognize a truth but to identify with it."[7] In this passage, Jesus calls for true discipleship that includes a public declaration of Him as Lord and a personal commitment of oneself—even to the point of death.

The greatness of Christianity has often been expressed in the number of its martyrs, the depth of their faith, and their willingness to surrender all for the cause of Christ. The long list of believers who gave their lives for Christ is the hallmark of church history. But such devotion is often lacking in the church, especially in America today. Whatever our circumstances, each of us must face the challenge of the Savior's call to true discipleship—no matter what the cost.

Study Questions

1. Have you ever noticed that the twelve disciples are always listed in three groups of four, and that the same person is always listed at the head of each group? Check it out.

2. How is Jesus' instruction as to whom to share the gospel message with different in Matthew 10:5–6 than it is in Matthew 28:19–20?

3. Why did Jesus tell the disciples in verse 6 to focus on the lost sheep of the "house of Israel?"

4. In what sense was the kingdom of heaven "at hand" in verse 7?

5. Why did Jesus tell the disciples not to take any provisions with them (vv. 9–11)?

6. What did Jesus mean by being "shrewd as serpents, and innocent as doves" (v. 16)?

7. Who did Jesus promise would assist the disciples in their witness (v. 20)?

8. Is it necessary to publicly profess faith in Christ (vv. 32–33)?

9. Verse 39 presents a puzzle. You find, you lose; but you lose and you find. What is the meaning of this?

10. What is a prophet's reward (v. 41)? How can you earn it?

CHAPTER 11

More than a Prophet
Matthew 11:1-30

Preview:

John the Baptist identified himself as the Messiah's forerunner, as seen in Isaiah 40:3 (Matt. 3:1–3). But now John has been imprisoned and has some questions for the Messiah. He is confronted with legitimate doubts. "If I am His forerunner, and He really is the Messiah, then why am I in prison?" Jesus answers the Baptist's questions and concludes that no one greater than John the Baptist ever preceded him. Yet dispensationally, the one who lives beyond John and enters the kingdom stands on a higher plane than even John.

John the Baptist and Christ (11:1-30)

John the Baptist had been imprisoned by Herod Antipas in the desert fortress at Machaerus, east of the Dead Sea. There in the middle of the desert, John was confined in a narrow dungeon, awaiting sentence for publicly condemning Herod for divorcing his wife and marrying his brother Philip's wife, Herodias.

Verses 2–19 parallel Luke 7:18–35. This imprisonment has already been mentioned in Matthew 4:12, but the circumstances leading up to it are not described in detail until 14:3–12, where the manner of John's death is also recounted.

Jesus was a preacher as well as a teacher. "The works of Christ" (v. 2) were His miracles, which attested to His deity and authority. It has often been said that God only had one Son, and He was a preacher/teacher/missionary. Certainly, we see in Jesus the epitome of personal ministry in every form. The

"Coming One" refers to the predicted Messiah of Old Testament prophecy whose coming had already been proclaimed by John. "The blind receive sight" is an allusion to Isaiah 35:5; 61:1, where it is stated that this will be one of the works performed by the Messiah. John would certainly have understood the allusion. The poor have the gospel preached to them is a clear citation of Isaiah 61:1. Hence, Jesus was clearly vindicating His messiahship to John, who may have begun to question why Jesus had left him in prison. This account helps us appreciate the vulnerability of even God's greatest servants. John had not expected this, and he wanted reassurance that Jesus was indeed the Messiah he believed Him to be. The Savior's response was to quote the messianic prophecies of Isaiah as proof of His claims.

"But what did you go out to see? A prophet? Yes . . . and one who is more than [Greek, *perissoteros*] a prophet." The quotation in verse 10 is from Malachi 3:1. John was recognized as the forerunner of the Savior and, technically, as the last of the Old Testament prophets. Thus he belonged to the Old Testament dispensation. This certainly emphasized the clear distinction between the Old Testament era (i.e., before the resurrection) and the New Testament era (after the resurrection). The weakest believer who has the knowledge of the glory of God in the face of the risen Christ is, therefore, in a more privileged position than the greatest of the Old Testament prophets. Church Age believers have a fuller message and a greater understanding than even John did, as seen in the previous verses. The expression "those born of women" means mortals, the idea being that the greatest of all in this life cannot be compared with the glory of the life to come.

Matthew is more careful and precise in making dispensational distinctions between the Old Testament and the New Testament than any other gospel writer. In this passage, he clearly places John the Baptist in a pre-Christian dispensation by listing him with the Old Testament prophets. This same idea is emphasized in Acts 19:1–5, where some of John's disciples who had moved to Ephesus were converted to Christ and were baptized again "in the name of the Lord Jesus." These distinctions tell us that John and his ministry belonged to the Old Testament dispensation, despite his being the forerunner of Christ.

John's ministry pointed the Jewish people to the Savior of all people— Jews and Gentiles alike. By calling the Jews to "repent and be baptized," he was following an Old Testament pattern. Heartfelt repentance was to be accompanied by the ritual of cleansing in the *mikveh* by immersion in water. While the form is similar to New Testament Christian baptism, the nature of it is pre-Christian. John's disciples were not baptized in the name of Jesus, identifying with His death, burial, and resurrection because Jesus had not yet died or risen from the dead. Baptism in Jesus' name would come after the resurrection on the day of Pentecost (Acts 2:38).

"The kingdom of heaven suffers violence" (Greek, *biazomai*). The meaning of this saying, and the connection of verses 12–14 with preceding and following contexts, indicates that John opened the kingdom of heaven to sinners and thus became the culminating point of Old Testament witness. Most commentators have taken "suffers violence" to be in the passive voice, indicating that the church has been suffering from the days of John until that of the author of this gospel (cf. also the parallel passage in Luke 16:16 where the same verb is used). The New American Standard Bible margin indicates that the kingdom "is forcibly entered," that is, violent men take it by force.

Ministries of John and Jesus

John the Baptist	Jesus Christ
Calls the Jews to repent and be baptized in order to prepare for the coming Messiah (Matt. 3:2–11).	Calls all nations to believe and be baptized (Matt. 28:19–20; Luke 16:15–16).
His message is distinctively Jewish and pre–Christian. Therefore, his baptized disciples were later rebaptized in the name of Jesus (Acts 19:1–5).	Baptism in Jesus' name is distinctively Christian (Acts 2:38–41) and publically identifies the believer with the death, burial and resurrection of Christ (Acts 8:35–39; 9:17–18; 10:47; 16:15, 33; Rom. 6:3–4; Col. 2:12).

Both Reformed and dispensational thinkers agree that this statement refers to people being saved under John's ministry and at the time of Christ. William Hendriksen comments, "But vigorous or forceful men, people who dare to break away from faulty human tradition and to return to the Word in all its purity, no matter what be the cost to themselves, such individuals are eagerly taking possession of the kingdom."[1] Similarly, William Pettingill says, "The meaning is that John had preached the Gospel of the Kingdom with such power that those who had received the truth had not counted any sacrifice too great to obtain the Kingdom. In spite of every obstacle and opposition and persecution they had entered violently into the Kingdom."[2]

Jesus' statement that John himself is Elijah indicates that He saw the ministry of John as the fulfillment of the prophecy of the coming of Elijah in Malachi 4:5–6. The meaning of Malachi 4:6 would be that John is a link between the Old and New Testaments. However, it might be better to see this expression as a contingency statement. If Israel would have received Christ, then John would have fulfilled the Malachi prophecy. But since God knew that Israel would reject Christ, He did not send the real Elijah to them, but rather sent John "in the spirit and power of Elijah," as Gabriel explained in Luke 1:17. This seems to be what Jesus meant when He said, "if you care to accept it."³ Later, after the Jews had rejected Jesus as Messiah, He still pointed forward to Elijah but also added that "Elijah already came, and they did not receive him" recognize to the ministry of John the Baptist (Matt. 17:11–12).

"This generation" refused to exercise its capacity to hear and made excuses for rejecting both John and Jesus. Some have likened the illustration of Christ to that of children playing a game of "wedding" and then a game of "funeral." The idea is that the children cannot decide which game to play, therefore, they decide to play nothing at all. The reference to the rejection of John's ascetic ministry brought the charge that he was demon-possessed. However, Jesus' open contact with sinners brought the equally untrue claim that He was a gluttonous man and a drunkard. The next phrase, that "wisdom is vindicated by her deeds," may be the correct reading, but it has very little manuscript support.⁴ Some texts (KJV) read "children" for "deeds." The meaning, however, is the same in either case. The differing lifestyles of John and Jesus were justified in either case by their results.

The denunciation of Galilean cities that follows is recorded also by Luke, but in a different context (see Luke 10:13–16). Chorazin was about an hour's journey on foot north of Capernaum into the hills. Bethsaida was on the northeast side of the Sea of Galilee, about four miles, or an hour's walk to the east of Capernaum. Tyre and Sidon were both on the Mediterranean coast beyond the northern boundary of Israel. The statement, "You shall descend to Hades," is an allusion to Isaiah 14:13, 15, where it is spoken of the king of Babylon and may refer to Satan himself. "It shall be more tolerable for Tyre and Sidon . . . Sodom" indicates there will be degrees of punishment. Some will receive harsher judgment than others, depending on the light they had. The Jewish cities of Chorazin, Bethsaida, and Capernaum saw a much greater light in Christ than did the now ancient ruins of Tyre, Sidon, and Sodom. They will therefore be judged more harshly. Hell will not be the same for everyone. Some will suffer far more than others. As a result of Jesus' prophecy about the Galilean cities, note that they are all in ruins today and none of the three has ever been rebuilt.

The words that follow in verses 25–30 are the response of Jesus to the circumstances just described. "I praise" (Greek, *exomologeō*) is literally to acknowledge. "Babes" refers to spiritual babes who receive God's revelation in simple faith. "My yoke" refers to the teaching of Christ, which is represented as being light in comparison with the burdensome teaching of the Pharisees (see 23:4).[5] Those who feel the Christian yoke is a hard burden should consider Proverbs 13:15, "the way of the unfaithful is hard" (NIV). "You shall find rest for your souls" comes from Jeremiah 6:16. The Septuagint has "ye shall find purification unto your souls" and is corrected by Matthew to the original meaning in the Hebrew. "Easy" means "good" or "kind." The entire passage is peculiar to Matthew's gospel.

The uniqueness of this chapter is seen in its stark contrasts. John the Baptist is in prison facing execution. The Jews are on the verge of rejecting their Messiah and His forerunner. The cities of Galilee face a judgment more serious than Sodom, Tyre, and Sidon. Yet Jesus dares to announce that submission to His lordship is easy and His burden is light! Indeed it is—in contrast to all that is wrong in the world. Following the Savior leads to the blessing of salvation, and thus it is an experience to be desired in contrast to facing His judgment. Only in Him do we find the true meaning and purpose of life.

Study Questions

1. Can you understand John the Baptist's predicament and his question posed in verse 3? He was supposed to be the forerunner of the Messiah, yet he found himself imprisoned. So, he wondered, was Jesus really the Messiah?

2. What two passages in Isaiah does Jesus cite in verses 5 and 6 in answer to John's question?

3. What passage in Isaiah does Jesus quote that He refers directly to John the Baptist? See verse 10.

4. When Jesus says in verse 14 that John the Baptist "is Elijah, who was to come," what does he mean? Is Jesus teaching reincarnation?

5. Do you believe that Sodom will fare better on the day of judgment than Capernaum? See verses 23–24.

6. What does Jesus' teaching about Chorazin, Bethsaida, Tyre, and Sidon tell us about degrees of punishment? Very simply, how would you phrase the argument for degrees of punishment?

7. Read verses 25–27. Do you think it sounds a lot like the Gospel of John? Why or why not?

8. Is the invitation in verse 28 for all or for just a few?

9. How is Jesus' yoke easy and His load light? Could it be in comparison to the way of the sinner, which is said to be hard?

CHAPTER 12

Who Do You Think You Are?
Matthew 12:1-50

Preview:

This chapter presents a pivotal turning point in Christ's ministry. He is rejected by the Jewish leaders. There are three disputed points concerning the Sabbath. The Jewish leaders also accuse Jesus of casting out demons by using Satan's power, and they demand a sign of Jesus, other than the miracles He performs. With this rejection, the Pharisees begin to close ranks to destroy Jesus. Jesus, in turn begins to teach in parables (chap. 13) and to introduce the new concept of the church (chap. 16).

A Disputer with the Pharisees (12:1-50)

By this point, opposition to Jesus' ministry was growing among the Jewish leaders. The Pharisees were upset with His interpretation of Mosaic Law whenever He contradicted their own views and traditions. The phrase "at that time" connects the previous events and the current chapter as being close in time. The Sabbath day, that is, the seventh day of the week, corresponding to our Saturday (cf. Mark 2:23–3:6; Luke 6:1–11). However, in New Testament times, it began at sunset on Friday and lasted until the following sunset. The Pharisees had burdened the Sabbath with a multitude of detailed observances that were not laid down in the Mosaic Law. Correspondingly, in this incident they had objected to the manner in which Jesus' disciples had plucked grain on the Sabbath, violating the command against reaping on the sacred day (Ex. 20:10).

In responding to their legalistic traditions, Jesus always referred to Scripture. "Have you not read . . . ?" The passage referred to is 1 Samuel 21:1–6.

The point that our Lord makes is that in the case of necessity the ceremonial law might be overruled. He uses the illustration of David eating the consecrated bread.[1] These loaves were placed on the table in the Holy Place in the tabernacle each Sabbath. They were to be eaten only by the priest and his family (cf. Lev. 24:5–9; Num. 28:9). The priests prepared the sacrifices on the Sabbath in spite of the general prohibition of work. If the necessities of temple worship permitted the priests to break the sabbath, there was all the more reason why the service of Christ would allow a similar liberty. The Old Testament permitted a hungry person to pluck and eat grain when walking through someone's field (Deut. 23:24–25). However, the Pharisees considered this to be reaping and threshing, which were against their Sabbath rules.

I desire compassion, and not sacrifice. The application of this principle is that ethics are more important than ritual. The passage clearly asserts that Jesus had the right to interpret the Mosaic ordinances in light of their spiritual intention, rather than their literal application. The Son of Man is "Lord of the Sabbath" indicates that Jesus is in charge of the Sabbath. The Sabbath was made for man's benefit. William Hendriksen observes, it was "to keep him healthy, to make him happy, and to render him holy. Man was not created to be the sabbath's slave."[2] This is in accord with verse 6, where Jesus said, "Something greater than the temple is here," and verses 41 and 42, where Jesus said, "Something greater than Jonah. . . [and] Solomon is here." Jesus was that "something" that was greater. He takes precedence over all others and all else.

Luke 6 shows that the incident of the healing of the man with the "withered" (paralyzed) hand occurred on a different Sabbath than that of verse 1. However, the objection of the Pharisees on this occasion was essentially the same. They were in opposition to Jesus' healing on the Sabbath. The reference to their synagogue indicates that in this particular synagogue the Pharisees were predominant. They asked Jesus the leading question, "Is it lawful to heal on the Sabbath?" The Old Testament made no such prohibition, but some rabbis considered healing to be work. Jesus' response was that what one would be willing to do for an unfortunate animal, in sparing its life on the Sabbath, ought to be extended as a gesture of mercy to people in physical peril as well. Thus, Jesus' conclusion was, "It is lawful to do good on the Sabbath."

The ensuing miracle only enraged the Pharisees further, and they immediately counseled together (lit., "took counsel"). The Old Testament reference to "My Servant" is here applied to the person of the Messiah Himself. William Pettingill notes, "This quotation from Isaiah 42:1–4 explains why Jesus did not smite His enemies before Him, instead of meekly turning from them. He had leaned on Israel and had found them a bruised reed. Their worship was so corrupt as to be a grievous offense unto Him, as smoking flax. But he had not yet come to judgment, and therefore He would not break the bruised reed nor quench the smoking flax, until at His Second Advent He should send forth judgment unto victory."[3]

The statement that He shall proclaim justice to the Gentiles is a prophecy that the righteousness of God would be made known to the Gentiles through the ministry of the Messiah. "Until He leads justice to victory" means until the final triumph of righteousness that shall be brought about by Christ Himself. Throughout Jesus' earthly ministry, He continually focused on His ultimate eschatological triumph. Whatever resistance He faced at His first coming would be removed at His second coming.

Messianic Titles in Matthew

The son of David (1:1)

The Anointed One (the Christ) (1:17; cf. Ps. 2:2)

Immanuel ("God is with us") (1:23)

King of the Jews (2:2)

The ruler (2:6; cf. Mic. 5:2)

God's beloved Son (3:17)

The Lord (7:21–22)

Son of Man (8:20; cf. Dan. 7)

God's Servant (12:18)

"Son of David" is definitely a messianic title (see 9:27). The crowd had this thought because of the tremendous miracle they had just witnessed. Demon possession sometimes exhibited itself in physical maladies. But the Pharisees would not accept Jesus as the Son of God, so they accused Him of being in league with the devil. "Beelzebul" refers to Satan. "Jesus knew" implies that He fully understood the true meaning and intention of their thoughts. Whenever the New Testament says that Jesus knew someone's thoughts, it always refers to His divine omniscience. His reference to your "children" meant the disciples of the Pharisees. Hendriksen explains that the sons of the Pharisees were also casting out demons, but by what power? If the sons were to say that Jesus used demonic powers to expel demons, "they would be condemning themselves. On the other hand, if they judge the charge to be false they are condemning their teachers and vindicating Jesus. Either way their verdict would be very embarrassing to Christ's opponents."[4]

Matthew's usual expression is the "kingdom of heaven" (e.g., 3:2), but in verse 28 he refers to "the kingdom of God." While some have attempted to distinguish between the meanings of the two, it is more likely that they mean the same thing. "Has come upon you" is literally "has come upon you unawares." The Lord's power over demons was evidence enough that He was the Messiah. Hence, to "carry off his property . . . house" refers to Satan as being defeated or ruined by the capture of souls from him by the gospel of Christ. As Pettingill notes, "Jesus had not been so foolish as to attempt to rob the strong man—that is, Satan—without first binding him. The very first act of His ministry was to overcome this 'strong man' in the wilderness, and now He was spoiling His [sic] house."[5]

Satan's Doom Foretold

The seed of the woman, Christ, will defeat Satan, "bruise his head" (Gen. 3:15).

He has already been judged and awaits the final sentencing (John 16:11).

He knows his time is short (Rev. 12:12).

In the Tribulation Satan will be "overcome" by the blood of the Lamb (Rev. 12:11).

He will bound in the abyss for a thousand years (Rev. 20:1–3).

His final doom will be in the lake of fire (Rev. 20:10).

The issue of the binding of Satan is often dismissed in relation to various views of eschatology. Jesus' presence on earth had already demonstrated His power over Satan, who was incapable of tempting Him to sin or preventing His miracles. However, Satan was still actively resisting His ministry as he continues to resist believers today. Paul refers to Satan "tormenting" his body (2 Cor. 12:7 NIV) and "thwarting" his ministry (1 Thess. 2:18). Peter adds: "Your adversary, the devil, prowls about like a roaring lion, seeking someone to devour" (1 Pet. 5:8). These references make it clear that the ultimate binding of Satan, described in Revelation 20:1–3, has not yet occurred. At that time, Satan will be bound for a thousand years and cannot escape to deceive, tempt, or hinder the believers during the millennial reign of Christ.

It must be noticed that the kingdom of God was already present in the person of the King—Christ Himself! Jesus' admonition "He who is not with Me is against Me" clearly states that there is no middle course in relation to the authority of Christ as King and Lord. In Mark 9:40 we have the converse truth stated. The present passage applies to any person or position that is definitely antichrist. While the passage in Mark indicates that there may be minor differences (e.g., denominational distinctives) among genuine believers, Matthew's passage indicates that there can be no departure from the doctrine of Christ. Those who fail to affirm Him as the divine Son of God are ultimately against Him, no matter what kind of "appreciation" they may claim to have for Him.

Blasphemy against the Spirit is mentioned in verses 31-38. Some hold that this sin is simply that of rejecting Christ and His salvation. In the final analysis, it is the ultimate sin that by its very nature puts a person beyond the opportunity of salvation. That would seem to be true if the person immediately died. However, Jesus makes a distinction between blaspheming Himself and the blasphemy against the Holy Spirit. Don Carson explains, "The first sin is rejection of the truth of the gospel (but there may be repentance and forgiveness for that), whereas the second sin is rejection of the same truth in full awareness that that is exactly what one is doing—thoughtfully, willfully, and self-consciously rejecting the work of the Spirit even though there can be no other explanation of Jesus' exorcisms than that."[6]

The Holy Spirit brings the offer of salvation to the hearts of people. To reject Him is to act "presumptuously" and thus to "blaspheme" God. Those who reject His offer of salvation are in reality blaspheming the very nature of God Himself and the genuineness of His grace. The act of blasphemy involves far more than cursing God. It involves attributing the word of God to the devil as the Pharisees did the work of Christ.

The reference to the tree being known by its fruit seems to be that the good works done by Christ were evidence of His personal goodness and should have prevented any such blasphemy by the Pharisees. However, this illustration is conversely applied to the Pharisees, who are known by their wickedness as well. "By your words" does not refer to justification or condemnation on the basis of what one says, but to the outward evidence of the inward attitude of the heart. While the Pharisees asked for evidence of Christ's claim, they overlooked the clear evidence seen in His miracles. At the same time, they also were blind to the obvious evidence of their own unbelief.

John MacArthur observes that "'the day of judgment' for unbelievers culminates at the great white throne judgment, the ultimate and eternal judgment at which all unbelievers shall be condemned."[7] Jesus was referring to this judgment as the consequence of all unbelievers—religious or irreligious.

The chapter ends with a severe denunciation of the Pharisees. By requesting a "sign," they were demanding that Jesus do a miracle to convince them that He really was the Son of God. Instead, Jesus called them an "evil and adulterous generation," meaning that they were unfaithful to God. This was a metaphor frequently used in the Old Testament for spiritual "adultery." Then He added that the only sign they would see was the "sign of Jonah" (v. 39). Here Jesus clearly referred to one of the most controversial stories in the Old Testament. Jesus uses Jonah's interment in the fish for three days and three nights as an illustration of the time that He would spend in the grave Himself. The actual period was either, minimally, from Friday evening to Sunday morning (covering parts of three days idiomatically) or, maximally, from Wednesday evening at sundown to Saturday evening at sundown (covering seventy-two literal hours).[8]

That Jesus was entombed for parts of three days, from Friday evening through early Sunday morning, best explains why He said He would rise again "on the third day" (Matt. 16:21; 17:23; 20:19), not *after* the third day. It would also be difficult to try to explain how with a Wednesday crucifixion the women waited four days to prepare and return with the spices to anoint Jesus' body, or how the two on the road to Emmaus could say that Sunday was only the third day since Jesus' death (Luke 24:21).[9]

By referring to "Jonah the prophet," Jesus affirmed one of the most criticized stories in all the Bible. He shows no hesitation in accepting the literal and historical account of Jonah's interment in the fish. In fact, He uses it as a prophetic picture of his own death, burial, and resurrection.

The reference in the King James Version to the "whale's belly" in verse 40 is unfortunate. The Revised Standard Version's "belly of the whale" was rendered "the great fish" in the English Standard Version and the New Living Translation. The New American Standard Bible's "belly of the sea-monster" is preferred. The New International Version has "a huge fish." The Greek word *kētos* means a great sea monster. The Old Testament references are to a "great fish" (e.g., Jonah 1:17). It should be noted that our Lord placed this entire account on the same level of historical reality as that with which He Himself was dealing. To imply that Jesus was the "victim of the ignorance of His day" is ludicrous. He certainly did not show such victimization in dealing with other issues of life. The Queen of the South refers to the Queen of Sheba (see 1 Kgs. 10). Here our Lord contrasts her eagerness to hear the wisdom of a man (Solomon) with the refusal of His listeners to hear one "greater than Solomon." Again, this statement must be taken in light of the deity of Christ, rather than as a presumptuous boast.

Jesus gives a striking parable of the precarious spiritual condition of the nation. The parable is that of a house well swept but unoccupied. The demon having been driven out but finding no place to rest, returns with seven other spirits, resulting in an even greater degeneration.[10] In using this illustration, Jesus clearly indicated that though the Jews had been cleansed from their idolatry by the severity of the Babylonian exile, their unbelief and hardness of heart were in danger of producing an even worse moral condition than when they were idolaters. The moral reformation that had taken place after the captivity should have prepared Israel for the ministries of John and Jesus. Unfortunately, in most cases it fell short in that Israel's spiritual house was "unoccupied." Only by inviting Christ to occupy the position of honored guest and head of the home could Israel know the full blessing of God.

The chapter closes with a reference to Jesus' mother and His brothers. Craig Keener notes, "Not only the religious leaders (12:24, 38), but Jesus' own family doubted him."[11] These brothers are presumably the children of Joseph and Mary born after the virgin birth of Jesus. While some have attempted to view them as cousins, this certainly is not implied in the gospel records. The names of Jesus' four brothers (James, Joseph, Simon, and Judas) are given in Matthew 13:55 and Mark 6:3. Kent believes that Jesus' preaching at Nazareth had already forced the family to move to Capernaum.[12] By asking, "Who is My mother?" Jesus called attention away from earthly relationships to more important spiritual relationships. A believer is even closer to Christ than a physical relative. This saying was not intended to be one of disrespect to Mary or to His brothers, for they too would come to share that spiritual relationship.

It should also be noted that there is no suggestion here at all that Jesus' mother had any special access to His presence or any particular influence over Him. Hendriksen observes that "He wishes to indicate that neither Mary nor these brothers must be permitted to divert him from his appointed task."[13] Keener adds, "Jesus followed the practice he had demanded of others . . . the kingdom of God comes first."[14] By using this startling question, Jesus prepares the crowd to receive the precious truth that "whoever does the will of My Father" is in fact, His mother, His brother, or His sister. Hendriksen suggests that it was to His disciples that He gave this loving and honored designation.[15] The "whoever," however, clearly designates the universality of the gospel offer.

The beauty of this passage can be seen in the fact that while the disciples had left all and followed Him and were still often "of little faith" (8:26), He was not ashamed to call them brothers (see Heb. 2:11). Those who trust Him as their personal Savior become adopted members of the family of God (see Rom. 8:17, 29). Thus, Christianity has always fostered a sense of family among true believers. We are all brothers and sisters in Christ's family. As such, we are to show love, care, and concern for one another.

Jesus makes several matters very clear in this chapter. First, he claims to be "Lord of the Sabbath." Second, He reminds his Jewish audience that the "kingdom of God" is being made available to them by the sincere and gracious invitation of the King. Third, to attribute His offer, words, and works to the devil is to blaspheme the Spirit of God by rejecting the Son of God. Fourth, the sign of His resurrection will be the ultimate proof of His identity. Fifth, anyone who believes may enter into His family by faith.

Study Questions

1. The Pharisees observed Jesus and His disciples of picking grain on the Sabbath and accused them of breaking the Sabbath (vv. 1–2). Did they break the Sabbath? Why or why not?

2. Jesus' reply was, "Have you not read what David did . . . ?" What did David do, and where is the story found in the Old Testament?

3. What does Jesus mean when He says the Old Testament priests break the Sabbath while working on the Sabbath?

4. Jesus quotes from what three Old Testament prophets in this chapter?

5. Do you suppose that the man with the withered hand in the synagogue was placed there by the Pharisees as a setup? Why?

6. "To cast out demons by Beelzebul" would mean what?

7. What is "blasphemy against the Spirit"?

8. What exactly was "the sign of Jonah the prophet" (v. 39) that Jesus mentioned?

9. Did Jesus' mention of Jonah's experience in the great fish mean that Jesus had to be buried exactly three full days and three full nights. Why or why not?

10. What are verses 43–45 talking about? Could it be self-reformation, which is really of no permanent benefit, because of the need for God to truly change things?

11. In verses 46–50 was Jesus renouncing all human relationships or was He pointing to relationships that surpass the mere human connection?

Parables of the Kingdom
Matthew 13:1–58

Preview:

This chapter marks an abrupt change in Jesus' message and in His method of teaching. The Jewish leaders have rejected Him. He will not inaugurate the kingdom with an unregenerate nation. Instead, Jesus begins to use parables to explain the mystery form of the kingdom. He would also announce a new entity—the church (chap. 16). Israel was to be temporarily set aside, but as Paul notes, they will later come to faith—"and thus all Israel will be saved" (Rom. 11:26).

Chapter 13 marks a significant and pivotal change in Jesus' message. He introduces a series of parables (illustrations) to communicate the spiritual nature of the kingdom and the "mystery" form that it will take in the interval between His first and second comings. Chapters 11 and 12 emphasize the impending rejection of the King by the leaders of Israel. They anticipate the postponement of a literal earthly kingdom. John Walvoord notes, "The concept of a Kingdom postponed must be understood from a human perspective. . . . What is contingent from the human standpoint, however, is always planned the from the divine standpoint."[1]

R. V. G. Tasker explains the transition in Jesus' message as deliberately intended. He writes, "Jesus deliberately adopted the parabolic method of teaching at a particular stage of His ministry for the purpose of withholding further truth about Himself and the kingdom of heaven from the crowds, who had proved themselves to be deaf to His claims and irresponsive to His demands."[2] From this point on, Jesus speaks to the crowds in parables and then interprets them for his disciples privately.

The issue that many dispensationalists have struggled with is whether these particular parables are about the church (mystery form of the kingdom) or whether they actually belong to the kingdom age. The principles taught in these parables—sowing and reaping, and so on—seem to point to the Church Age, whereas the order of judgment (tares before wheat) implies the entire inter-advent age (from Jesus' ascension to His return), which would include both the Church Age and the Tribulation as Walvoord suggests.[3]

His Mystery: Secret Form of the Kingdom (13:1–58)

On one of the busiest days of Jesus' earthly ministry, He gave an extended series of parables (seven in Matthew and four in Mark, including one not given in Matthew). Jesus went out of the house, where He could not minister to the crowds pressing in around Him. To accommodate the multitudes, He pushed off in a boat to teach from the water. This is the turning point in Matthew's gospel. Already sensing His impending rejection, Jesus now expressed the "mystery" form of the kingdom that would be the church.

Jesus' early ministry involved a proclamation of the spiritual principles of the kingdom. The Jews, however, seeking a political and nationalistic kingdom, were now rejecting Jesus' concept of a spiritual kingdom. To bring in a political kingdom before people were born again would be a travesty. Therefore, an interval was now announced between the Messiah's original appearance and His final return. That interval is the Church Age, during which believers are citizens of the kingdom that is "in their midst" (Luke 17:21). The distinction between the church and the kingdom is not that one is more spiritual than the other. The church is the present (realized) form of the kingdom of God. The millennial kingdom, which is to come in the future (Rev. 20:4) is another transitional form of the kingdom that will ultimately be presented to the Father to be the eternal kingdom of God (Rev. 21).

Speaking in parables was a common method of teaching in the Near East. It was used to convey spiritual truth through a series of earthly comparisons. Jesus was an expert at this form of teaching. It should be noted, however, that parables did not always convert unbelievers who were often confused about their meaning. Therefore, Jesus took time to interpret the parables for His disciples.

The Parable of the Sower *(13:3-23)*

The first parable is set in an agricultural context. The "sower went out to sow" refers to the ancient seed sower planting a crop. The Greek definite article here is generic. Jesus later interpreted this parable Himself. The seed depicts the Word of God (v. 19), and thus the sower is the gospel evangelist. The road is the path trampled through the field. It was hard-packed and the seed found no root, thus the birds (demons? v. 19, "evil one") snatched it away. Here there was no response at all to the gospel.

The second category is called "rocky places" or the rock ledge beneath a thin, shallow layer of soil. This thin crust would warm quickly, causing the seed to sprout initially but without adequate rootage or moisture. Thus the sun scorched the crop and it withered away. The third group of seeds fell among the thorns, and the wild growth choked out the crop.

The good ground represents well-plowed and prepared soil capable of producing a large crop. The statement "He who has ears, let him hear" goes beyond physical hearing and implies an inner spiritual reception of truth. This prompted the disciples' question as to why He had spoken to them in parables. Whereas before He had used parables to illustrate His messages, now they formed the basis of the message. Jesus used parables for several reasons. (1) Everyone likes a good story. (2) Truth is easier to remember in story form than it is in a regular sermon. (3) The truth would be made plain to believers. (4) The truth could be hidden from those who opposed the gospel. (5) Jesus could expose the Pharisees in a story before they could figure out that the story was actually about them.

The Savior's reply was that only the disciples were to know the "mysteries" of the kingdom of heaven. The mystery implies a secret into which one must be initiated in order to understand it. The mystery revealed would be the new form of the kingdom during the interval between the first and second advents. Homer Kent notes, "These parables describe the strange form of the kingdom while the King is absent, during which time the gospel is preached and a spiritual nucleus is developed for the establishment of the messianic reign."[4] This special revelation is given only to the apostles who will become the foundation of the church.

Those to whom this revealed secret has not been granted are those who have already rejected Christ. Thus the parable form leaves unbelievers without understanding. This is in accord with 1 Corinthians 2:14: "But a natural man [unsaved person] does not accept the things of the Spirit of God; for they are foolishness to him, and he cannot understand them, because they are spiritually appraised." One can only understand spiritual truth by and through the work of God's Spirit. The Pharisees' rejection of Jesus lead to His rejection of them.

THE PARABLES IN MATTHEW
Those in CAPITALS are Peculiar to Matthew

Parable	Reference
1. The Salt of the Earth	Matthew 5:3; Mark 9:50; Luke 14:34–35
2. The Light of the World	Matthew 5:14–16; Mark 4:21
3. The Adversary	Matthew 5:25–26; Luke 12:58–59
4. The Offending Members	Matthew 5:29–30; 18:7–9; Mark 9:43–48
5. The Mote and the Beam	Matthew 7:1–5; Luke 6:41–42
6. DOGS AND SWINE	Matthew 7:6
7. The Broad and the Narrow Ways	Matthew 7:13–14; Luke 13:24
8. Good and Bad Fruit Trees	Matthew 7:15–20; 12:33; Luke 6:43–45
9. The Wise and Foolish Builders	Matthew 7:24–27; Luke 6:46–49
10. The Physician and the Sick	Matthew 9:12–13; Mark 2:17; Luke 5:31
11. The Bride and the Bridegroom	Matthew 9:14–15; Mark 2:19–20; Luke 5:34–35
12. New Cloth on an Old Garment	Matthew 9:16; Mark 2:21; Luke 5:36
13. New Wine in Old Wine Skins	Matthew 9:17; Mark 2:22; Luke 5:37–39
14. Parables about Satan's Kingdom	Matthew 12:24–28; Mark 3:22–26; Luke 11:14–20
15. The Strong Man	Matthew 12:29; Mark 3:27
16. Good and Bad Treasures	Matthew 12:33–37; Luke 6:43–45
17. The Unclean Spirit That Returned	Matthew 12:43–45; Luke 11:24–26
18. The Sower and the Soils	Matthew 13:3–9; 18–23; Mark 4:1–9; Luke 8:4–8
19. THE WHEAT AND THE TARES	Matthew 13:24–30, 36–43
20. The Mustard Seed	Matthew 13:31–32; Mark 4:30–32; Luke 13:18–19
21. The Leaven in the Meal	Matthew 13:33; Luke 13:20–21

Parable	Reference
22. THE HIDDEN TREASURE	Matthew 13:44
23. THE PEARL OF GREAT PRICE	Matthew 13:45–46
24. THE FISH NET	Matthew 13:47–50
25. THE HOUSEHOLDER AND HIS TREASURES	Matthew 13:51–52
26. The Source of Defilement	Matthew 15:10–20; Mark 7:14–23
27. The Blind Leading the Blind	Matthew 15:14; Luke 6:39
28. RED SKIES	Matthew 16:1–4
29. The Lost Sheep	Matthew 18:12–14; Luke 15:3–7
30. THE UNMERCIFUL SERVANT	Matthew 18:23–35
31. THE LABORERS IN THE VINEYARD	Matthew 20:1–16
32. THE TWO SONS CALLED TO WORK	Matthew 21:28–32
33. The Wicked Husbandmen	Matthew 21:33–41; Mark 12:1–12; Luke 20:9–16
34. The Rejected Stone	Matthew 21:42–44; Mark 12:10–11
35. THE MARRIAGE OF THE KING'S SON	Matthew 22:1–14
36. The Sprouting Fig Tree	Matthew 24:32–35; Mark 13:28–31; Luke 21:29–33
37. The Householder and the Thief	Matthew 24:43–44; Luke 12:39–40
38. The Faithful and Evil Servants	Matthew 24:45–51; Luke 12:42–46
39. THE TEN VIRGINS	Matthew 25:1–13
40. THE TALENTS	Matthew 25:14–30

The quotation from the prophecy of Isaiah (i.e., Isa. 6:9–10) follows the Septuagint, emphasizing the obstinate unbelief of the people. As in Isaiah's day, the Jews had hardened themselves against God's truth and He had further hardened them in their unbelief. Their hearts had become dull, and they would not turn and be saved. The faith of the disciples was evidence of their conversion and caused them to see and hear the truth the prophets (v. 17) had desired to know (cf. 1 Pet. 1:10–12).

Jesus interpreted this parable Himself in verse 18–23. The sower is Christ working through the agency of His disciples to spread the gospel throughout the world. No longer is the message to be restricted to the house of Israel, but is to be declared to all people. The word of the kingdom is the gospel proclamation of Jesus the King and is not to be limited to an Old Testament Jewish-only message. Remember, these parables make it clear that the church is the present-day form of the kingdom. The key to interpreting the reception of the seed into the ground is the term "understand," meaning to comprehend by believing faith (cf. v. 32). Unsaved listener do not understand and do not receive the seed, whereas believers both hear and understand the message, and their lives produce fruit to prove it. The reference to the heart in relation to the ground indicated that the quality of the soil represents man's heart response to the message. The heart is the seat of belief and response to the gospel.

The rocky places are those shallow-hearted individuals who immediately, "at once," receive (outwardly) the message with joy—that is, with enthusiasm or excitement. These emotional converts are not truly born again, for they have no firm root and wither away. Those among the thorns (cares of this world) are carnal, worldly converts who never really break with their past. Worldliness and materialism choke the word in their lives and they are finally unfruitful (unsaved). Those who receive seed in the good ground are ones who both hear the Word and understand it, who indeed bear fruit (evidence of true conversion). While such evidence may vary in its amount, all true believers will produce some fruit. No fruit means no spiritual life. This parable does not teach that some are saved and then lose their salvation. The first three soils (hearts) were never saved in the first place. Only the good soil indicates salvation, because only it produced fruit.

However, the parable of the sower has been variously interpreted. Some hold that only the first one was lost, while others believe that examples two and three lost their salvation. To the contrary, only the last one was genuinely saved and produced fruit to prove it. The others fell away—not from salvation, but from their profession—and were unfruitful. Jesus said that the believers' fruit would vary, but He gave no one the option of being His follower and producing no fruit at all!

The Parable of the Tares (13:24–30; 36–43)

This parable serves as a warning to the laborers in the field (which is the world, v. 38). Unlike the Jewish form of the kingdom in the Old Testament where citizens could be easily recognized, during the Church Age, converts will be made from all over the world and received upon their profession of faith. Thus it will be easier to slip in some counterfeits who profess what they do not possess.

The kingdom of heaven must refer to the church, the mystery form of the kingdom, which is the subject of these parables. The enemy is Satan, and the tares (Greek, *zizanion*, denoting "darnel," *lolium temulentum*) are false converts. The darnel was a weed that resembled wheat but did not come to fruition. The wheat sprang up and bore grain, emphasizing that true converts produce fruitful lives. By contrast, false (professing) converts produce no lasting fruit. It should be noted that a "fruit" is something that God must produce in us by His power (cf. Gal. 5:22ff.), whereas, a "work" is something we can do by our own efforts. Singing, preaching, ushering, teaching, and witnessing are all works; by contrast, loving people, having a deep-seated inner joy, and being at peace with people are fruit of the Holy Spirit, as are righteousness and holiness. False converts may produce outstanding works but no real fruit.

The servants questioned what could be done with these tares. To uproot them would damage the entire crop, rooting up the wheat with them. The implication seems to be that too much criticism of people's genuineness of faith may damage the saved before the lost are exposed. "Allow both to grow together" indicates that there will always be some false professors among true Christian believers until the time of the harvest or judgment. Note that the tares are gathered, bound, and burned first, whereas the wheat is gathered into "my barn" (probably the millennial kingdom). The same progression of judgment then blessing follows in Revelation 19–22.

The parable of the tares is interpreted later by Jesus in verses 36–43. It should be observed that only the main details are symbolic in a parable, the minor incidents (e.g., the servants) merely give substance to the story. The field is the world, not the church. The sower of the good seed is the Son of Man, or Christ Himself, who will also be the final Judge who evaluates the fruit. The gospel is to be sown where lost people are and where converts need to be made in the world. As Lord of the harvest, Christ directs this sowing process, that is, the missionary mandate of the church. The sons of the kingdom are the saved believers of the Church Age, who are Christ's true followers. The harvest is the end of the age and the reapers are angels who play a decisive role in the final judgment. The fire of the parable is interpreted as actually being fire and represents hell, or the lake of fire, the destination of all unbelievers and false professors who deny Christ. By contrast, the righteous shall enjoy the eternal kingdom of their Father.

George Ladd, and others who hold a posttribulation view of the rapture are hard-pressed to explain this parable. The harvest, or judgment, is actually at the end of the Tribulation period, just before the millennial kingdom begins. But instead of the wheat (the saved) being gathered first, as will happen at the rapture, the tares are separated out beforehand. Ladd asserts, "Nothing is to be made of the fact that the tares are gathered first before the gathering of the wheat."[5] Contrary to Ladd, however, this parable corresponds perfectly with the pretribulation rapture view. In that scenario, the church is raptured just prior to the Tribulation period. The separation pictured in this parable is that of the good and the bad at the end of the Tribulation period, just before the kingdom age. It corresponds with the judgment of the sheep and the goats parable of Matthew 25:31–46. In that case also, the goats (the unsaved), will be cast into the fire, then the sheep (the saved) will be ushered into Christ's millennial kingdom.[6]

It should also be noted that the concept of postmillennialism, that the world will be converted before Christ returns at the end of the age, is hopelessly refuted by this parable. William Pettingill aptly remarks, "By it we learn that the Dispensation is to end without a converted world. The tares do not grow into wheat at the End-time, but they are gathered up and set aside for judgment. We shall be terribly disheartened and grievously disappointed if we are looking for the conversion of the world before the return of the Son of Man."[7]

Interpreting Parables

Look for the main or central idea in the parable.

Remember that parables may or may not teach doctrine.

Interpret the parables within the cultural context.

If the parable is in the Gospels, look for Christ's interpretation.

Look for the interpretative clues within the parable.

Look for Old Testament associations.

The Parable of the Mustard Seed (13:31–32)

The parable of the mustard seed can also be found in Mark 4:30–34; Luke 13:18–19. The mustard seed is fairly small, about the size of a common radish seed, and yet grows to a comparatively large size, large enough in fact for birds to build a nest in it. The idea seems to be that the tiny beginning of the church will eventually culminate in great growth. Garden plants (Greek, *lachanon*) refers to vegetables such as one would find in a garden. However, such numerical growth will come to harbor the birds of the air. In the parable of the sower, the birds represented evil ones. They could represent the same here or the wording may indicate that the plant was large enough to house birds. B. F. Atkinson holds that "The parable accordingly foreshadows the growth of the church into a world power. . . . We have here a perfect picture of the apostasy not condemned, as such, we are reminded that outward growth is not always a true picture of spiritual depth. Again, as with the tares, false professors clutter the branches of the true tree (Rom. 11) of God's fruitful people, seeking to benefit their own interest."[8]

The Parable of the Leaven (13:33–35)

"Kingdom of heaven" is the spiritual form of the kingdom in the church. Leaven is a lump of old dough in a state of fermentation that causes the bread to rise. Leaven is virtually always used as a symbol of evil (cf. Matt. 16:6–12; Mark 8:15; Gal. 5:9). Three, referring to the number of pecks of meal has no symbolic meaning; it was simply a common baking quantity (cf. Gen. 18:6), equivalent to one and a half gallons (Greek, *saton;* Hebrew, $s^{e'}\hat{a}h$). Kent sees the woman here as the false prophetess, elsewhere called Jezebel (Rev. 2:20) and the great harlot (Rev. 17).[9] Thus, the leaven is not just false profession of unsaved church members, but false doctrine that they will attempt to bring into the church.

    See notes on verses 24–30 above.

The Parable of the Hidden Treasure (13:44)

The tiny parable in verse 44 has been subject to widely diverse interpretation. Some see Christ as the treasure hidden in the field, for which the sinner must forsake all in order to obtain.[10] However, this view smacks of self-effort in obtaining that which only grace can give. It also violates the imagery of the other parables where Christ is the man. Others view the treasure, then, as representing Christ's treasured people, whom He bought and hid with Himself in God (Col. 3:3). Some see the treasure as Israel, made up of various pieces, in contrast to the pearl, which they identify as the church. Regardless, the point of the parable is that all must be forsaken in pursuit of the treasure.

The Parable of the Pearl of Great Price (13:45–46)

The merchant in the parable of the pearl of great price could be Christ, who comes to purchase, through His atonement, sinners who shall become fine pearls. The one pearl of great value would be the church for whom Christ gave His life—that is, all that he had. Another way to view the treasure and the pearl parables may be to see the treasure as something a person stumbles across when he is not even looking for it, while the person who found the pearl was diligently seeking it. Could this be contrasting how some persons come to Christ? But if the pearl is Christ, or the kingdom, for whom a person must give all in order to obtain, then no person has ever yet given all that he or she has for Christ. While we receive Him as Savior, we also progressively continue surrendering areas of ourselves to Him as we come to know better His will for our lives.

The Parable of the Dragnet *(13:47-50)*

The dragnet "was pulled between two boats or taken out into the water by a single boat and drawn to shore by ropes."[11] In such a process, all kinds of fish and other objects would be caught together. The good were put into containers, while the bad were cast away. Jesus' interpretation is similar to the parable of the tares. In both cases the angels separate the bad to be burned in the furnace of fire (in hell).

Excursus: The Use of Parables *(13:51-58)*

The disciples have been given the parables and the principles of interpretation. Thus they reply in the affirmative when Jesus asks them if they understand. Since they clearly understood these parables, we are to understand them as well. An informed disciple is a true scribe who comprehends new and old truths and can rightly discern between them.

Jesus then gave His disciples a firsthand opportunity to witness the truth of these parables in action by teaching at the synagogue in His hometown (Nazareth, not Capernaum). The people were "astonished," that is, greatly amazed or astounded. The "carpenter's son" refers to the family trade of Joseph, Jesus' legal guardian and earthly "father," being the husband of Mary. The word "carpenter" (Greek, *tekton*) may refer to either a carpenter or a stone mason. The indication is that Jesus had learned His family's trade. There is no valid reason for understanding brothers and sisters in any sense but the normal one. They are Jesus' half brothers, the children naturally generated by Joseph and Mary after Jesus' virgin birth.[12] Two of them, James and Judas (Jude), wrote New Testament epistles and played a prominent role in the early church. Some suggest that the family had moved to Capernaum but that the sisters had married and remained at Nazareth ("with us"). Because they took offense at His message He did not do many miracles there due to their unbelief. His power was not limited by people's faith, but was exercised in response to it.

John MacArthur writes: "As the Pharisees perfectly illustrate, when unbelief investigates the supernatural work of God, it comes up empty . . . It cannot recognize the works of God because it will not recognize the truth of God."[13] Thus, the entire chapter points to the contrast of two options—belief or unbelief. On that basis, Christ's response is one of acceptance or rejection. There is no middle ground. Either you believe in Him or you don't. It's that simple!

Study Questions

1. Which city was Jesus in when He told His parables, and who heard the parables?

2. What is a parable? Was Jesus the only person to use parables? How many parables did Jesus use in this chapter?

3. In the parable of the sower, is the number four significant, or could it just as well have been three or five soils?

4. What do the four soils represent?

5. What were some of Jesus' purposes in telling parables? How does the quotation from Isaiah fit into your answer?

6. When will the events pictured in the parable of the wheat and the tares finally culminate? What judgment does it speak of?

7. What similarities and differences do the parables of the treasure in the field and the pearl of great price have?

8. What message do you think each contains?

9. Does the parable of the mustard seed indicate something good or something bad? Why?

10. Is the leaven in the three pecks of meal good or bad? Do you think it shows the rapid and universal growth of the gospel or of evil?

11. In Jesus' explanation of the parable of the wheat and the tares, what does Jesus say the fire in the parable stands for? See verse 42.

CHAPTER 14

Miracles of the Messiah
Matthew 14:1-36

Preview:

After Jesus received the painful news of the death of John the Baptist, He sought to withdraw for a time for reflection and solitude. John was Jesus' cousin and forerunner. John's death prefigured Christ's own coming death and burial. But even as Jesus withdrew, the crowds still followed Him. Jesus could not avoid them, so He taught them. When evening approached, it became the occasion for the feeding of the five thousand.

The Death of John the Baptist (14:1-12)

The occasion of John's death signaled a time for Jesus to retreat, lest He pro-voke an early death, before the appointed time. Herod the tetrarch is Herod Antipas, a son of Herod the Great. He began ruling over Galilee and Peraea after his father's death in 4 B.C. and was banished to Gaul in A.D. 39. Thus he had been on the throne for about thirty-five years. His ignorance of Jesus prior to this time is probably due to his self-indulgent, luxurious lifestyle which gave him little contact with religious figures. His guilty conscience over John's death caused him to think Jesus was John the Baptist risen from the dead. His fear of the resurrection indicates its widespread belief in those days. Matthew, then, recounts the story of John's murder at Herod's hands.

John had been arrested for challenging the legitimacy of Herod's divorce and incestuous remarriage. Robert Mounce observes, "Earlier, Herod had arrested John and put him in chains in prison. Josephus identifies the place as the fortress of Machaerus on the east side of the Dead Sea and says that John was imprisoned because Herod feared the great influence John had over the people."[1] Herodias was the daughter of Aristobolus, a half brother of Antipas. She had been married to her uncle, Herod Philip, and had borne him a daughter, Salome. However, she divorced her husband and married Antipas, who was already married himself. The first-century Jewish historian Josephus records it this way: "Herodias . . . was married to Herod [Philip], the son of Herod the Great. . . . [Herodias] had a daughter Salome; after whose birth, Herodias took upon her to confound the laws of our county, and divorce herself from her husband, while he was alive, and was married to Herod [Antipas], her husband's brother."[2]

The king's own anger was already set against John, but he feared the multitude and kept him alive because the people believed John was a prophet. And indeed he was the last of the Old Testament prophets. Herodias was a guilty and vindictive woman who wanted John dead and devised a plan to get rid of him. At the king's birthday party, her daughter performed a provocative and sexually enticing dance that so appealed to the drunken Herod that he "promised with an oath" that she could have whatever she wanted. Urged on by her mother, she asked for the head of John the Baptist on a table platter.[3]

Moments of the Savior's Compassion	
Matthew 14:23	*Went alone to pray by Himself*
Matthew 15:32	*Moved with compassion for the multitudes*
Matthew 20:34	*Moved with compassion for the blind men*
Matthew 26:36–38	*Deeply grieved over His coming death*
Matthew 26:39	*Prayed that the cup of death might pass*

The weak king complied with the evil woman's request, and the forerunner of Jesus was slain. However, the vindication of the family was short-lived. Historical records confirm that the Herodian family never escaped bloodshed and violence.[4] John's loyal disciples came bravely and obtained his body for burial and then informed Jesus, who, when He heard it, withdrew into a "lonely place" by Himself. We cannot fully comprehend the pressure Jesus was under at this time. Jesus knew what His mission was. He knew He had to die for the sins of all humankind. The death of His own forerunner, however, from the human standpoint, brought the nearness of His own sacrifice into full view. Yet, in spite of His own heartache over John's death, Jesus performed two major miracles for the multitude, whom, loving, He could not avoid healing and feeding.

The Feeding of the Five Thousand (14:13–21)

The stage was now set for the miracle of the feeding of the five thousand, which is the only miracle recorded in each of the four Gospels (see Mark 6:30–44; Luke 9:10–17; John 6:1–13). "When it was evening" may refer to either three o'clock or sundown. Both times were used in Jewish reckoning and both may appear in the harmonization of the various accounts. While towns were nearby where food could have been purchased, it was getting late in the evening (cf. Luke 9:12). Jesus' suggestion to the disciples "You give them something to eat," placed the burden of responsibility on them. According to the Gospel of John, Andrew, who had brought Peter to Jesus, now brought a boy's lunch consisting merely of five loaves and two fish—that is, small baked rolls and dried fish (an adequate lunch for a boy, but hardly a crumb compared to the immense crowd). The lad offered what he had, and Jesus did the rest. When we give of ourselves freely and sacrificially to God, He is ever willing to multiply the results.

The simplicity of the story and its inclusion by all four evangelists eliminates any doubt of its true historicity. Old liberal interpretations are totally inadequate. Albert Schweitzer suggested that in actuality each person received only a small crumb or fragment and yet felt satisfied. William Barclay hinted that the boy's offering of his lunch convicted the crowd so that they all got out their previously concealed lunches and shared them.[5] None of these approaches is suggested in the text. Even Schweitzer's crumbs would have had to add up to gigantic, unbelievable loaves to feed five thousand! The obvious miracle was the result of Jesus' divine person and power. As the Creator-God, He multiplied the bread, so that as each piece was broken off, the original roll still remained intact. No wonder the crowd came back the next day seeking more. If the liberal interpretation of this passage were true, no one would have returned seeking more bread from Jesus (John 6:22–26)!

R. T. France points out the connection of Jesus' miracle to the Jewish mind. He says, "Two Old Testament passages come to mind: the miraculous provision of bread . . . recalls the manna of Exodus 16, and the details of the story echo Elisha's miracle of feeding a hundred men with twenty loaves (2 Kgs. 4:42–44)." He further observes that "Jewish expectation of a return of manna when the Messiah comes (2 Baruch 29:8; cf. Rev. 2:17) suggests it was a Messianic gesture."[6]

THE MIRACLES IN MATTHEW

Those in CAPITALS are Peculiar to Matthew

Miracle	Reference
1. Cleansing of a Leper	8:1–4
2. Healing of a Centurion's Servant	8:5–13
3. Restoring of Peter's Mother-in-law	8:14–15
4. Stilling of the Tempest	8:23–27
5. Deliverance of a Gadarene Demoniac	8:28–34
6. Healing of a Paralytic	9:1–8
7. Healing of a Woman with an Issue of Blood	9:20–22
8. Raising of the Daughter of Jairus	9:18–19, 23–26
9. HEALING OF TWO BLIND MEN	9:27–31
10. DELIVERANCE OF A DUMB DEMONIAC	9:32–33
11. Restoration of a Man with a Withered Hand	12:10–13
12. Deliverance of a Blind and Dumb Demoniac	12"22–23
13. Feeding of the Five Thousand	14:15–21
14. Walking upon the Sea	14:25–33
15. Deliverance of the Syrophoenician's Daughter	15:21–28
16. Feeding of the Four Thousand	15:32–38
17. Deliverance of a Lunatic Boy	17:14–18
18. FINDING OF THE COIN (statēr)	17:24–27
19. Healing of a Blind Man near Jericho	20:29–34
20. Withering of the Fig Tree	21:18–22

Not only is the miracle itself amazing, but its result is equally stunning. Twelve full baskets of fragments (one for each of the twelve disciples) remained over and above that which was eaten. The baskets (Greek, *kophinous*) were small baskets carried on the arm and used as a satchel. These may have belonged to the disciples, who now receive a basketful of blessing as a result of their labor to feed others. Collection of the fragments emphasized the adequacy and immensity of Christ's provision as well as Jesus' belief in conservation. He did not waste what He had created. Besides the five thousand men, a large uncounted group of women and children were fed. We can know that the count was accurate, because Luke tells us that Jesus had the crowd sit "in groups of about fifty each" (Luke 9:14). It would be easy and natural for one or more of the disciples to count the groups and multiple by about fifty to obtain the total figure. The magnitude of the miracle of the feeding was reinforced by the miracle of the collection of fragments. The participation of the disciples in the whole process was designed to picture their future involvement in multiplying the impact of the gospel.

Walking on the Water (14:22-36)

Following the miraculous feeding, which John relates to the discourse on the Bread of Life, Jesus made the disciples get into a boat to cross to the other side of the Sea of Galilee. Jesus dismissed the crowd and went up into a mountain by Himself to pray. This was one of several times that Jesus spent all night in prayer. A previous occasion was when He was about to select the twelve disciples. This time the crowd had sought to make Him king (John 6:15), and He had refused but needed to fellowship with His Father and to keep His eyes squarely on the goal before Him. That night the disciples encountered great difficulty from a "contrary wind." They were many stadia, or as John tells us, about three or four miles out in the lake (John 6:19). That was near the middle of this very deep and rough lake. During the fourth watch, 3:00 to 6:00 A.M., Jesus came to them "walking upon the sea"—another obvious miracle not to be explained away by His supposedly walking on stones out in the middle of the lake! The nearly exhausted disciples, who had been rowing for many hours, were afraid, thinking he was a "ghost" (Greek, *phantasma*), that is, a spirit or apparition. Jesus reassured them, "It is I," bracketed by a positive and a negative admonition.

Peter answered Him in his characteristically impulsive manner. This part of the story is recounted only by Matthew, on whom it must have made a deep impression. Remember that he was in the boat at the time. Perhaps he got wet when Peter climbed back in. The incident is not presented as a parable, but as an actual event involving three miracles: Jesus walking on the water, Peter temporarily doing so, and the wind ceasing immediately.[7] Peter urged Jesus, "Command me come to You on the water." This was not an unreasonable request for one who had just that day participated with the Savior in the miracle of the feeding of the five thousand! However, Peter took his eyes off the

Savior and fixed them on the surrounding conditions and began to sink. With the concentration of his faith broken, Peter came back under the control of the natural forces. Nevertheless, Peter knew what to do—call on Jesus! His prayer was one of the shortest in the Bible—"Lord, save me!" The incident served as a good lesson in spiritual truth for all the disciples, to urge them not to be of little faith and doubt. Yet, for the rest of his life, Peter could remember that he also walked on the water and came toward Jesus, if only for a few moments.

Jesus walking on the water supersedes all the Old Testament miracles involving miraculous crossings. Moses parted the Red Sea (Ex. 14:21–22). Joshua crossed the Jordan River on dry ground (Josh. 3:11–17) as did the prophets Elijah and Elisha (2 Kgs. 2:8, 14). But Jesus alone walked *on* the water! Both this miracle and that of feeding the five thousand are intended to present Him as One greater than Moses or the prophets.

The disciples worshiped Jesus and recognized Him as God's Son. Their spoken Aramaic of this phrase was a clear recognition of the deity of Jesus. No mere man deserved their worship, and no mere man could do what He had done. France observes that Matthew not only records the disciples' response, but repeats it in 16:16 and 27:54. He writes, "The disciples' reaction here does not upstage Peter's deliberately Christological use of the title in 16:16, but prepares the way for it."[8] It is no surprise, then, that the people of Gennesaret, on the plain to the northwest of the Sea of Galilee, were healed by simply touching the fringe of His cloak. This procedure may have been motivated by reports of the healing of the hemorrhaging woman that had previously occurred in this same region (cf. 9:20).

Study Questions

1. Who is Herod the tetrarch? Can you distinguish him from some of the other Herods?

2. Did you ever notice how Matthew uses a flashback here to give the story of John the Baptist's death?

3. Who were Herodias and her daughter (Salome)?

4. What seeming effect did John's death have on Jesus? See verses 12–13. Did Jesus need a quiet repose? Did not John's death cast a shadow forth toward His own death?

5. How many do you estimate Jesus fed with the loaves and fishes, based on verse 21?

6. Can you imagine the fellowship and conversation Jesus must have had with His Father alone on the mountain in verse 23? What do you think they talked about?

7. We make fun of Peter for being so bold, to ask Jesus to allow him to walk on the water, but what does the text say that Peter did? See verse 29.

8. How short, but effective was Peter's prayer in verse 30?

9. In verse 33, do we have recognition by the disciples of who Jesus really is?

10. What is the extent of Jesus' ability to heal, according to verse 36?

CHAPTER 15

Tradition! Tradition!
Matthew 15:1–39

Preview:

Matthew, along with the other Gospels, shows a rising tension and outright opposition to Jesus from Jewish religious leaders. Here the issue is over ritual cleansing and/or defilement. Do Jewish traditions, rules, and regulations carry more authority than God's Word? Jesus meets this challenge as tensions rise. Then, withdrawing for some rest and quiet, He continues to minister through healings and even another large feeding miracle.

The Conflict with the Pharisees over Ritual (15:1–20)

Religious traditions are usually embedded in a sincere desire to do the right thing. However, they often degenerate into mere human preference, with little or no regard for spiritual matters. As a result, Jesus often found Himself at odds with religious traditionalists who questioned His integrity as well as His methods.

A group of important religious leaders from Jerusalem came to investigate the ministry and teaching of Jesus (see also Mark 7:1–23). "The tradition of the elders" refers to rabbinic traditions that had evolved over a long period of time. The Jews of our Lord's time believed that, in addition to the written Law of Moses (*Torah*), an oral law (*Mishnah*) was given to Moses on Mount Sinai. This oral tradition passed down from Moses by word of mouth until it reached the Great Synagogue or Council of Elders that succeeded Ezra after the return from the Babylonian exile. This council lasted till 291 B.C. and seems to have been the source of the many accretions to the Law of God that have been found in Judaism, both ancient and modern.[1]

Initially, the rabbis attempted to protect and define the Law. But their constant reinterpretations and applications actually perverted the Law. As a result, Jesus rejected their traditional hand-washing rules (Mark 7:1–5) and Sabbath definitions (Luke 13:10–16; John 7:22–23). He especially criticized the corban rule that allowed one to donate money to the temple instead of using it to support one's parents. In this sense the tradition actually broke the Law instead of supporting it.

The argument over washing consisted of pouring a trickle of cold water over the outstretched hands. Leon Morris notes, "Washing the hands before meals was not required by the Old Testament, but it had become an essential part of the tradition of the Pharisees, which they regarded as possessing the same authority as the law itself."[2] The Jews were not as concerned with cleanliness as with the ritual itself. Jesus responded with another question, but His counter claim accused the Pharisees, scribes, and teachers of the Law of a much more serious omission. "Why do you yourselves transgress the commandment of God . . . ?" The Lord here shows that additions to the Word of God ultimately contradict it. "Honor your father and mother." This is the fifth commandment of the Decalogue (see Ex. 20:12; Deut. 5:16). "He who speaks evil . . . let him be put to death" is taken from the Septuagint of Exodus 21:17.

It was possible for a Jew by a legal quibble to dedicate his property to the temple, thus avoiding the necessity of supporting his parents, although he could continue to enjoy the proceeds himself. Notice that the Lord interprets the command to honor our parents in a practical sense. For children it means to obey them (Eph. 6:1–3), and for adults it means to support them. Our Lord condemns this common practice based on tradition since it completely defeats the purpose of the law. Jesus accuses these Jews of invalidating the Word of God by the use of this common tradition. Jesus calls His opponents "hypocrites." Jesus was not concerned with political correctness, but rather with personal holiness. See Matthew 23 where Jesus calls the Pharisees and scribes "hypocrites" seven times. Verses 8 and 9 are from Isaiah 29:13 and follow the Septuagint where it differs from the Hebrew.

The term "defiles"—that is, makes him profane—is a technical one. The idea in Judaism was that to eat the wrong sort of food deprived a man of holiness and ultimately, therefore, of acceptance with God. The Jewish leaders showed offense at this deliberate contradiction of their own teaching. In two vivid pictures (vv. 13–14) our Lord tells His disciples that the Pharisees have no real mission from God and are themselves blind. They and all that their religion stood for would be destroyed.

Christ's Responses to the Jewish Traditions

Tradition	Response
Giving alms in public	Give alms in secret (Matt. 6:2–4).
Praying in the streets	Pray with your door closed (Matt. 6:5–6).
Praying with repetitions	Pray without meaningless repetitions (Matt. 6:7–8).
Fasting with gloomy face	Fast with bright, clean face (Matt. 6:16–18).
Being judgmental and critical	Take care of your own sins first (Matt. 7:1–6).
Ritually washing before meals	What come out of the mouth defiles (Matt. 15:1–20).
Believing good works save	Only God can save (Matt. 19:16–26).

Peter, acting on behalf of the others, asked for an explanation of the saying that had given such offense. Our Lord proceeded to elaborate the teaching for their benefit. The word "eliminated" is a euphemism in the New American Standard Bible. The phrase means literally, "cast out into the latrine [Greek, *aphedron*]." The "those" is emphatic. That which comes out of the mouth, not what goes into it defiles a person. The reason is that our words come out of our hearts. A. T. Robertson says, "Spoken words come out of the heart and so are a true index of character."[3] "Evil thoughts" actually means "evil schemes." The Greek word here is *dialogismoi* from which we get the English word *dialogue*. A dialogue is not necessarily bad, but as Hendriksen points out, "it is worthy of note that in nearly every passage in which the word is used the activity described is clearly of a sinful nature."[4] "Blasphemies" refers to not only blasphemy in the modern, narrow sense of the word, but also criticism or libel of others. Adulteries and fornications are distinguished here, as they are in other places (Gal. 5:19 in the KJV). R. C. H. Lenski has rightly observed, "The fact that some of these sins are deeds and not merely words makes no difference when we recall Jesus' exposition of the Commandments in 5:21, etc."[5] Jesus teaches that the heart of man is essentially evil and can only be represented by God.

The Healing of the Canaanite Woman's Daughter (15:21–28)

Jesus' second withdrawal followed not only John's death, but also further rejection by the religious leadership of Israel. Thus Jesus actually left the country and went into parts of Tyre and Sidon, leaving Herod's jurisdiction to retire to Phoenicia for a time of seclusion, which was interrupted by a Canaanite woman. Mark 7:26 calls her a "Gentile of the Syrophoenician race." This is the only known occasion during our Lord's ministry that He went outside the boundaries of Israel. This Gentile woman was descended from the Canaanites who inhabited Syria and Canaan before the conquest of the latter by Joshua. The daughter was demon-possessed. The word (Greek, *daimonizetai*) literally means "demonized." The woman persistently sought Jesus' help, and He persistently kept quiet. Finally, He remarked that He was "sent only to the lost sheep of the house of Israel." Jesus was testing her faith. Leon Morris observes that Jesus clearly understood the nature of His mission to the "house of Israel." Until their final rejection came, He was committed essentially to them. "He would make no exception in the case of this Canaanite woman, until He was convinced that she fully understood what that vocation was, and until He had overwhelming evidence of her faith."[6] She prostrated herself in worship before Christ and pleaded for His supernatural aid, begging, "Lord, help me!"

By "children" the Lord meant Jews, and by "dogs," Gentiles. Our Lord's attitude was intended to test the woman's faith, which was rewarded by a miraculous healing. Jesus was not angry with her but was trying to teach the disciples a valuable lesson. Having been rejected by the Jews, He now turned to the Gentiles, a move that would later shock some of His followers. He had healed Gentiles earlier, but here in Phoenicia He did not want to give the impression that he had totally abandoned Israel. The term used for "dogs" (Greek, *kunariois*) means little dogs (pets), not wild, scavenging beasts. She replied that "even dogs feed on the crumbs which fall from their master's table." She knew what could be hers, even as a Gentile. Therefore she became an illustration of millions of Gentiles who would later be blessed by the Messiah of Israel. She considered the healing of her daughter to be but just a small crumb that Jesus would allow to fall her way. "Your faith is great," Jesus told her, again commending Gentile belief (cf. 8:10).

The Feeding of the Four Thousand (15:29–39)

The supposition that Matthew 15:29–39 is a confused duplicate account of the feeding of the five thousand must be rejected. Both Matthew and Mark (7:31–8:10) include the account of the two events and do so in such a way as to indicate that they quite clearly thought of them as two separate miracles. In fact, in Matthew 16:9–10, Jesus refers back to each of these feedings as separate miracles, mentioning both the number of men who were fed as well as the number of loaves used, and the resulting baskets of leftovers that remained, even using different words for the baskets used in each instance.

The occasion for this miracle was the healing of the lame, blind, dumb, and many others. The incident evidently took place on the southeast shore of Galilee, near the Gentile Decapolis. Therefore, many Gentiles seem to be among His listeners who "glorified the God of Israel." This feeding took place after the crowd had been with Him for three days and was fed with seven loaves and "a few small fish," which were then distributed in a manner similar to the other feeding.

Jesus thanked the Father for the provision, and the disciples distributed the food. This time seven full baskets remained. These baskets (Greek, *spuridas* or "hampers") were much larger than those in 14:20. In fact, this is the word used for the basket in which Saul (Paul) was lowered over the wall of Damascus to escape the Jews (Acts 9:25), translated as "a large basket" in the new King James Version and the New Living Translation. The distinct differences in these accounts and the inclusion of both in Matthew clearly indicates they are separate events.

The lesson to the disciples seems obvious: What you accomplish among the Jews will be duplicated among the Gentiles. Magadan is perhaps Magdala, a suburb of Tiberias, the major city on the western side of the Sea of Galilee. From here, Jesus would later cross the lake again to the eastern side and proceed to Caesarea Philippi near the Golan Heights. Hendriksen observes that Jesus labored in and around Galilee from December A.D. 27 until April A.D. 29. From this point onward, He turned His attention toward the Gentiles and the future fulfillment of His mission.

Study Questions

1. How many separate incidents or stories about Jesus are recorded in chapter 15?

2. Why was Jesus so hard on the Pharisees in verses 1–9?

3. Can you explain Jesus' argument about the difference between what goes into the mouth and what comes out of the mouth?

4. Explain Jesus' withdrawal in verse 21. What purpose do you feel He had in withdrawing?

5. Can you recall an earlier time in Jesus' life when He left the country of Israel? Remember what happened when He was an infant? What was the purpose of that travel?

6. In verse 26, what was Jesus' implication about the Canaanite woman in relation to the Jews?

7. How was the woman's faith shown in her remark about the little dogs under the table that eat the crumbs that fall? Was she asking for just a little crumb to fall her way?

8. What are the similarities and differences between the feedings of the multitudes in chapters 14 and 15?

9. What did Jesus do before He broke the bread and started the distribution? Should that not be an example to us as well?

10. Approximately where on the Sea of Galilee is Magadan? Use a map to point it out.

CHAPTER 16

The Great Prediction
Matthew 16:1-28

Preview:

The religious antipathy toward Jesus grows in this chapter. The Pharisees and Sadducees team up to test Him, and He warns His disciples about them. The climax, however, is when Jesus asks the disciples to clearly state who they believe Him to be. He is the Messiah, the Christ, the Son of God, Peter exclaims for the group. Then Jesus announces the church as a coming future entity, followed by a prediction of His own coming death and resurrection on the third day.

The Pharisees and Sadducees Rebuked (16:1-12)

The unbelieving Jewish leaders came seeking a sign from heaven, that is, an outward miraculous manifestation, of which Jesus had already given many. Notice that miracles alone never save anyone. They only serve to authenticate and call attention to the message, which must be believed in order for salvation to be experienced in the soul. Instead of another miracle, Jesus pointed them to the "signs of the times," eschatologically related to the sky and His second coming. He referred to their ability to discern the coming weather by the sky and implied that they should have been able to discern the time of His coming also.

Messianic anticipation was very strong among the common people of the first century. Yet the Jewish rulers seemed unconcerned. When they asked for a miraculous sign, Jesus reminded them that they had earlier asked for such a sign and He told them of the "Sign of Jonah," pointing to

His miraculous resurrection. By continuing to ask for "signs," the unbelieving leaders were admitting they did not trust Him.

The "adulterous generation" is used here in a spiritual sense, of being unfaithful to God. The "sign of Jonah" is one of Jesus' favorites, for it relates to His resurrection (see 12:38–40; John 2:18–22). This sign gives hope to the believer but is an indication of judgment for the unbeliever, who will be judged by the risen Christ at His second coming. Verse 12 says "the leaven of the Pharisees and Sadducees" (vv. 6, 11) is their teaching. According to Mark 8:10, the Pharisees questioned Jesus on the western shore near Dalmanutha. Now they proceeded by boat across to the sparsely populated eastern shore, having forgotten to take along enough bread. Robert Newman, a New Testament scholar who did an extensive study on this passage, believes Jesus' admonition is an aphorism, a short pithy statement of a principle. It is also a prophetic warning to beware of the kind of teaching and contrary conduct that characterized these two groups of religious leaders.[1] Walvoord notes that leaven is a "symbol of permeating evil" that expands in unbelief.[2]

False Teachings of the Pharisees and Sadducees

Pharisees	Sadducees
Believed that studying the Law was worship	Held that only Moses' writings had authority
Adhered to legalistically keeping the Law	Strictly observed the Law
Accepted oral law equally with written law	Believed that oral laws were obligatory
Believed in keeping all the rituals	Denied divine providence
Believed salvation was basically by law keeping	Denied eternal life and the resurrection
Believed in the existence of angels and demons	Denied the existence of angels and demons

Peter's Confession (16:13–17)

Peter's confession of Christ as the Son of God is found here in Matthew as well as in Mark 8:27–33 and Luke 9:18–21. Proceeding northeast, Jesus came into the "district of Caesarea Philippi." This was a town in the extreme northeast corner of Galilee, near the source of the Jordan. Today there are just ruins there, but the setting is very picturesque. A small stream emerges from beneath a two-hundred-foot cliff of solid rock. Small pebbles form the bed of the little stream, one of four primary sources that merge to form the Jordan River. This setting helps us understand the references to Peter and the rock in verse 18. Two things are evident about this location. First, Caesarea Philippi, named for Augustus Caesar and Herod Philip, was a very Gentile location. Second, the city sat in front of a large rocky cliff. It was here that Jesus would announce the formation of the church, which would include both Jews and Gentiles. Public opinion placed our Lord on the highest human pedestal by identifying Him with one of the Jewish national heroes of the recent past, John the Baptist. Herod himself was a victim of this particular superstition (see 14:2). From 21:26 we know that Christ was also held in high esteem as a prophet by the people. The coming of Elijah was prophesied by Malachi (Mal. 4:5), and the Jews often linked the name of Jeremiah with the prophet foretold in Deuteronomy 18:15. These identifications may have been popular among some of the people, but the disciples knew better. Speaking on their behalf, Peter announced the true identity of Jesus.

"Thou art the Christ," Peter exuberantly exclaimed. Simon Peter recognized and acknowledged openly the Lord's messiahship and deity. He may have been speaking for all the disciples. Verse 20 suggests that it was a conviction they all now shared. Peter further used the Greek definite article "the" to designate that Jesus was "the Son of the living God." Jesus was not merely *a* son of God; He was indeed *the* Son of God!

Hendriksen points out that in both the Gospels and Acts, Peter frequently represents the Twelve (Matt. 15:15–16; 19:27–28; 26:35–41; Luke 8:45; 9:32–33; 12:41; 18:28; John 6:67–69; Acts 1:15; 2:14, 37–38; 5:29).[3] He further adds that Peter's declaration of Jesus as the Christ (Messiah) means the long-awaited Anointed One, ordained by the Father and anointed with the Spirit to be the chief Prophet, only High Priest, and eternal King promised and predicted in the Old Testament. Peter's further declaration that Jesus is "the Son of the living God," uniquely distinguishes Him as the divine Savior in a sense that is not applicable to any mortal man. In response to the truth of this declaration, Hendriksen observes, Jesus' words are immediate, definite, warm, and commendatory.[4]

Jesus' Prediction (16:18–28)

"You are Peter, and upon this rock I will build My church," the Savior declared. The Greek word used for "rock" (Greek, *petra*) is played against the name of Peter (Greek, *petros*) in the original. The Roman Catholic interpretation of this passage is that Peter was the foundation stone of the church, that he had a primacy among the apostles, that he became the bishop of Rome, and that his primacy was passed on to his successors, the popes. The verse may bear the first of these propositions but certainly none of the others. Protestant interpreters, with some patristic support (Chrysostom, Justin Martyr, and Augustine), have tended to identify the rock with Peter's faith or confession, or with our Lord Himself.

The most straightforward interpretation seems to be that Peter is meant by the rock but that he is not the exclusive foundation.[5] For the twelve-fold foundation of the church, see Ephesians 2:20; Revelation 21:14. This view seems borne out by the fact that the same words are spoken to all the disciples in Matthew 18:18 as are spoken to Simon Peter in 16:19. Therefore, the rock or foundation of the church is the confession (ultimately, the doctrine) of the apostles, which became normative for the true church.[6]

The word here translated "church" (Greek, *ekklēsia*) literally means "a chosen or called-out assembly." Thus the use of the word as a technical term for an assembly or group of believers in Christ was quite natural. It was not viewed as an external organization, denomination, or hierarchical system. The New Testament church, therefore, is a local, autonomous congregation or assembly of believers, which is a "church," in and of itself. The same word was used in the Septuagint to translate "congregation" (Hebrew, *qâhâl*) again emphasizing the local independent function of both a synagogue and a church.

This is the first occurrence of the word *ekklēsia* in the New Testament and is used in prophetic anticipation. Jesus' prediction "I will build" (Greek, *oikodomeō*) could be translated, "I shall continue to build" (progressive future).[7] Since the commission in Matthew 10 sent the apostles only to the "house of Israel," and no further commission was given until chapter 28, there was no worldwide task for the disciples until the physical manifestation of the church at Pentecost. In the meantime, Jesus announces one of His greatest predictions. He will establish, build, and perpetuate the church continually as evidence of His authority.

Jesus also promised that the "gates of Hades" shall not overpower the church (assembly). Some have viewed this as the inability of hell to conquer the church and see the church as being on the defensive against Satan. However, the phrase "shall not overpower" (Greek, *katischusousin*) may be understood as meaning "shall not stand against." The imagery would then picture the church as being on the attack against the gates of Hades. Here Hades probably represents the kingdom of Satan, not just death and the grave. While Jesus' resurrection certainly will overcome the sting of death, it will also enable His church to aggressively and offensively attack the gates of Hades (cf. usage as Satan's kingdom in Job 38:17; Ps. 107:18; Isa. 38:10) by snatching out victims from darkness into His glorious kingdom of light. One does not attack with gates; he defends. It is the church that is on the attack here, and Hades, Satan's realm, is on the defensive.

Our Lord then promised Peter and the other apostles the "keys of the kingdom." This means that Peter would have the right to enter the kingdom himself and would have general authority therein, symbolized by the possession of the keys. Preaching the gospel would be the means of opening the kingdom of heaven to all believers and shutting it against unbelievers. The book of Acts shows us this process at work. In his sermon on the day of Pentecost (Acts 2:14–40), Peter opened the door of the kingdom for the first time. The expressions bind and loose were common in Jewish legal phraseology, meaning to declare forbidden or to declare allowed.

Peter and the other disciples (see 18:18) were to continue the work of Christ on earth by preaching the gospel and declaring God's will to people. Doing such, they were armed with the same authority as He Himself possessed. Christ in heaven ratifies what is done in His name and in obedience to His word on earth. There is also a definite reference here to the binding and loosing of church discipline, which is further explained in chapter 18. The apostles do not usurp Christ's lordship and authority over individual believers and their eternal destiny. They do, however, exercise the authority to discipline and, if necessary, excommunicate disobedient church members. The revelation was to remain the property of the disciples until after the Lord's resurrection. Thus, they were to "tell no one" until later.

The *great prediction* of Christ building His church is the basis for the Great Commission, which follows in 28:18–20. After the resurrection and ascension of Christ, the disciples would be empowered to take His life-changing message to the whole world. Jews and Gentiles alike would be gathered into the body of the church. From Pentecost until the rapture, the church will continue to grow. Therefore, it should not surprise us that churches are still growing today and new ones are being planted continually. This is exactly what our Lord predicted would happen. Until the trumpet sounds and the Lord calls His bride home to heaven, we have a job to do here on earth. We are to preach the gospel to all nations, making disciples and baptizing them in the name of Jesus Christ. The church is central to our Lord's plan for world evangelization. He has not given up on it, and neither should we. He will continue to build it until He calls us home to heaven.

Next, Jesus announced His coming rejection and death at Jerusalem. All this would be necessary to initiate the church as the spiritual form of the kingdom on earth. "From that time" He openly revealed His coming rejection, since the disciples' faith was now established enough to bear it. From this point onward, our Lord's ministry took on a different complexion as He sought to prepare His followers for the suffering that awaited Him and that would so disappoint their hopes. This was all the more ironic in light of the prediction He had just made. Jesus referred to the religious leaders as "elders." The word probably denotes members of the Sanhedrin and included the high priest and former high priests. The words "be killed" and "be raised up" on the third day clearly indicate the divine Messiah's awareness of His earthly mission and destiny. To predict His death in view of His rejection was human, but to predict a supernatural resurrection could only be done by the God-man! Jesus clearly understood that He must die and then rise from the dead to build His church, which would overcome both hell and death.

Peter's instantaneous reaction to our Lord's new teaching shows how foreign to his way of thinking was this conception of His suffering. "God forbid it, Lord!" Notice the marginal readings of both the King James Version and the Revised Standard Version. The sentence seems to mean literally "Have mercy on yourself." The New American Standard Bible margin says, "Lit., (God be) *merciful to You.*" The Lord recognized in Peter's words a repetition of the temptations of Satan to avoid the cross that He had undergone in the wilderness. This incident clearly indicates that Satan can tempt us even through the words of other believers.

The word translated "stumbling block" (Greek, *skandalon*) means a trap or snare. "Setting your mind" (Greek, *phroneō*) is very difficult to translate. It occurs in Romans 8:5 and Philippians 2:5, meaning to adopt and maintain an attitude of mind upon which one's life and actions are based. "Deny himself" means to refuse his own claims upon himself. Oswald Chambers says, "The characteristics of individuality are independence and self-assertiveness. It is the continual assertion of individuality that hinders our spiritual life more than anything else. . . . God wants to bring you into union with Himself, but unless you are willing to give up your right to yourself, He cannot."[8]

Jesus again challenges the disciples to "take up the cross." The meaning is "lift up." It is a stronger word than that used in 10:38 (Greek, *lambanō*), and implies a lifting of the cross on high, so that all may see it. This is the strongest statement in the New Testament about the disciple's need to crucify himself to the claims of self and submit to Christ's lordship over him. Jesus makes it very clear that discipleship is more than intellectual assent.[9] "Loses his life" (v. 25) means to lose one's life and perish. Jesus promises He will "recompense every man according to his deeds." The words are adopted from the Septuagint of Psalm 62:12 and Proverbs 24:12. This great fundamental moral principle of the Old Testament is made more explicit here by our Lord in explaining that it will find its fulfillment at His return.

Taking Up the Cross	
A sign of complete submission to God's will	Matthew 10:38
A sign of self-denial	Matthew 16:24
A sign of daily sacrifice	Luke 9:23
A sign of Christ's finished work to atone for the believer's sins	Colossians 2:14; 1 Peter 2:24
The cross of Christ is foolishness to the world	1 Corinthians 1:18

Jesus concludes by promising, "Some. . . shall not taste death until they see the Son of Man coming in His kingdom." This statement has caused much difficulty and needless misunderstanding. Its fulfillment may be looked for in the transfiguration, which immediately follows. On this occasion the apostle Peter asserts that the three disciples saw Christ's coming (cf. 2 Pet. 1:16ff.). They also saw it in the Lord's resurrection and subsequent glory. The preterist idea that this had to be fulfilled in the destruction of Jerusalem in A.D. 70 has no validity.[10] Jesus did not return in A.D. 70, Jerusalem was not spared, and the Antichrist was not overthrown at that time. Everett F. Harrison writes that Jesus' statement "seems to suggest that the transfiguration was intended as a foregleam of the glory of the Son of man as he would be in his consummated kingdom. This eschatological understanding of the event . . . answers well as a corollary to the suffering of the Messiah that was discussed on the mount. . . . The glory in anticipation was designed to offset the perplexity and pain that the announcement of the passion had brought to the minds of the disciples."[11]

Study Questions

1. What real purpose did the Pharisees and Sadducees have in asking Jesus questions?

2. In verses 6–12 Jesus warns against the "leaven" of the Pharisees and Sadducees, and then explains that He was warning against their teachings. In what ways do you think their teaching resembled leaven?

3. Can you find Caesarea Phillipi on a map? If not, look to the area just south of Mount Hermon.

4. Why did Jesus refer to Himself in verse 13 as the Son of Man? Did you know that no one else ever called Him by that title? Is there a connection of His usage with Daniel 7:13–14?

5. Why do you think some people thought Jesus might have been one of the men mentioned in verse 14?

6. Jesus asked, "But who do you say that I am?" How did Peter answer that question? What is your answer to that question?

7. Can you explain what Jesus may have meant when He said, "You are Peter, and upon this rock I will build My church" (v. 18)?

8. What is meant by the "keys of the kingdom of heaven" that Jesus gave to Peter? Did that make Peter the pope?

9. Was Jesus specific enough in predicting His own death and resurrection in verse 21? Why do you think the disciples were so shaken when it all came to pass?

10. How is verse 25 a "hard saying"? In what way is it also a paradox?

11. What do you think Jesus was referring to when He said that some of the disciples would see "the Son of Man coming in His kingdom"?

CHAPTER 17

The Glorious King
Matthew 17:1-27

Preview:

Christ's prediction of His own coming death weakened the disciples and deprived them of all courage. Now Christ reveals His glory and the reality of His coming kingdom by His own transfiguration. The disciples are stunned but no doubt reassured, Peter and John both mentioning the event in their later writings.

Christ's Manifestation: Special Transfiguration (17:1-27)

The transfiguration is one of the most spectacular events in the life of Christ. It is the only display of His divine glory recorded in the Gospels. For a brief moment, three of the disciples (Peter, James, and John) saw Him in all the splendor of heaven. They saw Him as He really is—the divine Son of God.

What the disciples saw that day on the mountaintop was deity on display. They already knew Jesus was no ordinary man. His miracles were proof enough of that. They had seen Him heal the sick, feed the multitudes, cast out demons, and walk on water. But in all those situations, He looked like a man. He walked, talked, and lived like a man. But on this special day, Jesus looked like God.

John Walvoord notes that "Matthew gives the most complete detailed account of the transfiguration, showing that he is not as dependent upon Mark's gospel as some have taught."[1] The parallel accounts can be found in Mark 9:2-13 and Luke 9:28-36. Only Luke mentions that Jesus went up the mountain "to pray," and that "while He was praying" the transformation occurred. We might wonder how the three disciples Jesus took happened to be there with Him. Could Jesus have said, "Who wants to go up the mountain to pray?" and only three responded? Peter and James and John represent the "inner circle" of leadership among the disciples (cf. Matt. 26:37; Luke 8:51) and serve here as ample witnesses according to Mosaic Law. They went into a high mountain by themselves. Tradition claims that the transfiguration took place at Mount Tabor, in the Jezreel Valley. Others suggest a more probable location would be Mount Hermon, near Caesarea Philippi, where Jesus and the disciples had been the week before this event.

Jesus was "transfigured before them" (v. 2). The verb (Greek, *metamorphoō*) indicates a transformation of essential form, proceeding from within. See Romans 12:2 and 2 Corinthians 3:18, where it is used of the spiritual transformation of the believer's new nature.[2] The witness of Peter in 2 Peter 1:17–18 verifies the testimony that this was a real experience, not a vision. In His transfiguration, Jesus was the personal manifestation of God's glory (cf. John 1:14, "We beheld His glory, glory as of the only begotten from the Father, full of grace and truth"). He revealed that glory temporarily to these key disciples. Later, in John's Patmos vision of Revelation 1, the risen, glorified Savior again appeared.

Moses and Elijah were the representatives respectively of the Law and the Prophets (see Jude 9, where Moses' resurrection is implied, and 2 Kings 2:11 for the account of Elijah's being taken up into heaven). Why these two in particular? Homer Kent notes that "some have seen in Moses (who had died) and Elijah (who had passed from this life without dying) representatives of the two groups that Christ will bring with him to establish his kingdom: dead saints who are resurrected and living saints who have been translated. Likewise, the three disciples are seen as representing men living on earth at the time of the Second Advent."[3] William Pettingill sees the three who are alive at the time the glorious kingdom of Christ is set up (Peter, James, and John) as representing Israel. He says, "These were not glorified in the picture, for they represent the Jews who will pass into the Kingdom as an earthly people."[4]

Moses and Elijah, the two witnesses representing the Law and Prophets on this occasion, were "talking with Him." Luke mentions the subject matter of that privileged conversation—"of His departure which He was about to accomplish at Jerusalem" (Luke 9:31). This shows that Messiah's death is in accordance with Old Testament revelation, as properly understood. "It is good for us to be here," Peter said as though his approval were somehow needed. Peter wished to retain the situation and so suggested building three "tabernacles" or tents. Actually, Peter has stumbled badly for a second time here; after upbraiding Christ about the crucifixion (Matt. 16:22), now he was suggesting that Moses and Elijah were of equal status to Christ. "A voice," that is, the Father's voice (for the words spoken, see 3:17), spoke "out of the cloud," indicating that Christ's authority superseded that of the Old Testament Law and Prophets. "Listen to Him!" is a good admonition at any time. The warning "Tell . . . no one," is to avoid a premature popular, but misdirected, awakening in Jesus' favor, as when some wanted to make Him King after He fed the five thousand (John 6:14–15). By this momentous event, Jesus assured the disciples that He is truly the Son of God, and that His kingdom will come in all the power, majesty, and glory just as He and all the Old Testament prophets have declared.

Moses and Elijah at the Transfiguration

Moses	Elijah
Brought forth the Law	Announced the coming of the Messiah
Brought Israel out of sinful Egypt	Announced the terrible Day of the Lord
Delivered the Jewish people	Will restore the Jewish people — father to son
Conflicted with the Egyptians	Conflicted with the priests of Baal

The point of the disciples' question in verse 10 seems to be that, supposing that Jesus' resurrection meant the end of the world and the inauguration of the kingdom, it would be necessary for Elijah to appear first. They had been reminded by seeing him on the mountain, so it was a natural assertion. Our Lord's answer is a quotation from Malachi 4:5–6, where the coming of Elijah was prophesied. "Restore all things" has reference to a ministry of preparing hearts to receive the Messiah. He then repeats what He has told them already—that the prophecy foretelling the coming of Elijah was fulfilled as a contingency in John the Baptist (see 11:14). That is, if the Jews had received Jesus, John would have fulfilled the prophecy of Malachi. Some, however, see John the Baptist as completely fulfilling the Elijah reference in Malachi.[5] Others, such as Walvoord, state, "The evidence that John the Baptist at least in part fulfilled the prophecy of Elijah is clear, but a future appearance of Elijah is debatable."[6] Still others hold that Elijah himself will one day appear to completely and finally fulfill the prophecy of Malachi 4.

Arno Gaebelein affirms, "His work is *exclusively* among the people who are the kingdom people. His witness is to the remnant of Israel. Like John's call to repentance, he will preach repentance and his testimony will be received; he will accomplish the mission of Malachi iv:5, 6."[7] Without naming John the

Baptist directly, Jesus recalls his suffering and compares with it the treatment He will receive (v. 12).

Upon returning down the mountain, Jesus came upon His remaining nine powerless disciples who were attempting to cure an epileptic. The King James Version has "lunatic," from the Latin, *luna*, or moon, because the Greek word (Greek, *selēniazomai*), literally means "moonstruck." Demonic possession and certain psychological illnesses have certain apparent affinities. However, when medication can bring a person back into his or her right mind, as with a chemical imbalance, that is not demon possession.

This case was very difficult, for the boy was extremely ill. The question, "How long shall I be with you?"—that is, "How long can I endure you?" showed Jesus' concern for their inadequacy. "Faith as a mustard seed" seems to mean that faith, once implanted in the heart, grows naturally like a living organism. True faith, though it be small, can achieve much with God. John A. Broadus observes that "their faith must therefore have been extremely minute, being less than this."[8] This mountain may have referred to the Mount of the Transfiguration, but it obviously means any seemingly impossible obstacle or difficulty that stands in the believer's way. Verse 21 is not found in a handful of Greek manuscripts (about five), considered by some to be the more reliable texts. Some believe it was interpolated from Mark 9:29. Nevertheless, H. A. W. Meyer comments, "If you have only a slender amount of faith, you will, no doubt, be able to accomplish things of an extraordinary and seemingly impossible nature; but, in order to expel spirits of so stubborn a character as this, you require to have such a degree of faith as can only be reached by means of prayer and fasting. You have neglected the spiritual preparation that is necessary to the attainment of so lofty a faith."[9]

The Power of True Faith	
Metaphorically speaking, faith can move mountains.	*Matthew 21:21*
Stephen was full of power and of faith.	*Acts 6:8*
Believers live by the power of God.	*2 Corinthians 13:4*
The gospel comes by the word and by the power of the Holy Spirit.	*1 Thessalonians 1:5*
For the believer, faith works with godly power.	*2 Thessalonians 1:11*

The purpose of this incident is obvious. Since Christ alone is the glorified Savior, the disciples' ability to work miracles depends totally upon His empowerment. "Bring him here to Me" clearly emphasizes this. Bringing people to ourselves to listen to our ideas is never adequate. The true Christian evangelist must bring people to Jesus Himself. Christ emerges from this scene as dominant, with the disciples dependent upon Him. They again were exceeding sorry or "greatly distressed" by His further announcement of His coming death. This so shocked them that His prediction of His resurrection did not even register in their minds. This is the second of three clear predictions Jesus makes of His coming crucifixion and resurrection.

Christ Predicts His Crucifixion and Resurrection	
The Son of Man will be raised from the dead.	*Matthew 17:9*
The Son of Man is going to suffer at the hands of evil men.	*Matthew 17:12*
The Son of Man will be killed and rise again.	*Matthew 17:22–23*
Jonah is a type of Christ's death and resurrection.	*Matthew 12:40*
Jesus will raise the temple of His body.	*Matthew 26:61; 27:40*

Excursus: Paying the Temple Tax (17:24–27)

Jesus, the glorified Son of God is greater than demons and also greater than the temple itself. The two incidents following the transfiguration clearly reassert His supremacy. The two-drachma tax is a technical term for the tax of half a shekel, which every Jew over twenty was expected to contribute to the upkeep of the temple (Ex. 30:12–14; 38:26; 2 Chr. 24:6, 9). William Hendriksen notes: "The drachma, a Greek silver coin, was about equal in value to a Roman denar[ius]. It amounted to a workman's average daily wage. Consequently the double-drachma was the amount a man would generally earn for two days' work."[10] The amount was collected, not by the Roman tax collectors, as Matthew had been, but by the Jewish religious hierarchy from Jerusalem.

The difficulty in making this payment, however, was that "the payment had to be made in the Jewish coin, half-shekel. Hence the money-changers did a thriving business in charging a small premium for the Jewish coin.[11] The actual question posed to Peter "indicates that these temple tax agents are attempting to elicit an affirmative response: 'He does pay the tax, doesn't he?' "[12] The subject races ("strangers") which were taxed first and most heavily. The sons, that is, the king's own race, were exempt. The Lord Jesus Christ was the Lord and owner of the temple, and therefore it was not for Him to pay tax. Action based on this fact might obviously be misunderstood, however, and under such circumstances, our Lord would not give offense by seeming to be a lawbreaker. But note that in any matter where a fundamental principle was at stake, our Lord did not tone down His message in order not to offend (cf. 15:10–14). A stater (Greek, *statēr*), was "the silver tetradrachma, equivalent to the shekel and therefore the exact amount of the tax for two persons."13

The respect Jesus showed to the temple and public worship clearly indicates that He was concerned about being a proper example to others. He was not an iconoclast, bent on violating religious beliefs and practices. When such were in violation of the truth, He clearly said so. But in this case, the Savior's concern was not to cause others to stumble.

In order to pay the tax, Jesus instructed Peter to catch a fish with a hook, the only such example in the New Testament. He was to open it up, and there he would find a coin in its mouth to pay the tax. A. T. Robertson observes: "It is not stated that Peter actually caught such a fish, though that is the natural implication."14

The unique feature in the story is the relation of Jesus to the temple. As Lord of the temple, He did not need to pay the temple tax. But as Lord of life, He paid it as an example to others (as in the case of His baptism). But even then, God miraculously provided the coin, demonstrating Christ's superiority over the whole matter.

Study Questions

1. How long after Jesus predicted that some would see Him coming in His kingdom (16:28), did the transfiguration occur?

2. Which disciples went with Jesus into the high mountain? Can you recall other times when only this group was present with Jesus?

3. What significance was there in the appearance with Jesus of two men who had been dead for centuries? Why these two particular men?

4. What was God the Father's testimony about Jesus?

5. Can you explain how John the Baptist was Elijah yet was not really Elijah? Is there still a future ministry for the real Elijah to perform?

6. What does the story of the demon-possessed epileptic boy teach us?

7. What does it mean to have faith like a little mustard seed?

8. Did you notice Jesus' second prediction of His coming death and resurrection? In what verse is it found?

9. Why are brackets around verse 21 in chapter 17? What do you notice when you compare this verse with Mark 9:29?

10. What does verse 27 teach us about the attributes of our Lord Jesus Christ?

CHAPTER 18

Forgive and Forget
Matthew 18:1-35

Preview:

This chapter is Jesus' third great discourse in Matthew. Jesus' disciples, and we ourselves, are often in need of teaching on these topics. The part about humility comes out of the disciples' efforts to determine which of them was to be the greatest in the kingdom. The teaching on forgiveness followed another question, this time by Peter, related to church discipline.

Christ's Mercy: Sanctification of Forgiveness (18:1-35)

Personal Forgiveness (18:1-14)

This chapter forms Jesus' longest recorded statement regarding the principle of forgiveness. (See also Mark 9:33-37; Luke 9:46-48.) The act of forgiving one who has wronged us is one of the most responsible and spiritual activities in our lives and must be repeated continually throughout our lives. This passage is Jesus' last great discourse before His journey to Jerusalem and is given in response to the disciples' jealousy of one another. It is also given to prepare them for the crucifixion, an act they would have to learn to forgive. Mark 9:33 indicates the message was given "in the house," probably Peter's.

The question "Who then is the greatest in the kingdom of heaven?" was elicited by Jesus' asking what the disciples had been discussing along the way. Apparently Jesus would lead the group along the road, and perhaps talk to one or two who would be walking with Him. The rest, however, lagged back a bit and "had discussed with one another which of them was the greatest"

(Mark 9:34). Mark tells us that when Jesus asked about their topic, "they kept silent" (v. 34). Finally one of them went ahead and divulged the issue. They were discussing who would be the greatest in Jesus' kingdom. It would be settled, however, by Jesus' emphasis that it was the one who was willing to forgive the most! He thereby cut down the basic human motivation of pride to be the greatest by calling for the "greatest" to be the one most willing to forgive, which is contrary to proud human nature.

B. F. Atkinson suggests that the child may have been a member of Peter's family,[1] but it could just as well have been any neighborhood child. "Converted" means a "turning" (Greek, *strephō*) of one's whole life and person toward God. This is the true biblical picture of conversion. It is a turning (repentance) from sin and self and, at the same time, a turning toward God (faith) with correct beliefs about Him. It is far more than mental acknowledgment of the truth or intellectual assent to certain ideas. He now speaks generically of humankind's need to turn to Him and of the evidence of that turning in an attitude of humility. Thus He challenges the disciples' selfishness by making them examine the reality of their own conversion. To "become like children" means to be born again (converted) as a newborn spiritual child, characterized by faith and humility.

Jesus apparently sat the child next to Himself in the position of privilege, which the bickering disciples preferred for themselves. However, the innocent child had no pride about his position, which he humbly accepted. Thus the child represents a new convert or young believer. Whoever receives such a fellow believer actually welcomes Christ Himself. Therefore, the basis of true Christian fellowship is established in Christ Himself. There can be no real fellowship with those who deny Him and have not been converted, but with any true believer, fellowship may exist. This, of course, does not overlook the discipline of an errant believer. "Stumblingblocks" are viewed as a reality that must be accepted in the present world, but "woe" (the prophetic condemnation to death) to the one who is the source of the offense. Jesus very definitely took this matter seriously. A heavy millstone is literally an "ass-stone," or a large grinding stone turned by an ass or a donkey.

Verses 8–9 repeat some of the same ideas as in the Sermon on the Mount (see note on 5:29–30). The foot, hand, and eye, are not the real source of temptation, nor are they the real cause of offending others. Even as temptation arises from within, so does offending others and being offended. It should be noted that this message is dealing with both aspects of the problem. We are most likely to offend others when we are selfish and proud. At the same time, however, we are also most likely to be offended when we are selfish and proud. This reference to hell fire is another time that Jesus speaks of literal fire in hell. The New International Version has "the fire of hell," but strangely, the New Living Bible omits the word fire altogether. The Revised English Bible says, "the fires of hell." Either way, the idea of real and continuous punishment is clearly indicated.

See that you "do not despise" (Greek, *kataphroneō*) means "literally, 'think down on,' with the assumption of superiority."[2] William Hendriksen explains, "At the root of all self-exaltation lies sinful pride, a looking down."[3] The reference to their angels of these little ones (v. 10) may support the idea of individual guardian angels for believers (not all children in general). We know that nations (Dan. 10:13, 20–21; 12:1) have angels assigned to them, and according to Revelation 1:20, so do each of the seven churches of Asia, whatever that might entail. Hendriksen has an extended passage on this subject, and he concludes that God's angels take a very special interest in God's people (Heb. 1:14).[4]

Some hold that verse 11, while legitimate in Luke 19:10, seems to be inserted here, since some ancient texts omit it.[5] F. C. Cook has carefully observed that this verse "can hardly have been interpolated from Luke xix. 10, in which case the words, 'to seek,' so appropriate to the present context would not have been omitted." He believes there is a connection with the "former part of the verse; the thought being, 'Take heed lest ye despise one of these little ones, and think lightly of causing them to offend; for in causing the loss even of one of the least of your brethren, ye destroy one whom Christ came to save."[6] The truth of the statement, therefore, is reinforced throughout Scripture.

Salvation is not just a privilege to be enjoyed by the elect, but is also to be shared with the lost that they too may be saved. Thus, it is not the Father's will . . . that any of these "little ones," perish. The immediate context in Matthew relates "little ones" to believers, but the cross-reference in Luke 15:3–7 clearly refers to lost sheep. Thus we may conclude that it is not the ultimate wish (or desire) of God that anyone should perish. While God permits people to perish through their unbelief, He does not elect them to such condemnation against their will. Rather, all of heaven rejoices over every lost sheep that is saved. The contrast of the imminent danger to the lost sheep and the safety of those in the fold (of faith) clearly expresses where the majority of our attention and concentration should be in the ministry and activity of the church as we fulfill our commission to the world.

Church Discipline (18:15–35)

The setting of these verses fits into the context of church discipline. If a brother offends someone or refuses to forgive someone, what must be done? Three basic views have been given here for the synagogue or the church (Greek, *ekklēsia*). In either case, the action is the same. The responsibility of action is threefold: (1) personal, "go and reprove him"; (2) "take two or three witnesses"; (3) corporate, "tell it to the church."

"Go and reprove him" means to honestly express the point of offense. This should not be done in vindictive anger, but it must be done in straightforward honesty. To fail to speak up is to be dishonest and will lead to harboring continued bitterness. The last phrase of verse 16 is taken from Deuteronomy 19:15, substantially from the Septuagint. This just and sensible principle of the Mosaic Law is thus brought over by our Lord into the New Testament and established for the advantage of the Christian church. Refuse carries with it some blameworthiness on the part of the offender. "Let him be to you as a Gentile and a tax-gatherer," means to let him be as one who would not be admitted into the church. The obstinate sinner is to be cut off, at least temporarily, from Christian fellowship. Examples of this are found in 1 Corinthians 5:4–5 and 1 Timothy 1:20. The promise is here addressed to all the disciples. The concept of binding and loosing should be explained in accordance with their meaning in Matthew 16:19. Christ will confirm what the church does when it is in accordance with His revealed purposes and will as expressed in His Word. We proclaim the message, the basis on which things are either bound or loosed, and leave the results with Him.

Guidelines for Church Discipline

Reprove the brother in private.	Matthew 18:15
If the brother does not listen, two or more other witnesses confirm the problem.	Matthew 18:16
If the brother does not respond, the issue. is shared with the church	Matthew 18:17
The brother is forgiven when he repents.	Luke 17:3
The brother who persists in his sins is to be removed from fellowship.	1 Corinthians 5:2
The repentant brother is to be restored to fellowship.	2 Corinthians 2:5–10; Galatians 6:1
Forgiveness should end the matter,	2 Corinthians 2:10

Verse 19 is one of the great gospel promises with regard to prayer. But note the close connection of the verse with those that precede and that which follows. The promise is specifically given to a gathering of disciples with Christ "in their midst" (v. 20), called to discipline an erring brother (v. 17). Their authority to do this is restated (v. 18), and the promise can be claimed because they are acting on behalf of the Father, in the name of the Son. "In My name" means to claim and use Christ's authority. Notice that the church in view here is operating in the future, in Christ's physical absence but by His authority. These words also teach the omnipresence of Christ, as do John 3:13 in the received text, and Matthew 28:20.

All this teaching on forgiveness seemed overwhelming to the disciples, thus prompting Peter's question: "Lord, how often shall my brother sin against me and I forgive him?" Peter wrongly assumed that seven times were ample to forgive anyone. Jesus responded that seven was not only insufficient but that one should forgive seventy times seven; in other words, unlimited forgiveness must characterize the true disciple, not retaliatory listing of others' offenses in an attitude of limited forgiveness. But how often do we miss the mark when we have the attitude, "I told you once," and want to hold someone responsible? By the standard we use to judge, we will be judged ourselves (Matt. 7:2).

The parable of the unforgiving servant (vv. 23–35) was used by Jesus to reinforce the power and importance of the principle of forgiveness. A "certain king" represents God, the sovereign Father (cf. v. 35), to whom the debt is owed. The "one who owed him" is a servant or satrap who had access to the king's money, and represents the individual sinner. Ten thousand talents was an insurmountable debt equivalent to millions of dollars in our society. It represents the debt of sin which the sinner cannot possibly pay by himself. The command that he "be sold . . . and repayment . . . be made" indicates him being placed in a debtor's prison. Still, an entire lifetime of service could never repay such a debt. The interpreter must stick to the main point of the parable and not be sidetracked by its minor details. That is, the compassion of the king releases him and forgives (cancels) the debt. The picture illustrates God's total forgiveness when dealing with our sins at the point of salvation. Christ has paid the debt, and we are set free from it forever!

The contrast in verse 28, where that slave is unwilling to forgive his fellow servant a debt of a hundred denarii (even though it is one hundred days' wages for a common laborer) is deliberately presented as a hideous hypothetical situation. Carson says, "The amount is utterly trivial compared with what has already been forgiven him."[7] As unbelievable as this action would be, that is how unbelievable it would be for a Christian disciple, who has been forgiven a lifetime of sin, to be unforgiving of others.

Forgiving Others	
Repentance should bring about forgiveness.	*Luke 17:3*
If there is true repentance, forgiveness should be "sevenfold."	*Luke 17:4*
Forgiveness should settle the matter.	*2 Corinthians 2:10*
Restoration should follow forgiveness.	*Galatians 6:1*
We are to forgive as Christ has forgiven us.	*Ephesians 4:32*

In the story, such an unforgiving servant is called a "wicked slave," because no true believer would do such. The unforgiving servant is not one who was saved and then lost his salvation. The story is merely hypothetical; no one forgiven a debt of millions would behave this way, therefore, the intention of the parable is to challenge the genuineness of the disciples' conversion with an example of extreme hyperbole. A truly saved man would never behave like the man in the story, who was delivered to the torturers (Greek, *basanistēs* or "jailer"). This is certainly not a reference to purgatory. One behaving in this manner falls into the condemnation of the lost. The searching threat of verse 35 does not mean that a true believer will be lost, but if he claims to be born of God, he will act like a born-again person. True forgiveness "from the heart" of a regenerate person is one of the true signs of genuine salvation and conversion (cf. Eph. 4:32). Saved people are both forgiven and forgiving. Unforgiving people prove that they have never been born of God.

Study Questions

1. What does it mean to "become like children" (v. 3) in order to enter the kingdom of heaven,

2. How serious is it in Jesus' estimation for someone to cause a little one who believes in Him "to stumble"?

3. Does verse 14 say anything about eternal security? Can a true believer ever be lost against the Father's will?

4. What steps are required for church discipline according to Matthew 18:15–17?

5. Can verse 17 speak of excommunication, meaning removing someone from the membership of a church after due process?

6. What is "binding" on earth and in heaven all about?

7. Have you noticed that Jesus' words in verse 20 actually speak of His omnipresence while still here on earth? Jesus continued to have all the attributes of deity while here on earth, even though He chose not to use some of them at times.

8. In verses 23–34, Jesus taught a story about forgiveness. What is the essence of His teaching there?

9. Verse 35 is very frank. What is it saying? How do you think this should this affect our daily walk with others?

CHAPTER 19

Marriage, Divorce, and Money
Matthew 19:1-30

Preview:

This chapter records Jesus leaving Galilee for the final time and passing through Peraea on His way to Jerusalem. Jesus is confronted by the Pharisees on the question of divorce in an attempt to catch Him teaching something unlawful. The story of the rich young ruler is recounted. He kept all he had, but went away sad. In contrast, the disciples have given up all, but they want to know what they will receive. Jesus answers their question.

Jesus' Teaching on Divorce (19:1-12)

Verse 1 of chapter 19 indicates the close of another division of the gospel (see 7:28). With verse 2 it describes briefly a journey from Galilee into the district of Judea beyond Jordan (i.e., Peraea). This must have taken considerable time, and the events of Luke 9:51-18:34 must largely be fitted into this time period. Matthew indicates that Jesus "departed from Galilee" and went "beyond the Jordan" (19:1); was "going up to Jerusalem" (20:18); and passed through "Jericho" (20:29). The teaching and incidents that follow in 19:3-20:43 also took place during the stay in Peraea. During the various movements on the way to Jerusalem, Matthew presents a varied series of events: Jesus' teaching on divorce, the confrontation with the rich young ruler, a parable, and a miracle.

Some Pharisees came testing Jesus with a difficult question. They wanted to test His wisdom with one of the most controversial questions of their day, and Jesus proved far superior to their expectations. They challenge Jesus' interpretation of Mosaic Law in Deuteronomy 24:1–5, where a "certificate of divorce" was allowed. The stricter school of Shammai held that divorce was lawful only upon a wife's shameful conduct. The more liberal school of Hillel gave the widest possible allowances for divorce. Homer Kent is correct when he explains, "Thus Jesus was being asked, 'Do you agree with the most prevalent interpretation?' (Hillel's)."[1] By asking "Have you not read . . . ?" Jesus refers them back to God's original purpose in creation that they be one flesh. The passage in Genesis 2:24 indicates that being one flesh is one "person," and is not to be limited to sexual union.[2] The Bible clearly indicates that sexual union does not itself constitute marriage, which is fundamentally a covenantal agreement between two partners for life (cf. Prov. 2:17; Mal. 2:14, "your wife by covenant").

The question "Why then did Moses command . . . ?" revealed the misuse of Deuteronomy 24 by the Jews of Jesus' day. Moses did not command divorce, he permitted it. Similarly, God did not command retaliation, but He permitted it. God had instituted marriage in the Garden of Eden. He is not the author of divorce; man is its originator. However, to protect the Hebrew woman from being taken advantage of by a verbal divorce, Moses commanded that it be done with a certificate, that is, an official written contract, permitting remarriage. The Jews tended to take the Deuteronomy passage as an excuse or license to get divorced whenever they pleased. The original provision was for the protection of the wife from an evil husband, not an authorization for him to divorce her at will. Therefore, Jesus gave one exception to the no-divorce intention of God. Immorality (Greek, *porneia*), or "sexual sins," is not limited to premarital sex only, but it includes all types of sexual sin: adultery, homosexuality, and even bestiality. Among the Jews, only the male could divorce, so Mark 10:12 reverses the statement for His Gentile audience. In that society, a woman could also divorce a man.

Since divorce, on any grounds, was common in those days (cf. rabbinical literature) the disciples wondered whether it was better not to marry. The severity of Jesus' statement was in total contrast to the society of that day and represented the true intention of God. While divorce appears to be allowed in both Testaments (cf. Deut. 24:1–5; 1 Cor. 7:15; 27–28), it is never encouraged, because it always violates God's original intention in marriage.[3]

Jesus' reply, "Not all men can accept this statement," indicates that some are called to be married and remain married; others (who cannot receive this) are called to be single (never to marry). If God calls you to be married, He will enable you to remain married. On the other hand, some are called to be single and never marry "for the sake of the kingdom of heaven." A eunuch was a person who never married and often served as a royal official. Some were born that way, due to physical or mental deficiency; some were made eunuchs by men, either by choice or by force; others deliberately chose to be single for the purpose of serving God without being tied to regular family responsibilities (e.g., Origen). Unfortunately, the early church began to take this statement to mean that it was more spiritual to be single than to be married, and eventually celibacy for priests became legislated within the Roman Catholic Church. The single life is not to be forced on anyone. Those who are called to it are able to accept it gladly.

The balance of Jesus' statements about marriage and singleness reflect His respect for people in both categories. He shows His respect for those who are unmarried, while fully expressing His commitment to the permanence of marriage. As a result, Christianity has held both in the highest esteem. At the same time, Jesus' comments about divorce were intended to preserve marriage, not bind burdens on those who have been divorced. His point to His Jewish listeners was that Moses' *permission* to divorce (because of hard-heartedness) was not meant to be a *promotion* of divorce but a *protection* of the innocent.

The Rich Young Ruler (19:13–30)

How does this next section fit in with what has preceded it? John Walvoord notes, "Although there is no definite connection between the discourse on divorce and the incident regarding children, it is obvious that one of the evils of divorce is the effect on the children."[4] The children, for whom Jesus cared so much, were evidently of sufficient age to respond to Him (not infants), and He told the disciples not to hinder them from coming to Him, revealing that, while all childhood professions may not be genuine, a child may follow Christ.

In contrast to the children's simple obedience came the complex, young, rich man with all of his "hang-ups," calling Jesus Teacher. Jesus wanted to impress upon this seeker the seriousness of his question. "Are you sure you really mean that?" would be a modern paraphrase. The young man's question, "What good thing shall I do . . . ?" implies that he wanted to perform some work that might gain him eternal life (salvation). Jesus' challenge was intended to elevate his concept of "good." The young ruler sought for something "good" that he might do to gain heaven. Jesus' concept of good was that which is divine. Therefore, only an act of God could grant eternal life. Jesus told him, "Keep the commandments." To his reply, "Which ones?" Jesus began to list some of the Ten Commandments—the sixth, seventh, eight, ninth, then the fifth, and the command to love your neighbor out of Leviticus 19:18. However, the young man interrupted Jesus with his claim to have kept all those. Keeping the commandments does not ensure one's salvation, because it is humanly impossible to do so. So why did Jesus say this? He was setting the young man up. Jesus knew the young man would insist that he had kept the commandments, and thus his self-righteousness would be exposed. Yet the man added, "What am I still lacking?" A. T. Robertson observes that this further question demonstrates "a psychological paradox. He claims to have kept all these commandments and yet was not satisfied. He had an uneasy conscience and Jesus called him to something that he did not have. He thought of goodness as quantitative (a series of acts) and not qualitative (of the nature of God)."[5] The Master's reply, "If you wish to be complete," implies that the young man was still spiritually inadequate.

The idea is this: if you want to gain eternal life, you must first of all enter it! The imperative "keep the commandments" (v. 17) was intended to hit the young man's point of pride—his self-righteousness. Jesus did not believe that mere outward keeping of the commandments of the Law brought anyone salvation. He had already told Nicodemus earlier that he must be born again (cf. Rom. 3:20; Gal. 2:16). Why, then, did He tell this young man to keep the commandments? The rest of the story reveals the answer. Jesus will go to great lengths now to show him that he has not kept the commandments and, therefore, is in need of God's grace.

This list of commands that Jesus enumerates in verse 18 centers on outward duties rather than inward nature, which was the young man's real problem. He protested that he had kept these outward demands. Jesus then revealed his real weakness. Later, when asked, "Which is the great commandment in the Law? Jesus would summarize the Law in two statements: "Love the Lord your God with all your heart" and "Love your neighbor as yourself" (Matt. 22:37–39). Herein was the young man's real failure. His wealthy self-centeredness and luxurious self-righteousness had blinded him to his real weakness. To expose this Jesus ordered, "Go and sell your possessions and give to the poor . . . and come, follow Me" (v. 21). This he would not do and went away grieved. What had Jesus done? Simply, He had shown him that he had not kept the commandments at all. He loved himself more than his neighbor (the poor), and he loved his possessions more than God, as evidenced by the fact that he refused to follow Jesus. This passage teaches the seriousness of true discipleship, but it in no way teaches average people that they must sell their possessions in order to be Christians, or even good ones. Not every person with possessions has that same problem, but from the further discussion that ensues, rich people often do have some obstacles to overcome.

The further comment, "It is hard for a rich man to enter the kingdom of heaven," shocked the disciples (note verse 25, "Who then can be saved?"). They accepted the common notion of the day that the rich were blessed of God and therefore certainly saved. To correct that misunderstanding, Jesus explained the human difficulty for the rich to be converted. "Hard" (Greek, *duskolos*) implies with extreme difficulty, though not hopeless. The illustration of a camel going through the eye of a needle has been interpreted as a camel hair rope going through a needle; as an actual camel squeezing through a small gate, "the eye of a needle," next to the main gate at Jerusalem; and so the absolute impossibility of a camel (Israel's largest animal) literally going through a tiny needle's eye. The latter usage is most likely, following a similar Talmudic proverb about an elephant. Note that they were not in Jerusalem at this time and that the first two suggestions, while very difficult, were within the realm of possibility, whereas the salvation of the rich is called humanly impossible (v. 26). In fact, all human nature is incapable of saving itself and must rely on God's efficacious grace for that which is humanly impossible to become possible with God. The salvation of a rich sinner is just as miraculous as the salvation of a poor sinner. Both are only possible with God!

Peter's response, "We have left everything . . . what then will there be for us?" was most ill-timed and certainly reflected a selfish motivation. Nevertheless, Jesus answered the question. "In the regeneration" (Greek, *paliggenesia*) refers to the renewed world of the future, the kingdom of righteousness is yet to come— "the new heavens and the new earth." While the term is used for individual rebirth in Titus 3:5, here it looks to the future millennial kingdom. Jesus makes this abundantly clear when He notes that He, the Son of Man will sit on His glorious throne. The Old Testament predicts this many times (see Isaiah 2:2–4; 9:6–7; 11:1–9; Jeremiah 23:5–6; 30:1–9; 31:31–34; Ezekiel 37:21–28; Daniel 2:44; 7:13–14, 27). The New Testament confirms Christ's earthly millennial rule in Luke 1:32–33 and Revelation 20:4–5. He will be the Judge of all humankind (John 5:22–23, 27; Acts 17:31).

When Jesus says that the apostles will sit upon twelve thrones, judging the twelve tribes of Israel, this is to be taken literally. There is no literary or logical reason to abandon a literal understanding of this promise in order to "spiritualize" this text. David L. Cooper enunciated the "golden rule of interpretation": "When the plain sense of Scripture makes common sense, seek no other sense; therefore, take every word at its primary, ordinary, usual, literal meaning unless the facts of the immediate context, studied in the light of related passages and axiomatic and fundamental truth, indicate clearly otherwise."[6]

Christ's Millennial Reign	
He will appear in the sky coming in the clouds.	Daniel 7:13; Matthew 24:30
He will defeat the Beast and the False Prophet at Armageddon.	Revelation 19:17–21
He comes back to the Mount of Olives.	Zechariah 14:4
The Jews will mourn when they see His return.	Zechariah 12:10
He will gather His elect from throughout the world.	Matthew 24:31
He will come in His glory and sit on His throne.	Matthew 25:31
He will judge the nations.	Matthew 25:32
His angels will come "in flaming fire."	2 Thessalonians 1:7
The resurrected Tribulation saints will reign with Him.	Revelation 20:4
He will reign for a thousand years (the Millennium).	Revelation 20:4–5

There is no reason to think that all these Old and New Testament prophecies would be fulfilled in any manner other than literally. To assert that the apostles' rule over the twelve tribes of Israel will all be spiritual, or in some other "matrix" is unwarranted and unfortunate. Forsaking earthly benefits will bring many times as much blessing and eternal life.[7] Yet, while rewards will be abundant, attitudes are still crucial, and many who would be first shall be last and the last shall be first. These final words of the chapter form a bookend with Matthew 20:16 surrounding the parable of the laborers.

Study Questions

1. Can you picture Jesus in Transjordan followed by huge multitudes, including many sick people? Do you think they flocked to Jesus primarily to be healed?

2. Why, according to verse 3, did the Pharisees approach Jesus? What was their motive for this kind of action?

3. What Old Testament book does Jesus quote from to demonstrate God's original purpose of permanence for the marriage bond?

4. Is divorce ever allowed in the Bible? Is there biblical evidence that divorce was ever permitted?

5. What grounds does Jesus give for divorce? Are there any additional grounds for divorce in the New Testament? See 1 Corinthians 7:15.

6. The rich young ruler was pretty good but not "complete" according to verse 21. How would his selling of all his possessions and his following of Jesus have made him "complete"?

7. Are we to sell everything and give all our money to the poor? Why or why not?

8. Did not Peter, in fact, claim in verse 27 that the disciples had "left everything and followed" Jesus? Would you be willing to do that if Jesus asked you to?

9. Do you believe Jesus' promise to the Twelve (with the exception of Judas, of course) that they would sit on twelve thrones judging the twelve tribes of Israel will be fulfilled literally? Why or why not?

10. What does Jesus mean in verse 30 when he talks about the first and the last? Notice the story that follows, and Matthew 20:16 as well.

Is It Really Worth It?
Chapter 20:1-34

Preview:

Jesus pauses here to further instruct His disciples about work and rewards. Peter had asked what they would get for forsaking all. Jesus' answer was direct and factual—rulership over the twelve tribes of Israel and much more. However, Peter's question exposed a spirit of bargaining and negotiation. There would be further bickering over who would be the greatest in the kingdom. The parable of the laborers in the vineyard helps dispel our inappropriate attitudes toward labor and rewards.

The Parable of the Laborers (20:1-16)

This parable reinforced Jesus' teaching regarding true Christian service and riches. The connection with what precedes is all important to note. It is an answer to Peter's question in 19:27, "What then will there be for us?" R. C. Trench has commented that this is "a parable which stands only second to that of the Unjust Steward in the number of explanations, and those diverging the most widely, that have been proposed for it; and only second to that, if indeed second, in the difficulties which it presents."[1] The landowner is Christ Himself, the Master of the vineyard, which is the field of labor (service to the world through His church). Early in the morning, the first workers were hired at dawn. Note here that these laborers made an agreement for their wages. They would not start work without knowing what they would be paid. A denarius was the Roman coin equal to a day's wages for a foot soldier or a common laborer. Others standing idle in the market place were not lazy but were in the common place of seeking employment. They simply had not yet been hired. No blame is placed on them for being there. From this unemployed group, the householder hired additional workers at 9:00 A.M., noon, 3:00 P.M., and 5:00 P.M. The pay scale, however, would be "whatever is right," indicating Christ's justice to His laborers.

When evening had come—that is, at the end of the day—every man was paid his wages. The ones hired last were paid first and received an entire denarius. Those who were hired first and had worked all day thought they surely would receive more, once they saw what the other workers had received. But instead, they received exactly what they had agreed upon. The first hired laborers then grumbled at the landowner. However, he reminded them that he had been just in paying them that for which they bargained. The statement "I wish to give to this last man the same as to you" is Jesus' interpretation of "The last shall be first and the first last" (v. 16). Jesus reminds the disciples that He is their Lord and He will deal fairly with them all, despite their different experiences serving Him.

All manner of interpretations have been given for this parable, since Jesus does not interpret it for us. Some suppose that the early workers are the Jews and that the workers hired later represent the church. Others have thought the connection is that some are saved early in life while others are saved at an old age or just before they die. Others hold that no matter how much work we do for Christ, we all get the same reward—salvation. However, that would suggest that salvation is based on works. Another view is that Christ here gives a sweeping view of church history, in which those working in the last hour are promised equal blessing to His original disciples. The key is in the bargaining situation. Jesus is saying to His disciples, "Don't try to figure out what you will get. Leave the rewards with God. He will be just and fair. He will give more than one might expect, or even deserve." Thus Jesus warns against jealousy and impurity of motive in serving Him.[2]

Verse 15 shows that everything being of grace, God has the right to give or withhold at will. We must take care that this goodness of God does not provoke us to complaint. One point that can be made of verse 16 is that all Christians receive everlasting life given on the ground of Christ's death for them. By earthly standards of judgment, expressed clearly in verses 11 and 12, such action is regarded as putting the last first and the first last. Of course, there will be infinite degrees of rewards as well. This is expressed in the parable of the talents in Matthew 25:14–30.

The Coming Suffering of Christ and His Disciples (20:17–28)

Jesus referred to being delivered up to be mocked and scourged and crucified. This is the third time in the Synoptic Gospels that Jesus has plainly predicted His own approaching death. He also says that on the third day He will be raised up. The disciples are puzzled by these revelations as can be seen in their responses to Christ later in the upper room, for example in John 16:16–20. (See the parallel passages of this prophecy in Mark 10:32–34; Luke 18:31–34.) Matthew emphasizes that Jesus knew full well what was coming in the future.

The journey to Jerusalem was now resumed after the ministry in Peraea. As the final events of His life drew nearer, our Lord again sought to enlighten His disciples. And again they failed to understand, as is evidenced by the request of Zebedee's sons that immediately followed. But the fulfillment of these detailed predictions would strengthen their faith when the time came. "The Sons of Zebedee" were the apostles James and John (Matt. 4:21). Their mother, speaking in their behalf, said to Jesus "Command that in Your kingdom these two sons of mine may sit, one on Your right and one on Your left." This bold request and the indignation of the others that followed show that the disciples were still thinking in terms of the setting up of an earthly kingdom, in spite of the clear prediction of suffering and death that our Lord had just made. The cup, as well as the baptism of the parallel passage in Mark 10:38, both refer to our Lord's suffering and death. James and John affirmed that they could accept that too, and Jesus confirmed, "My cup you shall drink." Indeed, James was the first disciple to lose his life in martyrdom by beheading (Acts 12:2), and John suffered persecution, banishment, and imprisonment (Rev. 1:9).

Jesus expresses the spiritual principle that "whoever wishes to become great among you shall be your servant." This is true in the church, in the home, in business, and in life in general. Jesus demonstrated servant leadership by His own example. One can exercise authority and leadership most effectively when serving others. Jesus made it clear that the "Son of Man did not come to be served." It is not wrong to accept ministry. Christ accepted it. Sometimes in order to allow a blessing to fall on someone else, you must allow that person to be of service to you or to another. But receiving service was not the purpose of His life and should not be the purpose of ours. His "life" (Greek, *psuchē*) literally refers to "his soul." Jesus' statement that he came to give His live as a "ransom" is one of the few times the doctrine of substitutionary atonement is mentioned in the Synoptic Gospels. It implies a price paid for the deliverance of captives.[3] The price lay in the necessity for His life to be laid down. His life thus became the cost of our redemption. The use of the word "many" does not necessarily restrict the extent of His death (as contrasted to "all"), but it does indicate that not all would accept His offer of salvation.

The Healing of the Two Blind Men (20:29-34)

(For parallel accounts of the healing of the blind men, see Mark 10:46-52; Luke 18:35-43.) Luke places this event on the approach to the city, whereas, Mark and Matthew say it was "as they were going out from Jericho" (v. 29). Homer Kent notes that the problems of harmonizing these texts prohibit any suggestion of "collusion."[4] In actuality there were two Jerichos. The Roman city lay about a mile east of Herod's winter headquarters (also called Jericho) where the wealthy friends of the Herodian family lived near the palace and fortress. The healing of the blind men evidently took place while Jesus was going from one city to the other. Luke's attention would be on the Herodian city, for his next recorded event, the calling of Zacchaeus, took place there. Also complicating the matter is the fact that ancient Jericho lay in ruins all around where they were.

Two blind men are mentioned by Matthew, while the other synoptists refer to only the more prominent Bartimaeus. Rebuked by the crowd, they cried the louder, "Have mercy on us, Son of David!" a messianic title earlier avoided by Jesus in public but now accepted as He approached Jerusalem. The miracle of restoring their sight was so total that afterward even they followed Him. What a contrast! The rich young ruler rejected Jesus for worldly possessions; Jesus' own disciples argue over who will be the greatest; the laborers in the parable murmur. Yet now two transformed blind beggars gladly follow Him! Of such is the kingdom of heaven!

Study Questions

1. At what times did the owner of the vineyard hire laborers to work in his vineyard?

2. What was the difference between the arrangement the owner made with the earliest workers he hired and the arrangement he made with the last workers?

3. What are some of the possible interpretations for the ones hired at different times?

4. Was the owner within his rights to pay what he desired to the last hired workers?

5. Where in Matthew is the third very plain prediction that Jesus made concerning His approaching death and resurrection?

6. What do you think of the attempt James and John made to seek a privileged position in Christ's coming kingdom?

7. In what way did James and John actually drink of the cup that Jesus was to drink? See verse 22.

8. Have you memorized Matthew 20:28 yet? What does this key verse teach us about service?

9. What is implied in the term "Son of David," which the blind men used to address Jesus?

10. What is the essence of being "moved with compassion" as Jesus was?

CHAPTER 21

Here Comes the King
Matthew 21:1-46

Preview:

Matthew's gospel climaxes with Christ's final Passover week in Jerusalem. Jesus comes to the city and is presented as king but is still rejected by the Jewish leaders. He cleanses the temple, defends His own authority, and tells two parables that embarrass the chief priests and the Pharisees. Tensions rise. No doubt Matthew's first readers would hurry through the remaining pages to find out how the drama would end.

The Messianic Arrival at Jerusalem (21:1–11)

This event is traditionally known as the "Triumphal Entry," in which Jesus officially offers Himself to the nation of Israel as their long-awaited Messiah. However, in many ways it is far from a triumph, for the day ends in Jesus' public prediction of His rejection by His own people (see Mark 11:1–10; Luke 19:29–44; John 12:12–15). The final week and passion of Christ occupy major portions of all four gospels, percentages ranging from about 25 to 38 percent of each gospel. Bethphage was a village between Jerusalem and Bethany, about a mile east of Jerusalem. This village was hidden from the view of Jerusalem by the summit of the Mount of Olives, the large hill on the east of Jerusalem.

The account of these closing events in our Lord's life shows that there were men and women in Jerusalem and its neighborhood who recognized Jesus as Lord. They may have become disciples during the earlier Jerusalem ministry described by John. The repetition of the phrase in Matthew, "this took place that what was spoken through the prophet might be fulfilled" actually makes up the key verse of the entire book. Since Matthew is writing to a predominantly Jewish audience, he uses this phrase sixteen times to show fulfillment of the Jewish Scriptures that pertain to the Messiah. The quotation in verse 5 is a combination of Isaiah 62:11 and Zechariah 9:9, taken substantially from the Septuagint. Hosanna is the transliteration of a Hebrew term meaning "please save," and occurs in 2 Samuel 14:4 and Psalm 118:25. From the following verse of this Psalm (v. 26), the acclamation "Blessed is He who comes in the name of the Lord" is taken.

"That It Might Be Fulfilled"

Reference	Fulfilled	OT Reference
Matthew 1:22	The Virgin Birth	Isaiah 7:14
Matthew 1:22	His name to be called Immanuel	Isaiah 7:14
Matthew 2:15	The calling of God's Son from Egypt	Hosea 11:1
Matthew 2:17–18	Weeping at the slaying of innocent children	Jeremiah 31:15
Matthew 2:23	Christ called a Nazarene (cf. Hebrew, **netser**)	Isaiah 11:1 **(branch)**
Matthew 3:15	Christ's baptism: fulfilling all righteousness	Psalm 40:7–8
Matthew 4:14–15	Gospel light brought to Zebulun and Naphtali	Isaiah 9:1
Matthew 5:17	Christ fulfilled the Law	Isaiah 42:21
Matthew 8:17	Christ carried our infirmities	Isaiah 53:4
Matthew 12:17–18	Christ the Servant of the Lord	Isaiah 42:1–4
Matthew 13:35	Christ would speak in parables	Psalm 78:2
Matthew 21:4–5	Christ the King comes to Jerusalem	Isaiah 62:11
Matthew 26:53–54	Christ could call down a legion of angels	2 Kings 6:17; Daniel 7:10
Matthew 26:55–56	Messiah cut off and the sheep scattered	Daniel 9:26; Zechariah 13:7
Matthew 27:9	The thirty pieces of silver	Zechariah 11:12
Matthew 27:10	Purchase of Judas's grave in the Potter's Field	Zechariah 11:12–13

In verses 10 and 11 there is a contrast between the men of the city, who were ignorant of our Lord's identity, and the multitude who were able to answer their question. There were probably many Galileans in the latter group who had come up for the feast and who already knew our Lord through His preaching and healing ministry in the north. In Jewish history and tradition the quoted Psalm was considered a messianic royal psalm, and the riding of an ass's colt (not a horse) marked the official entry of the king.[1] The crowd acknowledged Jesus as a prophet, some accepted Him as Messiah, and others rejected Him and would seek His death.

The Cleansing of the Temple (21:12–17)

(For parallel accounts of the cleansing of the temple, see Mark 11:15–19; Luke 19:45–47.) A similar cleansing is recorded at the beginning of Jesus' ministry (cf. John 2:13–22), indicating His disdain for the corruption of organized religion, which lacked purity of life and the power of God. Such a violent move was not to provoke a revolution, but to bring about true spiritual conviction. In light of the seriousness of what He had come to do, Jesus could not tolerate such gross perversion of the temple (Greek, *hieron*), that is, the whole temple area on Mount Moriah including all the precincts and courts.

Temple dues could be paid only in sacred coinage, and it was necessary to change one's money. The selling of doves was, of course, for purposes of sacrifice. This exchange became a source of extortion for the high priest's family who personally controlled it. In reality, it amounted to a public bazaar. As Don Carson nicely put it, "But letting these things go on at the temple site transformed a place of solemn worship into a market where the hum of trade mingled with the bleating and cooing of animals and birds."[2] In his condemnation, our Lord quotes Isaiah 56:7 and Jeremiah 7:11. It appears in the Septuagint form here in Matthew.

Jesus also healed the blind and the lame. He demonstrated His authority by casting out the sellers and moneychangers from the temple precincts, and His messiahship by the healings. They became indignant. It was not just our Lord's popularity that angered them; the title "Son of David," which the children kept calling out also implied messiahship. The cavils of the enemy were stilled, however, by the children's praise, as is suggested by the context of the psalm from which our Lord quotes (Ps. 8:2). Bethany was the village on the eastern shoulder of the Mount of Olives, about two miles east of Jerusalem. It was the home of Lazarus and his sisters, Mary and Martha.

The Cursing of the Barren Fig Tree (21:18–22)

(For a parallel to the cursing of the fig tree, see Mark 11:12–14, 20–26.) The fig tree fruit generally appears in an initial form in February, followed by leaves, which are not formed until late spring. Thus, there should normally have been some edible fruit on the tree when Jesus passed by, at least some green figs. Even though Mark 11:13 says, "it was not the season for figs," Gleason Archer notes that "this particular tree had gone into full foliage without developing any figs at all."[3] The fig tree was often used as a symbol of the nation of Israel (cf. Hos. 9:10; Joel 1:7), and while Jesus literally came upon a barren fig tree, which had leaves but no figs, He used the incident to fully illustrate Israel's desperate condition.

The curse "No longer shall there ever be any fruit from you" resulted in the almost immediate withering of the entire tree. While trees are nonmoral, like all of nature, they are subject to the word of Christ. Homer Kent remarks, "Although there is no statement that the situation should be regarded as parabolic, that seems to be the only reasonable explanation of the incident (for trees have no moral responsibility). It provided a graphic sequel to the earlier parable of Luke 13:6–9 regarding the Jewish nation, unfruitful despite every advantage."[4] The disciples marveled at how this could happen so fast. Notice that none of them questioned the morality of this incident, as have some misguided modern commentators.

Jesus told them how to do such astounding things: have faith, or absolute confidence, in the power of God. This mountain probably refers to the Mount of Olives, and the sea may refer to the Dead Sea, which is clearly visible from the top of the Mount of Olives. In any event, this would be an impossible task. But as William Hendriksen points out, "Both in the physical and in the spiritual sphere the apostles had already been doing things that would have been considered just as 'impossible' as causing a mountain to be lifted up and thrown into the sea."[5] Is it possible that the removal of the mountain may indicate eliminating obstacles to giving the gospel to the Gentiles? Such might be a likely meaning of the entire incident. Israel is the fruitless fig tree, and the Gentiles are the mountain that shall be moved for God by the power of prayer.

The Question of Authority (21:23–46)

On Jesus' third day of successive visits to the temple (i.e., Herod's temple), His authority was challenged by the ever-threatened chief priests.[6] They included the high priest, who was also president of the Sanhedrin, and elders, who were laymen or scribes and also served as members of the Jewish high court. In their own view, they were attempting to protect their laws and traditions against one who appeared to be a usurper who reinterpreted the Law, rejected tradition, and overthrew the moneychangers. Jesus had spoken with authority on matters they considered their responsibility. Jesus did not challenge their right to question Him, but their hypocrisy and insincerity in such questioning.

The chief priests and elders asked by what "authority" Jesus had done these controversial things. Knowing that they would never recognize any authority but their own, He refused to answer them. Instead, He asked them about the authority of the baptism of John, which they had never officially sanctioned. This placed these corrupt leaders on the traditional "horns of a dilemma." To acknowledge that it was from heaven would be to condemn themselves for not receiving it, and to claim it was of men (i.e., human origin) would upset the people. Their reply "We do not know" was begging the question and brought His clever response: "Neither will I tell you by what authority I do these things."

This incident forms the setting of the all-out attempt by the various religious authorities to expose and humiliate Jesus in chapter 22, which ends in their total frustration and embarrassment. The beauty and dynamics of these incidents reveal Jesus' mental prowess over the greatest minds of Israel. The divine Savior is a genius, with no human peer. He can stump the Jews, mystify the Romans, and challenge the mind of any mortal man!

The parable of the two sons (vv. 28–32) follows as an expose of the hypocrisy of the religious leaders and as a vindication of John's ministry and the true work of God in general. In some manuscripts, the two sons and their responses and actions are reversed.[7] Here the first son initially boldly said he would go (v. 29) but did not follow through with obedience. The second initially refused to go but later regretted it and went, representing the immoral disobedience of the publicans and harlots who later repented under John and Jesus' preaching. Notice again the connection between genuine repentance and changed action in verse 29 (regretted and went). No one who truly repents fails to show clear evidence of inner heart change by outward obedience. Jesus asked, "Which of the two did the will of his father?" By answering, "The latter," the religious leaders had condemned themselves. This very effective teaching method is commonly used in the Bible as the *juridical parable*, whereby the respondent condemns himself by the obviously implied answer (e.g., the parable of the good Samaritan, answering the prejudiced question, "Who is my neighbor?" Luke 10:29). John had preached the way of righteousness (cf. 2 Pet. 2:21), and the leaders had rejected him, even while claiming to be God's obedient servants.

Thus repentant sinners are more ready for the kingdom of God than disobedient religious leaders.

Juridical Parables in the Bible	
Jotham's parable of the trees	Judges 9:8–20
Nathan's parable of the ewe lamb	2 Samuel 12:1–10
Jesus' parable of the good Samaritan	Luke 10:30–37
Jesus' parable of the two sons	Matthew 21:28–32
Jesus' parable of the landowner	Matthew 21:33–44

Jesus quickly gave another parable, the parable of the wicked vine-growers, or tenants. Again, Jesus makes clear His divine authority by presenting Himself as the Son sent by the Father. The landowner represents God the Father and the vineyard is Israel, a symbol of the theocracy that was familiar to the Jewish leaders (cf. Ps. 80:8–16; Isa. 5:1–7). The vine-growers were the priests and religious leaders. The anticipated produce represents spiritual evidence of true conversion, which was to be the end result of the work of the tenants. Instead, the religion of Israel had degenerated into a formal system for the benefit of the priests who were now more concerned about perpetuating their own interests.

The slaves sent by the owner represent the Old Testament prophets who came to correct religious abuses in the nation and were also rejected by their contemporaries (though venerated by subsequent generations). "Afterward" indicates that Jesus was God's final emissary to Israel. None has ever appeared since Him, and none ever will until the Jews recognize Christ as their final Prophet and Messiah! The desire to kill the rightful heir of the Father had already been expressed by the Jewish leaders (cf. John 11:47–53). Jesus clearly foretold His coming rejection and death with the statement "They . . . killed him." We must remember that in interpreting parables, one should arrive at one basic lesson. Much of the rest could simply be "window dressing" to help tell the story. Thus, in the parable of the lost coin in Luke 15, one should not try to make something out of the broom the woman sweeps with. The moral is simply that something was lost, it was found, and there was rejoicing. Likewise, nothing should be made of the fact that the owner of the vineyard, who represents God, says "They will respect my son." This is not an indication that God was mistaken or that He does not have infinite knowledge of all future events, including the actions of free moral agents. A parable, as the saying goes, should not be made "to walk on all fours," Not everything in a parable is meant to have some particular meaning. The parable serves as an illustration of one basic meaning.

Verse 40 represents the condemning question of the judicial parable, "When the owner of the vineyard comes, what will he do to those vine-growers?" Their reply again unwittingly condemned their own attitude of rejection toward Jesus. The other vine-growers would be the Gentiles (v. 43). Jesus quoted Psalm 118:22-23 exactly from the Septuagint, relating His present rejection to His ultimate triumph (cf. Acts 4:11 and 1 Pet. 2:6-7, where the stone the builders rejected is also quoted in relation to Christ). The Sanhedrinists represent the builders of Israel's religion, who rejected the real cornerstone of the foundation of the church, Christ. Thus the vineyard will be given to a nation producing the fruit of it (cf. 1 Pet. 2:7-9, where the church is called a "holy nation"). Equating the vineyard with the kingdom of God, Alva McClain notes that this clearly shows the kingdom as mediated to Israel through divinely appointed kings and now being transferred (mediated) to the church during the interval between Christ's advents.[8]

The warning "the kingdom of God will be taken away from you" (v. 43) was fulfilled at Pentecost when the "kingdom" was mediatorily transferred to the church (cf. Rom. 9-11, which clearly promises Israel's restoration at the time of the Tribulation Period and the millennial kingdom). The image of falling on this stone is a difficult one to interpret. Some may see it as an offer of mercy within a warning of judgment: Jesus offers mercy by falling on this stone, that is, falling upon Him in repentance and faith. But it seems that it pictures judgment in two ways. Most, with Michael Wilkins, hold that it means, "Those who stumble over the stone and try to destroy it, such as the religious leaders who reject Jesus and will later condemn him, will be destroyed. In the end Jesus will come as judge and fall on those who have rejected him."[9] Hendriksen likewise says, "Anyone who opposes Christ is going to be 'pulverized' (cf. Matt. 3:12). If Christ strikes him with his judgment, the person so stricken will be crushed."[10] Christ's falling upon man in judgment will "scatter him like dust." John Broadus emphasizes that "By etymology and general use, it signifies to 'winnow,' to separate the chaff from the wheat; and derivatively to 'scatter,' like chaff or dust . . . it falls upon him, and scatters him like a puff of dust."[11] Finally, the Pharisees and chief priests understood that He was speaking about them and wanted to seize Jesus, meaning to kill Him. However, the Jewish leaders were afraid of the multitudes because they looked on Him as a prophet.

Matthew is developing his case. Jesus is the true Messiah of Israel. Gentiles know it. Blind men know it. The common people know it. But the leaders of

Israel do not. They are blind to the truth and to the true Messiah. As a result, Israel will be temporarily set aside in the days ahead. One cannot read these chapters consecutively without feeling the anger and the frustration of the leaders of religion. The Messiah has come, and they have missed Him!

Study Questions

1. At what little town did Jesus obtain a colt on which to ride?

2. How many disciples were sent to fetch the colt?

3. What was Jesus' first act after entering Jerusalem on Palm Sunday?

4. To what town did Jesus return each evening from Jerusalem?

5. From what kind of tree did Jesus seek fruit?

6. Why did Jesus place a curse on the tree? Should it have had something edible growing on it at that time of year?

7. In verse 23, what action of Jesus did the chief priests and elders question?

8. Which of the two sons in verses 28–31 did the will of the father?

9. Examine different translations of these four verses. What variation can you observe? Is there any real difference in meaning if the order of the sons is switched in some of the manuscripts?

10. In the final parable of chapter 21, what is the surprise reaction of the chief priests and Pharisees? Might this indicate that one of the purposes of speaking in parables could be to hide understanding from those who were spiritually blind and insensitive?

11. What did the elders and chief priests answer when Jesus asked them whence the baptism of John came—from heaven or of men?

CHAPTER 22

Answering the Critics
Matthew 22:1-46

Preview:

The Passover lamb had to be kept for four days to make sure it was perfect. So also, Jesus, our Passover Lamb, was subjected to intense scrutiny before the sacrifice of Himself for us. On this particular day, Jesus first told a parable to quiet the Pharisees. Second, He answered the Herodians. Then He sparred with the Sadducees over the doctrine of resurrection, which they denied. Fourth, answered a lawyer's question. And finally, He finished with the Pharisees once again. In all this Jesus was shown to be the perfect Son of God.

The Parable of the Marriage Supper (22:1-14)

In preparation for the major confrontation that was coming, Jesus gave the parable of the marriage supper. While similar to the parable in Luke 14, this one differs in its occasion and details. Again, the kingdom of heaven must refer to the mediatorial aspect of the kingdom in the Church Age and through the Tribulation period. The king is God the Father and Christ is the son. The marriage, pictured by the wedding feast must be taken in the full aspect of salvation, including union with Christ, culminating in glorification at the marriage supper, which inaugurates the millennial age. Rejection of the invitation to attend constitutes disloyalty to the King, as well as discourtesy to the Son, and accounts for the severe treatment of the rebels (vv. 6-7), which included the fact that the king's armies set their city on fire, an obvious reference to the coming destruction of Jerusalem in A.D. 70.

The invited guests are the people of Israel, whereas those in the main highways are Gentiles. "Both evil and good" refer to moral and immoral sinners who alike need God's gracious invitation. The "highways" implies crossroads, as opposed to back roads. History has revealed the success of urban evangelization, which may be implied here. The man without the wedding clothes came to the feast but had disregarded the propriety of the king's provision, since such garments were normally supplied by the host. The reference seems to be to the "robe of righteousness," which we must receive from the Lord in order to enter the marriage feast. The garment must actually be worn on the heart, since nothing is made of the fact that servants had not refused him entry. Casting the unclad guest into outer darkness symbolizes the eternal judgment of the lost.

Again the phrase "many are called, but few are chosen" is repeated to emphasize to the Jewish audience, who considered themselves to be God's chosen people, that the outward call of God was not sufficient for salvation apart from responding to that call of grace in an effectual manner. There will be, as F. C. Cook notes, "the entire rejection of many."[1] No one should think that because he is Jewish, Catholic, Muslim, or Hindu that he will be received by Christ. Everyone has to come to Jesus Christ for his soul's salvation, no matter what his or her religion may be.

The Herodians: Question of Tribute (22:15–22)

Beginning at this point, Jesus deals with all three major Jewish sects: Herodians, Sadducees, and Pharisees—all in one day. In each case, we see His personal brilliance on display. (See Mark 12:13–17; Luke 20:20–26.)

Major Jewish Sects in Jesus' Time		
Herodians	Political	Promoted cooperation
Pharisees	Legalistic	Emphasized strict adherence to the Law
Sadducees	Liberal	Denied the resurrection and the miraculous

The Herodians were a party that favored the dynasty of Herod and backed the Roman connection. They promoted compromise with the Romans for personal and political gain. They cared little or nothing for religion and normally were bitterly opposed by the Pharisees. The statements recorded in verse 16 were insincere and intended as hypocritical flattery. Their question about paying taxes was intended to place the Lord on the horns of a dilemma. If He said yes, pay taxes to Caesar, He could be held up to the people as a traitor. If He said no, do not pay Roman taxes, He could be denounced to the Roman authorities.

Caesar was the family name of Julius Caesar, the first Roman who aspired to autocracy. The title was taken over from him by his adopted son, Octavian, who afterward became Emperor Augustus Caesar. The title Caesar referred to the head of the Roman state. The Caesar at the time of Christ was Tiberius, as both history and Luke 3:1 declare. The name soon came to be regarded as a title. The Jews were using the denarius coin to pay (Greek, *kēnsos*; Latin *census*) "either the annual head tax or one of the more general taxes, such as the poll-tax."[2] Caesar's likeness and inscription were on this coin. Jesus' answer was crafted marvelously: "Render to Caesar the things that are Caesar's." The Lord means that we are to give the civil magistrates all that is due to them, so long as it does not interfere with the honor due to God.

Jesus had broken the Herodians' dilemma by making light of the ultimate significance of Caesar's claim. The idea is, "If the coin is his, let him have it!" Jesus' response, "[render] to God the things that are God's" exposed the spiritual failure of the Herodians. John Walvoord comments that the Herodians "marveled at the adroit way in which He had solved their problem, and they had nothing more to say. It they used Roman coins, then they were subject to Roman tax."[3] In essence, Jesus made light of Caesar's temporal claim in favor of God's greater claim over people's lives. Believers have duties to perform in both the secular and the sacred realms. We are to be good citizens of both kingdoms.

The Sadducees: Question of the Resurrection (22:23–34)

The Sadducees made the next attempt to discredit Jesus and were even more severely humiliated. As the liberal party within first-century A.D. Judaism, they rejected belief in the supernatural, especially angels and the resurrection of the dead (see Paul's encounter in Acts 23:6–9). "Moses said" is a reference to Deuteronomy 25:5, where the practice of levirate marriage called for an unmarried brother to take his widowed brother's wife to be his own (cf. Gen. 38:8). This ancient practice was recognized by the Jews but rarely followed in those days. The absurd hypothetical case that follows represents another theological dilemma, this time attempting to discredit the legitimacy of the resurrection, which the Sadducees rejected. Thus their question "Whose wife of the seven shall she be?" This extreme example must have been thought by them to be the ultimate proof of the foolishness of this doctrine. All seven brothers had been married to her, presumably, from "the case of a woman known to them."[4] However, A. T. Robertson surmises that "it was probably an old conundrum that they had used to the discomfiture of the Pharisees."[5] They must have snickered as they asked such a ridiculous question, but the smile would soon be wiped off their faces by Jesus' reply. "You are mistaken, not understanding the Scriptures," He said. Jesus had extreme contempt for the Sadducees because they made light of the Bible and the power of God (i.e., His resurrection power, cf. Phil. 3:10). This is His strongest recorded rebuke of this Jewish party.

Jesus then explained that in the resurrection men do not marry but are asexual "as the angels in heaven."[6] The infantile illustration of the Sadducees showed that they had no confidence in the power of a glorious resurrection to a new life. They thought that a resurrection would be the same kind of life as on earth and probably "spiritualized" their rejection of such a concept. Alfred Plummer aptly comments, "In the life beyond the grave there are no wives and no husbands, and this disposes of the supposed difficulty."[7] To be as the angels means that resurrected believers will have a glorified nonmortal body (capable of neither reproduction nor destruction). The reference is not intended to imply that glorified people become angels nor that all earthly family relationships are lost in heaven.

All resurrected (or raptured) believers will be in a state of perfect glorification and fellowship without any clannish prejudice. As R. V. G. Tasker notes, Jesus' argument teaches "that marriage and the propagation of the race, which it is one of the objects of marriage to secure, are supremely necessary in a world where death is a permanent factor; but they are completely unnecessary in an existence whose main characteristic is that it is deathless."[8] The Mormon teaching about God being married, having a physical body, and reproducing in a carnal fashion—and that man will do the same in heaven—is totally out of keeping with the Word of God.

Jesus further attacked the Sadducees' major belief in no resurrection at all by quoting Exodus 3:6, a statement from the Pentateuch, the only part of the Old Testament which the Sadducees unquestioningly accepted. He explained that God's use of the phrase, "I am the God of" the patriarchs (Abraham, Isaac, and Jacob) demonstrated that they were still alive, or in existence. God is the eternal "I AM." He is the God of the living (a ploy probably used by Sadducees to limit God's activity to the living, but here cleverly reversed by Jesus to apply to the patriarchs). "[God] is not the God of the dead" does not mean that He has no relationship to those who have departed. It means that the departed are not really dead and are thus still responsible to the living God (cf. Heb. 10:31). Walvoord points out that "In His reply, Jesus not only affirmed resurrection but also continuance of personal identity, in that Abraham would be Abraham, Isaac would be Isaac, and Jacob would be Jacob, an identity related to the resurrection of their bodies."[9] Thus the crowd was astonished and the Sadducees were put . . . to silence, (Greek, *ephimōsen*), "muzzled."[10]

The Pharisees: Question of the Law (22:35–23:39)

Each group came with their most difficult question, representing their expertise and their point of departure from Jesus' doctrine. In other words, each came representing their own "hang-ups." Remember that each of these groups normally hated each other but were united in their rejection of Christ. Among the Pharisees, the next group to challenge Jesus, there was a lawyer, that is, an expert expounder of the Old Testament Law, equivalent to a Doctor of Theology today. He asked Jesus, "Which is the great commandment in the Law?" The phrase "testing Him" implies that he was trying to draw Jesus into an argument regarding the Pharisees' extensive interpretations of the more than six hundred separate laws in the Pentateuch. Instead, Christ summarized the two tables of the Law: that is, (1) responsibility to God, in commandments 1–4; and (2) responsibility to others, in commandments 5–10. Jesus did this by paraphrasing Deuteronomy 6:5 and Leviticus 19:18: love the Lord your God and love your neighbor as yourself. The phrase "with all your heart," indicates the total being of a person in Hebrew thought and is part of the "shema," the Jewish confession of faith consisting of Deuteronomy 6:4–9; 11:13–21; and Numbers 15:37–41. As the greatest commandment, it was of supreme importance and priority.[11] No Pharisee could fault such an answer. William Hendriksen observes that even though the law expert came to test Jesus, "we receive a favorable impression of this man, not only because he asked a worthwhile question, for which Jesus does not rebuke him in any way (contrast verse 18), but also because he of his own accord approvingly repeats Christ's answer, for which he received praise (see Mark 12:32–34)."[12]

Jesus' Summation of the Law

1. Love God with all your heart, soul, and mind. Covers the first four commandments and restates the **shema** (Deut. 6:5).

2. Love your neighbor as yourself. Covers commandments 6–10, which deal with our responsibilities to our fellow human beings.

Jesus then counterquestioned the Pharisees: "What do you think about the Christ, whose son is He?" By asking them who the Messiah was, He gave them a clear opportunity to acknowledge Him. Tasker notes, "By the nature of His question, He seems to imply that the questions the Pharisees and Sadducees have asked Him pale into insignificance before the all-important question 'What is *your* view of the Messiah?'"[13] The question is similar to the one Jesus asked earlier of the disciples in 16:15, where they gave the correct answer. The

Pharisees' response, "The son of David," was the common teaching of the scribes who accepted the Davidic lineage of the Messiah (cf. Mark 12:35).

Jesus, therefore, called their attention to Psalm 110, which they already recognized as messianic.[14] Jesus affirms the Davidic authorship of this psalm, and that it was given "in the Spirit," that is, by inspiration of the Holy Spirit.[15] In this psalm David refers to the Messiah as his Lord, thus He is more than just David's "son." The verse says: "The LORD [Jehovah God] said to my Lord [the Messiah], Sit at My right hand, until I [God] put Thine enemies [the enemies of the Messiah] beneath Thy feet" (the final messianic victory over all who oppose Christ). Jesus totally stumped the Pharisees who wanted to believe in a human Messiah but not a divine Messiah. However, Psalm 110 indicated both, and they were speechless. Thus, "no one was able to answer Him," that is, defeat Him by question or debate and, therefore, no one dared ask Him another question. In one day Jesus had annihilated and humiliated the wisdom and craft of the leaders of each of Israel's religious organizations. "Hallelujah, what a Savior!"

Study Questions

1. What group told Jesus the story of a woman married successively to seven brothers?

2. Fill in the blank. "You are mistaken, not understanding the Scriptures, or the —— of God."

3. What was the matter with the wedding guest who was expelled? What does his action indicate, or what was it a sign of?

4. How was Jesus on the horns of a dilemma with the question put to him about the tribute money?

5. What two groups asked James the tribute money question? Define who these people were.

6. In what way was Jesus' answer perfectly crafted? How does that answer still apply to us today?

7. What two groups sought to lay hands on Jesus but feared the multitude?

8. What Old Testament passages did Jesus use to answer the question about which commandment was the greatest?

9. What relationship do the two passages have to each other in content and meaning?

10. List as many different groups of people as you can that are mentioned in chapter 22.

CHAPTER 23

Denouncing the Pharisees
Matthew 23:1–39

Preview:

This is another of Jesus' six great discourses found in Matthew. It is unique to this gospel. The Pharisees have left Jesus. Unable to ensnare Jesus in His words, they reject Him and now move to have Him killed. Jesus warns His disciples about these wicked men in this moving and colorfully illustrated speech. Matthew records seven times that Jesus says, "Woe" to the scribes and Pharisees, whom He also calls hypocrites, because they often teach one thing but do another.

Jesus' final condemnation of the Pharisees fills the entire twenty-third chapter of Matthew. This now represents His final and official rejection of them at the temple, their very own stronghold of influence and security. The true character of the Pharisees and scribes can easily be shown by comparing several texts that show they sought to kill Jesus. John 18:3 notes that Judas, on his way to betray Jesus, came from the chief priests and Pharisees. After Jesus' crucifixion and burial, it was the chief priest and again the Pharisees who went to Pilate to make sure Jesus' tomb was well guarded (Matt. 27:62–63).

Our Lord exposes the true hostility and hypocrisy of these religious leaders of Israel. (See several parallel verses in Mark 12:38–40; Luke 20:45–47.) The "chair of Moses" (Greek, *Mōuseōs kathedras*, seat of Moses' authority) represented the synagogue chair that symbolized the origin and authority of their teaching. John Walvoord observes, "While not saying it in so many words, He implied that they were usurpers who were not truly successors of Moses."[1]

Christians, likewise, should refrain from speaking ex cathedra, as though their pronouncements were the very words of God.

"All that they tell you, do and observe," Jesus advised. Bearing in mind the Scriptures that follow, it seems clear that this means all lawful things—that is, it depends on the extent to which they teach that which is in accord with the real content and intent of Moses' Law and other Old Testament writings. It cannot include, for example, the traditions of the elders (see the condemnation of some of these in 15:1–20). But, as the verse goes on to show, the sin of the Pharisees lay more in their evil practices than in their teaching, for they themselves did not practice what they preached.

"They broaden their phylacteries" refers to strips of parchment on which were inscribed certain portions of the Pentateuch. They rolled these up and placed them in small metal cylinders inside square leather cases. The cases were attached with straps to their foreheads and to the back of their right hands, following a strictly literal interpretation of Deuteronomy 6:8–9. They were normally worn only during prayer, but the Pharisees appear to have worn them always and to have made them especially conspicuous. The word *phylactery* (Greek, *phulaktērion*) comes from an adjective that means to guard, and so came to mean "a fortified place, station for garrison, then a safeguard, protecting charm or amulet."[2] The "tassels" of their garments were the fringes worn in obedience to Numbers 15:38–39.

Jesus reminds us that man-made titles often engender pride and arrogance. "Rabbi" is from a Hebrew word (lit., my teacher). "Master," also means "teacher." "Do not call anyone on earth your father," that is, in a spiritual sense. This appears to condemn the use of the word *Father* used in addressing the clergy in the unreformed churches, and to render of doubtful propriety the use of the word *Padre* (Italian for "Father") as a synonym for a chaplain. "Servant' means "minister or attendant." Verses 10–12 are very typical of our Lord's teaching (cf. Luke 14:11; 18:14). Titles are sometimes used as a means of promoting oneself. However, Jesus' ethic was one of humility. Verse 12 is a short proverb. That thought is found in Isaiah 57:15 but is also preserved by Jesus' brother in James 4:10.

By "You shut off the kingdom of heaven from men," Jesus was saying that they put stumbling blocks in the way of sinners coming to repentance and conversion. "You devour widows' houses" means that they were extorting money from the helpless and bringing them into debt and bondage, while making an outward show of religion. You shall receive greater condemnation, that is, a more severe sentence. Degrees of punishment for larger groups, such as cities, is taught in Matthew 11:21–24, but here that are applied to individuals. The Jews recognized two sorts of "proselytes" (converts): those who agreed to the so-called seven precepts of Noah, and those who submitted to circumcision and became full Jews by religion. William Hendriksen comments, "It was not the purpose of the Pharisees merely to change a Gentile into a Jew; no, he must become a full-fledged, legalistic, ritualistic, hair-splitting Pharisee, one filled with fanatical zeal for his new salvation-by-works religion."[3] Don Carson adds, "But whether the scribes and Pharisees were winning raw pagans or sympathizers of Judaism, they were winning them to their own position. The converts in view, therefore, are not converts to Judaism but to Pharisaism."[4]

Woes to the Scribes and Pharisees	
Shut people out of the kingdom of heaven	Matthew 23:13
Mistreat widows	Matthew 23:14
Place heavy burdens on their converts	Matthew 23:15
Swear by the gold of the temple but renege on their promises	Matthew 23:16
Sticklers on external cleanliness but are polluted by sin internally	Matthew 23:25
Pretending external holiness but are like dead men's bones internally	Matthew 23:27
Honor the ancient prophets but are like those who murdered them	Matthew 23:29–31

Verses 16–22 give illustration of the Pharisees' casuistry with regard to oaths. They used trickery to avoid telling the truth. Jesus called them "fools and blind men," "because of their perversions of truth in oath taking. It is bad enough," notes Homer Kent, "that a man's word cannot be trusted apart from an oath. But the Pharisees had taught that there were distinctions in the binding force of various oaths."[5] "Temple" (Greek, *naos*) here is actually the "sanctuary." Our Lord teaches that all oaths are equally binding, and no man can expect to escape their consequences before God by making distinctions such as these. R. V. G. Tasker adds that Jesus "also exposes the folly of those who imagine that inanimate things can witness an oath."[6] In the Sermon on the Mount, Jesus commented on the use of oaths in 5:33–37 and urged His hearers to let their yes be a yes, and their no be a no. When someone says, "I swear

I'm telling you the truth," we have to wonder what he or she has been telling us up to that point.

In verse 23, Jesus commends tithing but urges that it be done with the right heart attitude. A "tithe," or tenth, of all produce was, by the Mosaic Law, to be given for the use of the priests and Levites (e.g., Lev. 27:30). Several species of mint grow in Israel. Dill (Greek, *anēthon*) grew both wild and cultivated, its fruits being used for medicine. The seeds of cumin, which resemble caraway, were used as spice in seasoning. In little matters, such as counting the tiny seeds of these plants, the Pharisees were careful to keep the Law, yet they had completely overlooked its more important precepts. Jesus said, "These are the things you should have done." Is Jesus here promoting tithing? One would have to say yes, but also remember that He was speaking of doing it unto the Lord and not for one's own glorification. Whatever was commanded by the Law ought to be exceeded under grace. Old Testament believers were required to tithe; we ought to do so as well, but out of gratitude for God's grace.

"Strain out a gnat" refers to straining (Greek, *diulizō*) wine before drinking it so as to avoid touching or swallowing anything unclean. Jesus uses sarcasm and hyperbole here by saying the scribes and Pharisees "swallow a camel!" The Pharisees were meticulous about washing hands, pots, vessels, and cups, but inside they were "full of robbery and self-indulgence." For "of" read "from"—they are full as a result of the robbery or extortion they practiced. The Pharisees' living was obtained by extorting wrongfully from others.

An explanation for "whitewashed tombs" can be found in Numbers 19:16, which says that anyone who "touches one who has been slain with a sword or who has died naturally, or a human bone or a grave, shall be unclean for seven days." Since this contact with a dead body, or even a grave, rendered a person unclean, it was the custom to paint graves white to make them conspicuous and give the opportunity to avoid contact with them. The outside looked great, so clean and tidy. But, of course, the inside of these tombs, so prominent on the Mount of Olives for pilgrims to see, was filled with dead men's bones and all uncleanness. This is the comparison Jesus was making with the Pharisees and scribes. Outwardly they "appear[ed] righteous" to men, but inside they were full of hypocrisy and lawlessness. They garnished the tombs of the slain prophets of old, but Jesus notes that they would have murdered the prophets if they had been living then. "Brood of vipers" speaks of their "offspring." They will not be able to escape the sentence of hell, that is, of being judged worthy of Gehenna.

The generation to which the words "that upon you may fall the guilt of all the righteous blood shed on the earth . . ." were addressed represented the culminating point of the whole sinful history of the nation, beginning with the murder of Abel by his brother Cain (see Gen. 4; Heb. 11:4) and going on to the murder of Zechariah, the son of Berechiah. Thus, the mention of "this generation" was not limited to the first century. In 2 Chronicles 24:20–21 we find the account of the murder of Zechariah the son of Jehoiada "in the court of the house of the LORD." Since the books of Chronicles closed the Hebrew Old Testament canon, if this is the incident here referred to, the mention of Abel and Zechariah may be intended to cover the whole Old Testament revelation.

The difficulty is that the Zechariah murdered in 2 Chronicles 24 was not the son of Berechiah. Zechariah the son of Berechiah was the prophet (Zech. 1:1). Though he lived after the exile and toward the close of Old Testament history, there exists no tradition or record that he was murdered. Another possibility is that the Zechariah referred to here is identical with "Zechariah the son of Jeberechiah" mentioned in Isaiah 8:2, but nothing further seems to be known of him. This passage is also recorded by Luke (Luke 11:49–51) and was evidently understood by His listeners. Gleason Archer concludes, "Since Jesus referred to Zechariah as the *last* of the Old Testament martyrs, there can be no legitimate doubt that it was the eleventh of the twelve minor prophets He had in mind. Therefore we can only conclude that the later Zechariah died in much the same way the earlier one did, as a victim of popular resentment against his rebuke of their sins. . . . In the absence of any other information as to how the prophet Zechariah died, we may as well conclude that Jesus has given us a true account of it and add him to the roster of noble martyrs of biblical times."[7] Jesus' statement that they would "not see Me until . . ." foreshadows His death, resurrection, ascension, and return in glory.[8] Following His resurrection, Jesus appeared only to His followers and not to the world in general. From now on He must be received as personal Savior by faith. Only at the time of His visible return (second coming) will the world ever see Him again.

Study Questions

1. How many different "woes" are there is chapter 23?

2. Who were the individuals or groups upon which Jesus pronounced the woes?

3. How serious were the matters Jesus condemned? Can you give several examples?

4. Are we sometimes guilty of any of the issues Jesus spoke against in this chapter?

5. Does Matthew 23:23 teach that tithing is imperative for believers today? Why or why not?

6. Jesus said that some strained out a gnat from their drink but would swallow what instead? What was he teaching with that illustration?

7. Name one Old Testament saint mentioned in chapter 23 who was murdered.

8. Can you name a second Old Testament saint whose blood was also shed by wicked men? Is that second murder actually mentioned in the Old Testament?

9. What did Jesus mean when he spoke about gathering Jerusalem's children like a chicken does her baby chicks?

10. When will the event Jesus spoke of in verse 39 actually take place?

CHAPTER 24

Signs of the Times
Matthew 24:1–51

Preview:
The sixth and final sermon of Jesus recorded by Matthew is found in chapters 24–25. Only the Sermon on the Mount is longer than this one. In the present chapter, Jesus gives signs regarding the destruction of Herod's temple, His own coming again in glory, and the end of the age. The major focus of this chapter is Jesus' glorious appearing after the Tribulation period.

This section forms Jesus' last major discourse and His most prophetic and apocalyptic message of the coming of the end of the world (or the present age). Homer Kent warns, "This discussion contains some of the most difficult of Jesus' utterances. The apocalyptic nature of the material resembles some of the prophetic discourses of the OT, where the mingling of historical and typical elements makes interpretation difficult."[1] John Walvoord steers a correct course when he says, "If the details of this discourse are observed and interpreted literally, it fits best with the view that the rapture is not revealed in this discourse at all, but is a later revelation, introduced by Christ in John 14 and revealed in more detail in 1 Corinthians 15 and 1 Thessalonians 4."[2]

The message of the Olivet Discourse includes a prediction of the imminent fall of Jerusalem. It also goes far beyond this to point us to the distant future, during which the "times of the Gentiles" (Luke 21:24) will continue until the end of the Great Tribulation. The entire discourse involves our Lord's response to three questions asked by the disciples in verse 3. Jesus took two whole chapters to answer these questions, while providing a series of warnings and applications in chapter 24, as well as three illustrations in chapter 25.

The incident unfolded as Jesus and the disciples walked through the temple complex one last time. Josephus describes the ornate beauty of the elaborate temple area.[3] This prophecy of the very stones of the temple being cast down was fulfilled in the time of the emperor Julian, who removed even the stones that had been left at the time of its destruction by Titus in A.D. 70.[4] Jesus' prediction of the destruction of the temple shocked His Jewish disciples. They respected the temple as the house of God and could not imagine that it would be destroyed. Jesus then left the city, crossed the Kidron Valley, and went east of Jerusalem to the Mount of Olives, from which He could look down on the temple courtyard. Here His disciples asked Him three questions: (1) "When will these things [i.e., the destruction of the temple] be?"; (2) "what will be the sign of Your coming [Greek, *parousia*, technical term for the coming of the King]?"; (3) ". . . and of the end of the age [Greek, *aiōn*]?". Therefore, the entire discourse must be looked upon as answering all three of these questions. On the significance of the signs of the end of the age, see Walvoord's *Matthew: Thy Kingdom Come*.[5] He comments, "Premillenarians, accordingly, interpret the discourse as an accurate statement of end-time events, which will lead up to and climax in the second coming of Christ to set up His millennial kingdom on the earth."[6]

Interpretation of the Olivet Discourse ranges widely from *liberal* (Allen, Moffat, McNeile, and Kee) to *conservative* (among whom there is variation from *amillennial* Hendriksen, to *posttribulational* Carson, to *preterist* Sproul, to *pretribulational* Walvoord). Difference of interpretation may even be noted between pretribulationists who view Matthew 24:4–14 as events of the Church Age leading up to the Tribulation period and those who view it as part of the Tribulation.

The key to interpreting this section rests in one's view of the "gospel of the kingdom" (vv. 13–14). Since Matthew has already shown in his selection of parables that the present form of the kingdom of heaven is the church, it seems more proper to view the events in these verses as relating to the entire Church Age and culminating especially at the end of it (thus John could say in general that he was a "fellow partaker in the tribulation and kingdom," though he was still in the Church Age of Revelation 1:9). Therefore, the "signs" of the end are general characteristics of the present age that will be intensified as the age moves on to its conclusion. These are followed by more specific signs (vv. 15–26) of the Tribulation Period and the final return of Christ in judgment (vv. 27–31).

Signs of the Present Age (24:5–14)

"Many will come" refers to the parade of false messiahs who have now spanned the centuries of church history, and even of recent Jewish history, and have led many astray into false religious cults. "Wars and rumors of wars" refer to peace being taken from the earth and the constant wars that have continually marked the "age of the Gentiles." Jesus warns the disciples that two major challenges will face them and us in the years ahead: 1) false prophets and 2) the threat of war. He reminds all of us that we are still living in a fallen world. While we may expect His blessings, we have no promise that living out our faith will be easy. Jesus speaks also of an increase in famines and earthquakes. Have there been more earthquakes in the last century than at other times in history, or is it just easier to detect and report them? The answer is that quantitatively there have actually been more in recent times than ever before. These events only mark the "beginning of birth pangs [Greek, *ōdinōn*]". Like a woman's contractions, which grow closer and severer as the time of birth approaches, these signs also will increase in number and severity. The seal, trumpet, and bowl judgments of Revelation will gain in intensity in the same manner. R. T. France acknowledges that "birth pangs" is a "technical term in apocalyptic for the period of suffering which must lead up to the new age."[7]

Olivet Discourse: Signs of the Present Age
Matthew 24:4-14

The disciples must avoid being misled (Matt. 24:4).

Many christs will arise (Matt. 24:5).

People will hear of wars and rumors of wars (Matt. 24:6).

Nations and kingdoms will go to war (Matt. 24:7).

There will be famines and earthquakes (Matt. 24:7).

Believers will be killed and hated of the nations (Matt. 24:9).

There will be apostates and hatred (Matt. 24:10).

False prophets will arise (Matt. 24:11).

Lawlessness will increase (Matt. 24:12).

Those who stand firm will survive (Matt. 24:13).

The gospel of the kingdom will go forth as a witness (Matt. 24:14).

These signs are followed by martyrdom, the rise of false prophets, and the abounding of iniquity. While Kent makes an interesting parallel of these events to the seven seals in Revelation, it still remains that the "gospel of the kingdom" refers to the missionary expansion of the church in the whole world. It is hardly reasonable to hold that the Jews will spread the gospel throughout the entire world during the first half of the Tribulation (three and a half years) when most conservative scholars view their coming national conversion at about the middle of the Tribulation (cf. Ezek. 37–39; Dan. 9; Zech. 12:10; 13:1–6). The challenge for pretribulationists involves the balance of holding to the imminent coming of Christ in the rapture, while accepting the challenge of worldwide evangelization prior to the rapture. The gospel shall be preached in all the world (Greek, *oikoumenē*), that is, the inhabited world, and unto all the nations (Greek, *ethnos*), "Gentile nations," as contrasted with the Jews. "Then the end shall come" certainly points to both the completion of the church's worldwide mission as well as the final aspects of global evangelism by the remnant during the coming Tribulation (see Rev. 7).

Signs of the Great Tribulation (24:15–28)

"You" must be taken generically, since the disciples have not lived to see this take place. The "abomination of desolation" refers to Daniel 9:27; 11:31; and 12:11, where Antiochus Epiphanes' profanation of the Jewish temple worship would foreshadow a similar and severer act by the eschatological Antichrist of the end times. Whereas Antiochus offered a pig on the sacred altar of the temple, the Antichrist will present himself and demand to be worshiped (2 Thess. 2:4)! The action of desecration by Antiochus, which Daniel had predicted, will now be repeated in the future by the Antichrist as the signal of the beginning of the Great Tribulation and the breaking of the covenant "in the middle of the week" (Dan. 9:27). The length of the seventieth week of Daniel's prophecy is found under three different terminologies: forty-two months (Rev. 11:2), 1,260 days (Rev. 12:6), or "time, times, and half a time" (Dan. 7:25; Rev. 12:14). Each of these should be taken literally, meaning three and one-half years.

The "holy place" will be in the rebuilt temple. Kent rightly observes that this cancels the limitation of Daniel's prophecy to just the days of Antiochus, since Jesus, in His day, was still awaiting further future fulfillment. It likewise goes beyond the catastrophe of A.D. 70, since it is called the greatest tribulation of all time (Matt. 24:21).[8] Preterist attempts to limit the tribulation prophecies to A.D. 70 seem ludicrous in light of Jesus' clear prediction of a powerful and visible return, which did not happen in A.D. 70.

The warning to flee into the mountains eschatologically looks beyond the first century to the Jews' flight from the persecution of the Antichrist (cf. Rev. 12:6–17). This is a warning to the Jews who will be living in Judea at the time of the tribulation spoken of here. Every Jew must flee and not look back, as any delay could cost one his or her life. The woe to those who are pregnant or nursing is because they may lose their lives by not being able to flee far enough or fast enough. The reference to the Sabbath day indicates that these events will occur in a Jewish area, where such restrictions would be observed. Hesitation to move on the Sabbath could be fatal.

"Then there will be a great tribulation" makes our Lord's reference to Daniel 12:1 clearly evident as taking place just prior to the resurrection in Daniel 12:2, when Old Testament saints will be raised up—that is, after the Tribulation period. The terrible days of that time will be "cut short" by the sudden return of Christ to destroy the "lawless one" (2 Thess. 2:8). The "false Christs" may even refer to the False Prophet who aids the Antichrist with his miracle-working powers (Rev. 13:11–17).

Olivet Discourse: Signs of the Great Tribulation
Matthew 24:15–28

The temple will be desecrated by the Antichrist (Matt. 24:15).

Those in Jerusalem are to flee the coming terror (Matt. 24:16–20).

There is nothing like the Great Tribulation (Matt. 24:21).

No one would survive if the tribulation was not stopped (Matt. 24:22).

Many will say the Christ has come (Matt. 24:23).

Many false christs will perform signs and wonders (Matt. 24:24–26).

The Son of Man will come to earth suddenly to judge (Matt. 24:27–28).

The phrase, "so as to mislead, if possible, even the elect" clearly indicates that those who have been truly saved cannot be deceived and fall away. For even if it were humanly possible, the Lord will stop it by shortening (hastening) His coming. The exclamation, "Behold, I have told you in advance," indicates Jesus' belief in the predictive nature of this prophecy. The lightning shining from the east even to the west is intended to describe the public nature of Christ's return after the Tribulation. The concept is that "the coming of the Son of Man will be visible to all people everywhere."[9] This refers to the final aspect of Christ's return (not the rapture) in judgment upon the earth. In 1 Thessalonians 4, Jesus comes in the clouds *for* the church; in 2 Thessalonians 1–2, He comes to the earth *with* the church to judge the world.

The mention of the corpse and the vultures has elicited various interpretations. Hendriksen, who takes an allegorical view of the judgments in the

Apocalypse, says, "When morally and spiritually the world has degenerated to such an extent that it resembles carrion, in other words when the Lord judges that the world's cup of iniquity is full . . . then, and not until then, Christ shall come to condemn that world."[10] The word for "vultures" (Greek, *aetoi*) can mean eagles, but they usually do not feed on carrion. If eagles are meant, then the swiftness of the coming would be in view. Either way, it could refer to swiftness, because as soon as the corpses are there, so are the vultures. The parallel passage in Luke 17:37 seems to have vultures literally feeding on the corpses of those who have been carried away to judgment at the end of the Tribulation.

Signs of the Coming Son of Man (24:29–41)

The reference to the events "immediately after the tribulation," such as the sun being darkened, the moon not shining, and the stars falling, refers to the cataclysmic events that will accompany Christ's return at the end of the Tribulation period to establish His millennial kingdom on earth.[11] Various attempts have been made by numerous groups (Adventists, Mormons, Jehovah's Witnesses, and even some evangelicals) to relate these signs to current events (earthquakes, comets, meteorites, etc.)[12] These signs described here will occur in the future. Jesus' return will be marked by "the sign of the Son of Man in heaven" which will identify His coming to the tribes of the earth. What this sign (Greek, *sēmeion*) will be is not explained here. Ancient commentators (e.g., Chrysostom) thought it to be the appearance of a cross in the sky, whereas Lange suggests it will be the shekinah glory of Christ Himself.[13] In some way a visible manifestation will mark the visible (cf. Acts 1:11, "in the same manner") return of Christ in judgment at the end of the Tribulation. As the earth revolves, the various nations and tribes will be able to see this sign. Instead of repenting, though, they shall mourn (Greek, *kopsontai*). This indicates a severe, ritualistic mourning (cf. also Zech. 12:10–12).

The clouds of heaven indicate that Christ will come from heaven to the earth (cf. also Dan. 7:13–14; 2 Thess. 1:7–9). The angels are the same agents of judgment as in chapter 13. The elect are the saved who have come to faith in Christ by the grace of God and are gladly anticipating their Lord's return. Some have taught that this is the rapture. However, the rapture will not require angel transportation. These people will continue in their earthly mortal bodies into the millennial kingdom of Christ. Here they are being gathered for His inauguration. The mention of a great trumpet also causes some to jump to the conclusion that this must be the rapture, because 1 Corinthians 15:52 and 1 Thessalonians 4:16 both mention a trumpet in connection with the rapture. But there are numerous trumpets in the end times. God is free to have a trumpet blast at the rapture, and He has said there will be one. But He is also free to have a trumpet blast to signal the return of Christ at the conclusion of the Tribulation as well. Notice what is missing from the mention of a trumpet in verse 31. "There is no mention of resurrection. There is also no mention of transformation of living believers. Indeed, an instantaneous transformation and a split second meeting with Christ in the air would counter the stated gathering work of Christ's angels."[14]

The illustration of the fig tree is referred to as a "parable." The immediate context seems to refer to the fig tree in a natural (not symbolic) sense. Walvoord says, "Because the fig tree brings forth new leaves late in the spring, the budding of the leaves is evidence that summer is near."[15] Walvoord notes that "while the fig tree could be an apt illustration of Israel, it is not so used in the Bible. . . . [and] while this interpretation is held by many, there is no clear scriptural warrant."[16] Instead, here the usage simply seems to be that as these events reach the apex of their fulfillment, the actual and ultimate return of Christ follows immediately. Just as God has built into nature certain time indicators (e.g., trees budding), so He has built into history certain time indicators of coming future events.

Jesus' saying, "when you see all these things" has caused some to speculate that these predicted events relate only to the coming destruction of Jerusalem in A.D. 70, within the disciples' lifetime.[17] In general, it is best to hold that "all these things" refers to the preceding tribulational context of the Olivet Discourse.[18] Tom Ice points out several significant factors in the debate over "this generation."[19]

The generation that "will not pass away" is the generation in whose lifetime all these signs occur, and it is that generation that will not pass away until "all these things take place." While some have attempted to relate "generation" (Greek, *genea*) to the race of the Jews, indicating the survival of their race until Christ's return, this may be somewhat stretched.[20] W. F. Arndt and F. W. Gingrich prefer "age" or "period of time."[21] In other words, the previously listed signs will continue to multiply throughout the Church Age and reach their ultimate climax at the end of the age in the generation of those who will live to see the entire matter fulfilled in their lifetime.

Carson, who believes Jesus' initial hearers are the generation in view, argues, "All that v. 34 demands is that the distress of verses 4–28, including Jerusalem's fall, happen within the lifetime of the generation then living. This does not mean that the distress must end within that time but only that "all these things" must happen within it."[22] However, no time indication of length is clearly given so that all may anticipate the imminent return of the Master. Those who object that the "last days" began at Pentecost should also see 2 Timothy 3:1, where "last days" are yet coming in the future. On the one hand, the final age began with the manifestation of the church and continues today.

On the other hand, the final aspect of this age will be a last day of perilous times that will occur at the end of the age. Even Filson agrees that Matthew certainly understood Jesus to be saying that "all these things" referred to the end of history in the distant future.[23]

Verses 35–36 warn against attempts to set an exact date for Christ's return at the end of the Church Age (a warning unheeded by the Adventists in 1844, the Jehovah's Witnesses in 1914, Edgar Wisenant in 1988, and many others). To speculate that "day" and "hour" do not eliminate "year" is a gross oversimplification.[24] The Father alone knows the time of Christ's return, since it has been set by His authority (cf. Acts 1:7). The obvious intent of Jesus' warning is against date setting. The best way to express this is to say, "Don't waste your time trying to guess the time. Be ready all the time, because Jesus could come at any time!" We are given a comparison to the days of Noah (and the Flood) that illustrates and prefigures the condition of humanity at the time of Christ's return. The last generation, like the one of Noah's day, is pleasure-oriented and self-gratifying by "eating and drinking." The reference to "marrying and giving in marriage" may refer to carrying on the normal course of life without heeding the impending judgment. However, the indication may even be stronger in that Noah's generation was judged as the result of the collapse of a godly line, as seen in Seth and others like him, by spiritual intermarriage with the ungodly line of Cain's descendants and those like them (see Gen. 4–6 for the setting of the Flood story). The drastic destruction of the godly families of Noah's day set the stage for the divine judgment of the Flood. Thus Jesus' warning is that the last generation will also be so pleasure-oriented that its families will collapse (a shocking observation in view of the current failure of the family in Western culture).

Olivet Discourse: Signs of the Second Coming
Matthew 24:29-41

At the end of the Tribulation there will be additional cosmic phenomena (Matt. 24:29).

All the earth will see the Son of Man returning (Matt. 24:30).

The Son of Man will gather His elect from throughout the world (Matt. 24:31).

Various signs will indicate that "all these things" are about to take place (Matt. 24:32–35).

Judgment will come with the Son of Man as in the days of Noah (Matt. 24:36–41).

The statement that the people of Noah's day did not understand the severity and suddenness of the coming destruction indicates that this last generation will be totally unprepared for the coming of the Son of Man (i.e., the return of Christ to judge the world, see 2 Thess. 1:7–8). "Took them all away" (Greek, *paralambanō*) is a significant phrase. It can mean to be "taken away" in the sense that a bride is taken by her husband. However, in verse 39 it seems to speak of being carried away to judgment. That seems to be its meaning in verses 40–41 also. The reference to two being in the field or at work at the time of Christ's return implies the suddenness of Him coming to separate the lost and the saved. The one taken and the other left has been variously interpreted as one being taken in the rapture and the other left to impending judgment, or as the taken one being taken to judgment and the one left being spared. Walvoord and Kent hold that the taking away is to judgment, not the rapture.[25] Kent notes that this separation occurs after the Tribulation (v. 29) and correlates with "took them all away" (to judgment) in verse 39. In the parallel passage in Luke 17:34–37, after Jesus says "one will be taken, and the other will be left," the disciples ask Him, "Where, Lord?" Jesus' reply is "Where the body is, there also will the vultures be gathered." Clearly, He was speaking of being carried away to judgment.

The Parable of the Two Servants (24:42–51)

The parable of the two servants follows to illustrate the seriousness of Christ's second coming, a fact that Jesus never allegorized or spiritualized. He spoke in the most serious terms: "cut him in pieces . . . weeping . . . and the gnashing of teeth." Kent notes that the evil slave (a usurper and impostor) "mistakes the uncertainty of the time of coming for a certainty that it will not be soon."[26] At Christ's return, however, all hypocrites will be suddenly exposed and judged by the Lord. There are several beatitudes in the New Testament besides those in Matthew 5:1–11. One is here in verse 46. The one who, at the time of His master's return, is doing what His master asked, will receive a blessing.

Chapter 24 ends with three words of *application*, answering the question of how we ought to live in light of our Lord's return. (1) "Be on the alert" (literally, "be on guard") translates a present imperative. Here the rapture is in view. We are to keep watching for Jesus to come. The only eschatology that fulfills the command is the pretribulational view. Midtribulationalists and posttribulationalists are looking for the coming of Antichrist and the beginning of the Tribulation. Pretribulationists alone are looking for the coming of Jesus Christ to take this bride home to heaven. (2) "Be ready." John MacArthur says,

"In this context, being ready seems to refer primarily to being saved, of being spiritually prepared to meet Christ as Lord and King rather than as Judge."[27] (3) Keep serving. The final beatitude is for the servant who remains faithful until Jesus returns. Here is the balance of the Christian life in the present age. We are to keep watching for Jesus to come. We are to be ready for Him to come. We are to keep serving Him until He comes.

Study Questions

1. What Old Testament prophet wrote of the abomination of desolation?

2. What did Jesus say to do when the abomination of desolation is seen in the temple? Why?

3. How many questions was Jesus asked at the beginning of chapter 24?

4. In what way do these questions form an outline for the material Matthew presents in this chapter?

5. Precisely what did Jesus predict would happen to the Jewish temple?

6. Was this a hyperbole, or was this prophecy literally fulfilled?

7. When was the time of fulfillment of the temple prophecy, and what were the circumstances surrounding it?

8. When did Jesus say the Son of Man would appear in heaven with power and glory?

9. Finish the sentence, "This generation will not pass away until — — — —."

10. Two women shall be doing what when Jesus returns? Which woman would you rather be, the one taken or the one left? Why?

11. What tree did Jesus speak of in a short parable? Why that kind of tree?

CHAPTER 25

Parables of the Second Coming Matthew 25:1-46

Preview:

With three parables, Jesus now illustrates the truths about His coming and the judgment that it will bring. The parable of the ten virgins demonstrates the necessity of being prepared when Christ comes. The parable of the talents portrays the need to do the Master's will while He is absent from us. The parable of the sheep and the goats shows the separation that will take place when Christ comes to establish His millennial kingdom on the earth.

The Parable of the Ten Virgins (25:1-13)

Jesus concludes the Olivet Discourse with three parables that amplify His words of admonition in 24:42-51. To illustrate these imperatives, He provides three stories that emphasize the need to be watching, be ready, and keep serving until He comes. He begins with the parable of the ten virgins. Homer Kent notes that "some [evangelicals] explain the virgins as the professing members of the church awaiting the return of Christ. Others apply the parable to the Jewish remnant in the Tribulation. Though the central theme of watchfulness is applicable to either group . . . the latter interpretation meets the demands of content and context more precisely."[1] The parable of the ten virgins explains the place of Israel's true converts of the Tribulation period in relation to the church. These "virgins" (Greek, *parthenos*; cf. 1:23) are the attendants at the wedding, not multiple brides. The church is the bride of Christ, John the Baptist is the best man (John 3:29, i.e., friend of the Bridegroom), and the prepared virgins are the saved believers of the Tribulation period. While all share as the people of God, the church is accorded a unique relationship to the Master.

In the parable, no account is given of whether the wedding ceremony has already taken place. According to Jewish custom, the bridegroom may pick up his bride from her parents' home, then proceed to his own home to continue the festivities. The ten virgins are awaiting the arrival of the bridegroom. The number five in each group does not necessarily indicate that half of humanity will be saved, but rather that there are two types of people. The lamps seem to refer to their lives, which are either prepared or unprepared. The oil refers to that which prepares them to give forth light and may properly be illustrative of the regeneration of the Holy Spirit.

The fact that they "all got drowsy and began to sleep" implies a period of Jewish inactivity during the Church Age, while the Bride is gathered. "Foolish" (Greek, *moros*) means "stupid" and is the designation for those who are carelessly unprepared. They had no oil at all, not an insufficient amount. Thus they are pictured as unregenerate. The refusal of the five prepared virgins to share with those unprepared must not be taken as cruelty. If the oil represents personal possession of the Holy Spirit, He cannot be shared but must regenerate each person individually. Thus the Lord responds, "I do not know you" (v. 12), indicative of 7:23. This does not mean that Jesus did not know they were out there or that He did not know their names. Rather, He did not "know" them, in the most intimate sense of that word, because they did not have a relationship with Him. False profession will save no one and only brings the final judgment of Christ upon the unsaved. As William Hendriksen reminds us, "the main lesson [is]: Preparedness is essential, for the time is coming when getting ready will no longer be possible; the door will be shut."[2]

The Parable of the Talents (25:14-30)

The parable of the talents further emphasized the need for personal preparation and faithful service to the Master. The talents represent monetary values and are distributed to three individuals "each according to his own ability" (v. 15). The similar parable of the minas (KJV, "pounds") has ten recipients who are each accorded an equal amount to trade with (Luke 19:11-18). The talents parable shows that there are differing abilities among Christ's servants. But the minas parable teaches that each one has an equal responsibility to use what God has entrusted to him. The journey indicates the time between Jesus' first coming and His final return, during which He is in heaven. The three slaves are typical of three types who are entrusted various tasks in accordance with their own ability. Not all are expected to produce the same results, but all are to be faithful with what they have had entrusted to them. The first two double their money, while the last one hides the one talent in the ground.

The phrase "after a long time" gives a veiled indication of the length of Christ's departure to heaven during the present age. This is the only place in the Gospels where it is implied that Jesus will be gone for a "long time." Notice in the parable that He goes on a long journey (back to heaven) and is gone for a long time before He returns (second coming). This does not eliminate the idea of an imminent return at any possible moment, but it does give a glimpse into the distance future when He will actually return at a time least expected. Each of those producing results is commended by the master: "Well done, good and faithful slave." Each is promised to be put in change of "many things," with a view to continued service in the millennial kingdom.

The great mistake of the unfaithful servant was in misjudging the character of his master: "I knew you to be a hard man." He could not have known the master well to assume him to be severe and merciless. B. F. Atkinson observes, "The slave seems to have thought that whatever he did his master would be unjust to him."[3] He failed to understand the real generosity of his master who wanted him to experience the joys of service. Whereas the parable of the ten virgins emphasized being wise with personal preparation for the coming of Christ, the parable of the talents stresses the importance of faithful service during His present absence.

The fact that the latter man is called a "wicked, lazy slave" and a "worthless slave" (v. 30) who is cast out into outer darkness certainly indicates that he was not a true disciple of the Master. The idea of this illustrative parable is that all true believers will produce results (elsewhere, "fruits") in varying degrees. Those who produce no results are not truly converted. Those who reject soul winning, personal evangelism, and church growth will find no comfort in this story. Those who hide their treasure (probably the life-changing message of the gospel) because of a harsh view of the Master's sovereignty over them, reveal that they do not really love people, and therefore, their own salvation is questionable! Alfred Plummer observes that some might feel that the foolish virgins made a pardonable mistake, and that "to keep a deposit safe, but fail to increase it, might seem to be pardonable also. But the failure in each case, whether it be regarded as great or small, is proof that there is something radically wrong with the characters of those who fail, and the result is outer darkness."[4] It is instructional to note that the one who utterly failed was the one entrusted with the least. If someone says, "Well, I just can't do much for God," he had better be careful lest he squander his time and talent for God.

The Judgment of the Nations (25:31–46)

The judgment of the nations concludes our Lord's prophetic discourse. Christ's return in His glory to be enthroned on His glorious throne marks the great interruption of history as He brings the Tribulation period to an end and ushers in the millennial kingdom. John MacArthur points out, "The judgment of the sheep and goats is not mentioned in any of the other gospels, no doubt because they do not focus on Christ's kingship, as does Matthew. For that same reason Matthew places much greater emphasis on all aspects of the Lord's second coming than do the other gospels, because it is at His return that He will manifest Himself as King of Kings and Lord of Lords."[5]

Judgment of Nations	Great White Throne
Takes place at the beginning of the kingdom reign (v. 31).	Takes place at the end of the final judgment of Satan (Rev. 20:7–10).
Christ will judge seated on the Davidic throne (v. 31).	Takes place at the end of the kingdom reign (Rev. 20:11).
The nations will be divided for the judgment (v. 32).	The unbelievers of all ages are resurrected for judgment (Rev. 20:12a–13).
The nations will be separated like sheep from goats (v. 33).	It is a judgment based on deeds not on lack of faith in Christ (Rev. 20:12b).
The righteous will inherit the kingdom (v. 34).	Death and the grave (Hades) are finished — thrown into the lake of fire (Rev. 20:14).
The basis of the judgment is how the nations treated the Jews (vv. 35–44).	Those not written in the book of life are also thrown into the lake of fire (Rev. 20:15).
The living unrighteousness will be slain (vv. 41, 46).	The resurrected unrighteous will face the final end — the second death (Rev. 20:14).

This judgment of all nations must be distinguished from the Great White Throne Judgment at the end of the Millennium. The nations (Greek, *ethnos*) are those peoples living through the Tribulation on earth at the time of Christ's return. This is a judgment of separation: sheep on His right . . . goats on the left. At this judgment all nations (better, "all Gentiles") stand before Christ, who then separates the sheep (the saved) from the goats (the lost) in a manner reminiscent of the wheat and tares parable. Some view this as the last general judgment,[6] whereas most premillennial commentators see this as the judgment of the nations who have survived the Tribulation period, with the saved going into the millennial kingdom.[7] Note that these are living nations, whereas the Great White Throne Judgment involves the wicked dead whose bodies are resurrected to face the final judgment of the lost. In this parable, the saved are invited to come into and share the blessings of God's kingdom: "Come, you who are blessed of My Father, inherit the kingdom." The basis of their acceptance seems to be their treatment of "one of these brothers of Mine," that is, the saved of the Tribulation. The acts of kindness (vv. 35–38) were done by these sheep individuals unto the persecuted Jewish believers and their converts during the reign of the Antichrist and now bring the blessing of God's salvation upon these persons. The acts of kindness do not themselves merit salvation apart from the atonement of Christ. Since the nations are the Gentiles and "my brethren" are neither, they could be the Jews. William Pettingill, for example, says, "These 'brethren' are doubtless the Jewish Remnant who will have turned to the Lord during the terrible scenes of The Great Tribulation."[8] Arno Gaebelein agrees, "They are the brethren of the Lord according to the flesh, in other words they are Jews."[9] John Walvoord argues, "In mentioning 'my brethren,' He is referring to a third class, neither sheep nor goats, which can only be identified as Israel, the only remaining people who are in contrast to all the Gentiles."[10]

The goats are banished into everlasting fire or hell. Both the judgment and the blessed life are designated by the same adjective, "eternal" (Greek, *aiōnios*), clearly indicating their equal duration. This eternal judgment is in keeping with Revelation 14:11 and 19:20. No unsaved adults are admitted unto the millennial kingdom when it is begun on earth. A natural and legitimate conclusion, then, is that the rapture must occur before this event. Thus the rapture precedes the Tribulation period, which itself precedes the millennial kingdom.

Study Questions

1. How many of the ten virgins are said to have slumbered and slept?

2. What did the slumber of the virgins represent?

3. What did the oil stand for, or was it just the idea of preparedness? Remember that all ten of the lamps began to go out.

4. How many total talents were distributed to the men in the parable of the talents?

5. In what ways does the parable of the talents compare and contrast with the parable of the pounds in Luke 19?

6. Do you think the servant with the one talent was saved? Why or why not?

7. At what point in the future does the enthronement of Christ pictured in verse 31 occur?

8. What does the judgment of the nations mean? Will some whole nations go to heaven while other whole nations go to hell? Why or why not?

9. Can we tell who the "least of these my brethren" are?

10. Does it not seem that the punishment of the lost and the blessedness of the saved will both last for the same amount of time, according to verses 41 and 46?

Rejection of the King
Matthew 26:1-75

Preview:
Chapter 26 is the longest chapter in Matthew's Gospel. It brings together both affirmation and denial of Christ, the latter by both friend (Peter) and foe (Judas). Jesus conducts the Passover with His disciples and institutes the Lord's Supper. Jesus foretells Peter's denial and then prays in Gethsemane where He is captured by Judas's mob. He is tried by the Sanhedrin while at the same time being denied by Peter.

These chapters describe the priests' plot, the Lord's anointing in Bethany, Judas's betrayal, the institution of the Lord's Supper, Jesus' agony in the garden, His arrest, His trial before the priests, Peter's denial, Jesus' trial before Pilate, and finally His crucifixion and resurrection.

Jesus' Denied by His Disciples (26:1-56)

The final preparations were made for the last week of Jesus' life. See also Mark 14:1-2; Luke 22:1-2. Jesus made a final prediction of His death two days before Passover, which was eaten on the evening of Nisan 14. Thus the prediction was made on the twelfth of the month (April). The Passover was the first feast on the Jewish yearly calendar and was kept in commemoration of the national deliverance from Egypt in the exodus under Moses. Passover takes its name from the Hebrew term related to the death angel passing over those who had applied lamb blood to their homes (cf. Ex. 12). The Hebrew root *pesach* was transliterated into "paschal," from which Christ's suffering is

often referred to as His "passion." Passover time was a great high day among
the Jews, and thousands of pilgrims flocked to Jerusalem to observe it each
year. Our Lord's death was the ultimate fulfillment of which the annual feast
had been a shadow. Paul even said, "For Christ our Passover also has been sac-
rificed" (1 Cor. 5:7). The Passover was followed by the seven-day Feast of
Unleavened Bread (Nisan 15–21). Sometimes the entire period was generally
referred to as Passover.

Jesus also predicted His betrayal. "Son of Man" is His favorite designation of Himself. It emphasizes His humanity and His identification with the
human race. "Delivered up" (Greek, *paradidōmi*) means "given over," or
"handed over." It is a word for betrayal. The assemblage of the Sanhedrin
took place at the court (Greek, *aulē*, meaning the courtyard of his residence).
Caiaphas was a Sadducee who had been appointed high priest a few years
earlier, about A.D. 18, about ten years before Christ's earthly ministry began.
The recent archaeological discovery of his burial box (ossuary), with the
inscription JOSEPH CAIAPHAS, confirms his historical existence. They plotted
together to seize and kill Jesus. There is no way that this action by the Jewish
elders and chief priests can be cast in a good light. Jewish leaders even today
readily admit Jesus should not have been killed. Nevertheless, it was because
of the sins of the whole world that Jesus had to die. It was God's eternal purpose and plan to bring about the death, burial, and resurrection of Jesus.
"Not during the festival" means "not during the feast." Since many of Jesus'
supporters from Galilee would be in Jerusalem during this time, the leaders
did not want to upset the crowd, whose emotions were high anyhow. God
ultimately foiled their plan, and Jesus died at the very hour of the slaying of
the Passover lambs.

The anointing at Bethany (cf. Mark 14:3–9; John 12:1–8) is related by
John as taking place six days before Passover, indicating that John's version is
chronological, and the other is topical, since neither Matthew nor Mark dates
the event. The chronological problems with the crucifixion have long been
wrestled with by scholars, but the detailed accounts of factual material relating to such highly emotionally material make their veracity all the more certain. These are no mere legendary accounts, embellished by church tradition.
They are highly factual and readable accounts of the most sublime narratives
in Scripture.[1]

Simon the leper is mentioned only here and in the parallel account in
Mark 14:2. Simon is still called by the old designation, "the leper," to distinguish him from many other Simons who lived in the region. Presumably he
had been healed by Jesus. Otherwise, all who were in the room were in violation of Mosaic Law. By a comparison with John 12:1–8, some have thought

it to be a reasonable deduction that Simon was either Lazarus or the father of Lazarus, Martha, and Mary. However, as John Walvoord notes, this could very well have been in another home since Jesus had many friends living around Bethany.[2]

The woman with an alabaster vial is thought to have been Mary. Alabaster is a translucent stone. Such jars are still made today in the Near East. The value of the contents is said to be "over three hundred denarii" in both Mark 14:5 and John 12:5. Not only Judas, but all of the disciples were indignant at the supposed waste of the precious, very costly perfume. "She did it to prepare Me for burial," Jesus explained. The point seems to be that the action was appropriate in view of His burial, which was soon to take place, and that it might be regarded as symbolic or prophetic of the burial. Mary had keener spiritual insight than any of Jesus' disciples. This gospel, that is, the good news of the Lord's death and resurrection would be preached in all the world, and her good deed and its true intention would be told worldwide (see also Mark 14:9; Luke 24:47). No one had done anything like this before. Mary Magdalene had washed Jesus' feet with her tears (see Luke 7:37–38), but this Mary had broken open the alabaster jar containing her most precious ointment and poured it all on Jesus' feet. It was an act of worship and devotion. And why not? He had recently raised her brother Lazarus from the dead. It was a way for Mary to express her gratitude. She gave the most expensive thing she had to say thank you to the Savior. She could not contain herself. Filled with awe and worship, she poured out her heart and soul as well as the perfume. Had she hesitated or waited until another day, she would have lost her opportunity to express the wonader and adoration of her soul.

Judas Iscariot (see Mark 3:19) was probably from Judea. He was the only disciple who was not a Galilean. Perhaps he was embarrassed by the reaction Jesus received in Judea. Perhaps he was personally upset by Jesus' obvious claims of deity. Whatever his human motivation, the Bible clearly indicates that Satan entered his heart (John 13:27). As a result, Judas made arrangements with the priests to deliver Jesus to them for thirty pieces of silver. The amount they gave Judas represented about a month's wages or the price of a common slave.[3] These words are substantially from the Septuagint of Zechariah 11:12. "Betray Him" meant to hand Jesus over. The same verb is translated "deliver" in verse 15.

The Last Supper is also related in Mark 14:12–31; Luke 22:7–38; and John 13:1–38. The Synoptics agree in the basic details and seem to assert that this was the Passover meal, whereas John clearly indicates that it was eaten before the Passover lambs were slain (John 18:28; cf. 1 Cor. 5:7). Liberal interpreters see the accounts as contradictory;[4] others suggest that Jesus followed the Essene custom of the Qumran community in taking the Passover meal on Tuesday.[5] However, it seems most likely that John, writing later, is simply clarifying the ambiguous points in the chronology, as he does elsewhere in his gospel in regard to other matters. It should be remembered that "the Passover" can refer to the entire Passover week, the Passover meal, or the paschal lamb itself. Homer Kent's material on the chronology of the passion week is excellent and should be thoroughly considered.[6]

The first day of the Feast of Unleavened Bread was the fourteenth of Nisan (cf. Mark 14:12; Luke 22:7). The day actually began at sundown on the thirteenth. While Jesus said, "I am to keep the Passover," the cross-reference in Luke 22:16 notes that He added, "I shall never again eat it until the kingdom of God comes," implying an interruption, perhaps after this meal was completed. Perhaps He did not want Judas to be aware of His certainty of the details. Only Jesus and the Twelve were present. At this crucial time, Jesus announced, "One of you will betray Me." We cannot imagine the shock with which this statement must have jolted the disciples. For the first time, Jesus clearly indicated that the betrayer would be one of the Twelve!

Passover Meal in Christ's Day	
Bread	Unleavened bread commemorating the night of deliverance
Cup	Symbol of the blood of the atonement
Lamb	Unblemished male for the sacrifice for sin
Bitter Herbs	Reminder of their years of bondage in Egypt

The disciples were deeply grieved, indicating their sorrow over such an announcement. In the original language, the question "Surely not I, Lord?" suggests that a negative answer was cautiously expected by each one—"It is not I, is it?" Coupled with Peter's later defensive protest and subsequent failure, it seems clear that the entire group feared the possibility of failure. What a transformation would have to take place to change these cowards into the mighty apostles of the book of Acts! Jesus warned, "It would have been good for that man if he had not been born." These words can well be used to discredit the false doctrine of annihilation, the belief that hell's punishment will be brief and complete by burning up the guilty sinner in an instant. It that were true, then these words of Jesus would have little meaning. There will be degrees of guilt and therefore various degrees of punishment as well.

Judas repeated the same question, and Jesus' reply, "You have said it your-self," meant "yes." Jesus' statement, "He who dipped his hand with Me" (v. 23), reveals the personal and intimate nature of the betrayal. Jesus took bread as the head of the Jewish household was accustomed to doing this during the Passover feast and gave a completely new significance to the action. "This is My body," He said. If the Lord had intended to convey that the bread was transformed into His body, He would have said, "This has become my body." During the Passover feast the Jewish householder took bread in his hand and said, "This is the bread of affliction which our fathers ate in the land of Egypt," meaning, of course, that the one represented the other. By His words the Lord changed the whole significance and emphasis of the feast from looking back to the typical redemption from Egypt to faith in the redemption from sin accomplished by His death. (For a clear example of the use of the word "is" as "represents," see Galatians 4:25.) The bread and wine were only outward symbols of our Lord's death and a reminder to us of the cost of our redemption during our Lord's absence (cf. Luke 22:19). Nothing in the Gospels indicates that these were to be viewed as a means of grace or as sacraments, or that they were physically necessary for one's salvation.

Three cups were passed around by the Jewish householder during the Passover meal. The third, which is probably that referred to here, was known as "the cup of blessing." Each of the disciples drank from the same cup; however, John seems to indicate that Judas had already departed before this institution of the Lord's Table (John 13:26–30). "My blood of the covenant" is taken from the Septuagint of Exodus 24:8 with allusions to Jeremiah 31:31–37 and Zechariah 9:11. The covenant in Exodus 24:8 was sealed with blood. The word "covenant" (Greek, *diathēkē*) did not mean an agreement between equals, but a settlement by a great or rich man for the benefit of another. As the most common form of settlement was, and still is, by testament or will, the word came to have this meaning almost exclusively.

The word "new" is applied to this covenant in Luke 22:20 and probably should be seen here (v. 28) as well. The textual evidence for including the word "new" is broad as well as ancient, and includes every ancient version, which the omission does not. "Poured out for many for forgiveness of sins" is a clear statement that the death of Jesus was necessary to enable God to forgive sins. It, in fact, made it right or morally justifiable for Him to do so. "Until that day," that is, until Jesus comes again in glory, He will not drink of the fruit of the vine. This may be an indication that the Marriage Supper of the Lamb will not be in heaven, but will take place on His return to earth after the Tribulation. The only announcement of that "supper" is in Revelation 19:9–10 after the marriage in heaven and just before Christ mounts a horse to return with the saints to fight at Armageddon. Thus it is probably best to place that event as a regal supper near the beginning of the millennial kingdom.

The quotation in verse 31 is taken from the Septuagint of Zechariah 13:7. By "I will go before you to Galilee" Jesus was saying that He would lead His disciples as their head, as an eastern shepherd leads his sheep. He did not mean that He would go first to Galilee in the sense that the disciples must go there to find Him, but rather that He would appear to them at Jerusalem and lead them to Galilee. Peter protested, "Even if I must die with You, I will not deny You." Peter's boast sets the stage for his later bitter denials of his Master. He promised to be more faithful than the others, thus later provoking Jesus' question, "Do you love Me more than these?" (probably referring to the other disciples; cf. John 21:15).

The scene in the Garden of Gethsemane is one of the most moving in all the New Testament. Gethsemane means "olive press" and was a lush garden east of the city, just across the Kidron Valley, at the base of the slopes of the Mount of Olives. Jesus often went there for peace and quiet. He took the same inner circle, as at the transfiguration (Peter, James, and John), further into the garden. "My soul is deeply grieved" is found in the Septuagint of Psalm 43:5. The imperative "keep watch" means to keep awake in order to be prepared for whatever might come.

Jesus' prayer for the cup of suffering to pass was not due to His fear of death. Many martyrs have faced terrible deaths without great fear. Jesus questions the will of the Father as to the necessity of drinking the cup. While this may refer to death ("He might taste death for everyone," Heb. 2:9), it is more likely that the cup represents the wrath of God against sin, which would be poured out on Christ on the cross as man's sin-bearer. In the awful anguish of that moment, the sin of the world was poured on Christ, and He became "sin on our behalf" (2 Cor. 5:21). Isaiah 53:6 says quite literally that God caused all of our sin to come crashing down upon Him. His total submission to the will of the Father caused Him to be obedient, even unto a substitutionary death. The innocent and righteous One died for the guilty. Herein was His ultimate exaltation as Lord (Phil. 2). "Not as I will, but as Thou wilt" is as clear an indication as we have that Jesus had two wills, a human and a divine, in His one person. Jesus always submitted His human will to His Father's will.

In the meantime, the disciples were sleeping due to emotional fatigue and physical exhaustion. Again Jesus urged them to "keep watching and praying, that you may not enter not into temptation" (v. 41). Several commentators unnecessarily relate this temptation to Christ, whereas in the context, He relates it to the disciples.[7] Because they are not prayerfully watching, they will not be prepared for the tragedy that is about to happen. He reminded them that "the spirit is willing, but the flesh is weak." Man's regenerated spirit may have good intentions, but it must control his body in order to gain spiritual victory (cf. Rom. 12:1). The Greek present imperative indicates that the disciples were to "continually keep watching." When Jesus returned and found them sleeping again, He asked, "Are you still sleeping and taking your rest?" This could either be a question (NIV, REB, RSV), or an imperative, as the New American Standard Bible marginal note has it (also KJV, NJB, ESV). If it is the latter, their fatigue may have caused the remark, "Keep on sleeping." Alfred Plummer calls it "mournful irony."[8] A. B. Bruce terms it "not ironical or reproachful, nor yet seriously meant, but concessive; you may sleep and rest indefinitely so far as I am concerned; I need no longer your watchful interest."[9] The immediate interruption of the soldiers causes Him to awaken them, saying, "Arise, let us be going."

Jesus' arrest took place in the garden during the middle of the night as a mixed mob led by the temple guards, arrived to take Jesus. There can be little doubt that Jesus saw them approaching, as there is always a full moon at Passover, and they probably also carried lighted torches.[10] "One of the twelve" refers to Judas. This terminology is found in each of the Synoptic Gospels. A. T. Robertson points out, "The very horror of the thing is thus emphasized, that one of the chosen twelve apostles should do this dastardly deed."[11] The Roman soldiers carried swords, and the Jewish temple police had clubs. A sign was necessary to identify Jesus to the Romans to whom He was unknown, so Judas kissed Jesus as the sign of betrayal of the One he still glibly called Rabbi (cf. Matt. 7:23ff.). In response, Jesus either said, "Friend, do what you have come for" (ASV, NASB, NEB, NIV, NJB), or asked, "Friend, what have you come for?" (KJV, NKJV, RSV). If a question, this convicting query was far more effective than an accusation, since Judas could not answer it.

Peter drew out his sword (John 18:10), probably one of the short swords referred to in Luke 22:38, and attempting to defend Jesus, struck the slave of the high priest, cutting off his ear. In a typically impetuous move, Peter had struck the one person who could have embarrassed them the most at the trial. Luke, a physician (22:51) tells us that Jesus healed him by replacing the ear (His last miracle), and John (18:10) tells us that the man's name was Malchus. Jesus' rebuke, "Put your sword back," clearly revealed that His kingdom would not be brought in by force at that time. "All those who take up the sword shall perish by the sword" is a statement of fact, but it cannot be taken alone to teach nonviolence in all situations. Jesus had no lack of power by which to deal with these few enemies. Twelve legions of angels could be called to His aid. Each Roman legion has six thousand soldiers. Christ's restraint was due to His willingness to obey the will of the Father and so fulfill the Scriptures. Even a well-intentioned defense by one of His disciples would not deter Jesus from the cross and His ultimate destiny.[12]

Jesus' Denunciation by the Sanhedrin (26:57–75)

Jesus was whisked away in the dark and taken to an illegitimate trial in the middle of the night at the home of the high priest (see Mark 14:53–72; Luke 22:54–65; John 18:12–27). The courtyard, was an open court around which the main buildings were built. The Greek word for "officers" (*huperetes*) can also mean "servants," as per the NASB marginal note. The "whole Council" refers to the Sanhedrin, the group of seventy elders of Israel who acted as a religious supreme court. However, they were not all there. Rather, a select group of them assembled, determined to condemn Jesus by obtaining false testimony. The entire proceedings were rigged. Injustice abounded. The "evidence" that was eventually brought forward (v. 61) was based upon the Lord's words recorded in John 2:19, 21, nearly three years earlier!

"I adjure You by the living God," was a statement that put a man on his oath and compelled an answer. The high priest was seeking an admission that could be the foundation of a charge of blasphemy. To the command "Tell us whether You are the Christ, the Son of God," Jesus replied, "You have said it yourself," meaning "yes." He added, "Hereafter you shall see the Son of Man sitting at the right hand of power, and coming on the clouds of heaven" (v. 64). The session at God's right hand began at the ascension (even, perhaps, at the resurrection). Note the allusion in our Lord's reply to Psalm 110:1 and Daniel 7:13. The second part of the phrase may refer as much to the ascension as to the second coming. The Jewish religious leaders would be witnesses of the victories of Christ after His resurrection. "He has blasphemed!" they shouted. Jesus' claim to be the Son of Man was a claim to be deity. They knew Daniel 7:13–14 well enough to see that. "They beat Him with their fists," or punched Him. Verse 68 is a sarcastic demand to be told the names and identities of those who were strangers to Him as a sign of supernatural knowledge. The incident ends with the indictment that He is "deserving of death." There can be no doubt that the Sanhedrin understood Him to be claiming to be a divine Messiah, a claim they violently rejected.

Peter's three denials occurred during the trial proceedings. Peter was sitting outside in the courtyard. We know from the other Synoptics and John that he was warming himself by a fire prepared by servants of the priests. Peter's first denial was prompted by a servant-girl, or young maid, and the porters who had admitted him and John. Somehow she recognized him from an earlier meeting. The form of the denial, "I do not know what you are talking about," was merely a pretense of ignorance on Peter's part, similar to, "I don't know what you mean." Feeling the pressure of the interrogation, Peter went out to the gateway, a passageway leading to the street. Then he was confronted by another servant-girl, probably the outer gatekeeper who alerted the men (thus Luke's reference to a man as the interrogator) that "this man was with Jesus of Nazareth." The terms "Galilean" and "Nazarene" were probably used in a derogatory manner by these Judeans. This time his denial was stronger, with an oath, in spite of Jesus' earlier warning against oath taking (5:34). "I do not know the man!" Peter exclaimed definitely and deliberately.

The third denial came a little later (less than an hour) when he was accused because his accent or dialect gave him away ("makes you evident," ASV, "Your accent betrays you," ESV). Under the mounting emotional pressure and fear of being condemned along with Jesus, Peter began to "curse and swear." This emotional and sinful outburst was intended to make him appear unattached to Jesus. Weeks later, this last great outburst of denial would be corrected by an emotion-packed reaffirmation of loyalty to the Savior (cf. John 21:15–18). "And immediately a cock crowed," probably refers to "cockcrowing" (i.e., the end of the Roman watch from midnight to 3:00 A.M.), verifying the illegitimacy of the trial that was being conducted during the middle of the night. And Peter remembered, not because he heard the noise, but as Luke (22:61) records, "the Lord turned and looked at Peter" with a convicting glance from the balcony of the high priest's house. Then Peter remembered the Savior's warning and went out and wept bitterly. All these events related to the betrayal, arrest, and trial of Jesus show that He was completely in control of each situation even while in the hands of His captors.[13]

Peter's Three Denials	
Ignorant	*"'I do not know what you are talking about'" (v. 70).*
Insistent	*"He denied it with an oath" (v. 72).*
Indignant	*"He began to curse and swear" (v. 74).*

In the darkness of that night, Peter came face-to-face with the Savior. As Jesus glanced at him with a look of love and a broken heart, Peter's heart broke as well. We cannot fully comprehend such love. It turns our worst mistakes into magnificent displays of His grace. The very next day Jesus did the unthinkable—He went to the cross and took all our failures upon Himself. He nailed our sin to the cross and said, "It is finished!"

Study Questions

1. In whose house was Jesus when a woman anointed Jesus' head?

2. In what city or town did the anointing occur? How close was this town to Jerusalem?

3. Who commented about the anointing, "To what purpose is this waste?"

4. Jesus was betrayed for how many pieces of silver? How does this compare with how many pieces Joseph brought his brothers when they sold him into slavery? See Genesis 37.

5. Which disciples accompanied Jesus to supposedly "watch" with Him?

6. How many times did Jesus find His disciples sleeping after He had prayed?

7. Whose ear was cut off by one of Jesus' disciples?

8. How many legions of angels did Jesus claim His Father would send if He asked?

9. How many angels would that have been? Would that have been enough to destroy the world and set Him free? Why or why not?

10. What was the name of the high priest in Matthew 26?

CHAPTER 27

Crucifixion of Christ
Matthew 27:1–66

Preview:

Even with their illegal trial, the Sanhedrin could not legally sentence Jesus to death. Only a Roman official could do that. So they took Jesus to the Roman procurator, Pilate. Pilate interrogated Jesus briefly, and then swayed by an angry crowd, handed Jesus over to be crucified. He died and was buried in a borrowed tomb.

Jesus' Deliverance to Pilate (27:1–31)

In order to have Jesus executed as a common criminal, the priests had Him taken to Pilate the governor. (See also Mark 15:1–15; Luke 23:1–25; John 18:28–19:16.) Pontius Pilate was the Roman procurator of Judea from A.D. 26 to 36, holding his office under the Prefect of Syria. His usual place of residence was Caesarea on the Mediterranean coast, but he was in Jerusalem during the festival to deal with any insurrection or trouble.

Before proceeding further with the story of Jesus, Matthew concludes the case of Judas the traitor. When Judas saw that Jesus had been condemned, which would be evident from seeing Jesus being taken to Pilate (a move that Judas may not have anticipated), he "felt remorse" (Greek, *metamelomai*, "to regret"). This word is different from the term meaning repentance to salvation (Greek, *metanoia*). Judas showed every indication of still being unsaved: he betrayed innocent blood for money, became guilty, returned the money, and committed suicide. These are the actions of a guilty conscience, apparently not a forgiven and regenerate one. Judas' admission "I have sinned" is not necessarily a true confession that indicates faith. The reply of the priests reveals the real cruelty of their hearts: "What is that to us? See to that yourself!" A. W. Tozer calls this the "great double-cross," wherein Judas betrayed Christ in collusion with the priests, who in return, rejected him![1]

Judas threw the money into the sanctuary, that is, the temple, but the priests would not put the money into the temple treasury (Greek, *korbanas*), because it would pollute the sanctity of it. As A. T. Robertson aptly remarks, "The rabbis knew how to split hairs about *Korban* (Mark 7:1–23; Matt. 15:1–20), but they balk at this blood-money."[2] Judas then hung himself. It is generally supposed that "falling headlong" (Acts 1:18–19) happened while he was attempting to do this. Perhaps, hanging himself over the ledge, he then fell into the valley below, or perhaps the branch on which he hung broke or the rope broke. In such cases, the purchase was made in the name of the man to whom the money had been paid and to whom the money by a legal fiction was supposed all the time to belong. By law, therefore, Judas himself purchased the field (see Acts 1:18).

Some have expressed concern over the mention of Jeremiah in this passage on the basis that the quotation apparently comes from Zechariah. While there is an allusion here to Zechariah 11:12–13, the actual words do not agree with either the Hebrew or the Septuagint. The major difference is the addition of the word "field," upon which the fulfillment claimed is based. This word, and the conception behind it, comes from Jeremiah 32:6–9, where the prophet refers to the purchase of a field for certain pieces of silver. It is obvious that Matthew's concept of prophetic fulfillment rests upon both passages. Thus, he combines both passages into one quotation, giving credit to Jeremiah as the older and more predominant of the two prophets. William Hendriksen draws the same conclusion, noting that in the Greek text, a major prophet is preferred over a minor one in a similar double reference in Mark 1:2–3.[3] There Isaiah is credited instead of Malachi (see Mal. 3:1). Similarly, 2 Chronicles 36:21 quotes both Leviticus 26:34–35 and Jeremiah 25:12, but only says it is from Jeremiah.[4] This is certainly to be preferred to Alfred Plummer's suggestion that "a slip of memory is much more probable."[5]

Pilate asked Jesus, "Are You the King of the Jews?" Pilate's question was to ascertain whether Jesus was a threat to the Roman authority. Michael Wilkins comments, "Pilate would not be concerned with the religious implications of the Sanhedrin's charge of blasphemy, so the Jewish leaders focus their allegation on challenges to Roman rule."[6] He apparently thought the charge was baseless and sought to release Jesus. Nevertheless, Pilate kept the accusation that Jesus was the Jews' king and placed it over His cross, perhaps as a mocking gesture against the despised Jews he had to rule over. Jesus made no answer.

He was perfectly in control of Himself. He was gentle and meek, fulfilling Isaiah 53:7, "And like a sheep that is silent before its shearers, so He did not open His mouth." Of this event in Christ's life, Peter later wrote, "while being reviled, He did not revile in return; while suffering, He uttered no threats, but kept entrusting Himself to Him who judges righteously (1 Pet. 2:23).

Pilate announced several times that Jesus was innocent. Even after all the accusations, Pilate still asked, "What evil has He done?" Pilate's wife called Jesus a "righteous Man," and urged her husband to let Him go. Barabbas means "the father's son" in Aramaic and must be seen in contrast with Jesus, the Father's Son. Pilate's question, "Why, what evil has He done?" comes late in the trial and represents a personal, though unofficial, acknowledgment of Jesus' innocence. Thus Pilate attempted to shift the blame for Jesus' death to the Jews themselves. As a symbolic gesture, Pilate even washed his hands, declaring his innocence from what would follow. The Jews' (Greek, *laos*, "people"; instead of *ochlos*, "crowd"), dramatic answer, "His blood be on us and on our children!" may eventually have brought the wrath of God upon His own people. Certainly their subsequent suffering must be viewed in light of this self-condemnation.[7]

Encouraged by their willingness to take responsibility for Jesus' death, Pilate then scourged Jesus in hope that a bloody beating would appease them (cf. John 19:1–6), but it did not. Instead, they yelled, "Crucify Him!" all the more. It was this beating that left Jesus extremely weak and eventually caused His early death on the cross (some survived on crosses for several days). The scourging was a whipping with a leather whip with sharp pieces of bone and metal embedded in its thongs. The statement that Pilate delivered over Jesus means he officially turned Him over to his soldiers for execution. They took Him into the governor's quarters (Greek, *praitōrion*, from Latin, *praetorium*), probably in the Antonia fortress that bordered the temple area. They mocked His claim to be King by clothing Him with a scarlet robe (Greek, *chlamus*). A military robe, probably fastened at the shoulder, it mocked the purple worn by royalty. The crown of thorns and the reed for a scepter added to their mockery. Changing Jesus' clothes once again, the soldiers led Him out to be crucified.

Jesus' Death for Humankind (27:32–66)

A certain Cyrenian named Simon helped carry Jesus' cross. Cyrene was a Roman province in North Africa where many Jews lived. They had a synagogue in Jerusalem (Acts 6:9), indicating that many of them lived there. His sons, Alexander and Rufus, later became well-known Christians (see Mark

15:21, and Paul's greeting to Rufus in Rom. 16:13). Simon was pressed into service (Greek, *aggareuō*, a technical term for being requisitioned) to bear His cross. The transverse piece of the cross was generally carried by the prisoner, which John 19:17 indicates was at first the case with Christ. Evidently, the weight was more than He could bear, due to His severe scourging. This carried piece was brought to the place of execution separately by the prisoner and attached by rope to the vertical pole that remained there.[8]

Golgotha was the "Place of a Skull." The name is a transliteration of the Aramaic word for skull and is equivalent to the Latin *calvaria*, probably due to the physical appearance of the hill. Presently two sites have been claimed as Golgotha: (1) the site of the Church of the Holy Sepulchre (which at that time was outside the wall) and (2) the nearby hill across from the Damascus Gate of Jerusalem known as "Gordon's Calvary" (which definitely resembles a skull, even until this day). They gave Him wine to drink mingled with gall, an allusion to Psalm 69:21. This was customarily given to condemned prisoners to serve as a kind of anesthetic or anodyne. It was literally a drugged "wine" (Greek, *oinon*). The statement that He was unwilling to drink indicates that our Lord refused any mitigation of His sufferings on our behalf. Jesus took all the pain and suffering the cross inflicted.

Crucifixion was a common means of execution in the Roman world, although it was generally limited to criminals and foreigners, not Roman citizens. Jesus' hands and ankles were probably nailed to the cross by spikes. A 1968 discovery in Jerusalem of the bones of an early first-century crucified man named Jehohanon demonstrate that this was the pattern followed.[9] The victim's legs were bent to allow him to push up against the nails in his ankles and pull up against the nails in his wrists, in order to gasp for breath, while literally standing on the nails of the cross. Several hours of this left the victim exhausted so that he would collapse, suffocate, and die of a massive heart attack.

The soldiers had to make sure that those who were crucified were not rescued by friends and that the sentence was completely carried out. Pilate had a placard placed over Jesus' head with the accusation: THIS IS JESUS THE KING OF THE JEWS. Little did he realize how true this intended mockery of the Jews really was. Indeed, as Matthew shows, Jesus was the King of the Jews, whom they had rejected. Jesus was placed in the middle, whether by accident or as another gesture of mockery. Ironically, Matthew "bookends" his gospel with Gentiles (the magi and Pilate) proclaiming that Jesus is the "King of the Jews."

Those who went by were wagging their heads, an allusion to Psalm 22:7. Some said, "You who are going to destroy the temple . . . save Yourself!" However, that was the one thing Jesus could not and would not do. To save Himself would have meant the loss of the entire world. No wonder He had to have endured Satan's earlier temptation to satisfy Himself, for now He would conquer Satan's power forever by denying Himself! The further accusations, "He saved others. . . . He trusts in God, . . . He said, 'I am the Son of God'" were actually true in the opposite sense in which the priests intended them. The robbers (Greek, *lēstai*) were brigands, the same word used by Jesus to describe those who attacked, robbed, and left for dead the man on the road to Jericho in Luke 10:30. Perhaps they were cohorts of Barabbas. The statement "were casting the same insult at Him" means they repeated similar taunts to Him.

Chronology of the Crucifixion

Before Dawn	Arrested in the Garden of Gethsemane
Before Dawn	Trial by Annas, the former high priest
Before Dawn	Condemnation by Caiaphas and elders
Before Dawn	Peter denies Jesus three times
Early Morning	Formal condemnation by the Sanhedrin
Early Morning	Suicide of Judas Iscariot
Early Morning	First trial by Pilate
Early Morning	Appearance before Herod Antipas
Early Morning	Second trial by Pilate
6:00 A.M.–9:00 A.M.	Scourging by Roman soldiers
9:00 A.M.	Crucifixion at Golgotha
9:00 A.M.–Noon	Mockery of Jewish leaders
Noon – 3:00 P.M.	Three hours of darkness
After 3:00 P.M.	Death and burial of Christ

Based upon A. T. Robertson, *A Harmony of the Gospels*

"From the sixth hour . . . unto the ninth hour" means from noon until 3:00 P.M. Mark (15:25) indicates that Jesus had been placed on the cross at the third hour (9:00 A.M.). Whether this is Jewish or Roman time is uncertain. The darkness was evidently supernaturally imposed, since an eclipse of the sun at noon is impossible, the two heavenly bodies being on opposite sides of the earth. God's wrath was poured upon His Son during this time of darkness. At the ninth hour (3:00 P.M.), Jesus cried, *"Eli, Eli, lama sabachthani?"*—Aramaic for "My God, My God, why hast Thou forsaken Me?" a quote from Psalm 22:1. Here we have the high cost of the atonement to Christ, who was accursed of God for us as our sin-bearer (cf. 2 Cor. 5:21; Gal. 3:13) and suffered the agony of spiritual death for us. Jesus was spiritually separated from God the Father and the Holy Spirit. The sense of being forsaken was not necessarily caused by God the Father looking away from Him, but from His looking at Him in wrath, as He would look in judgment at a condemned sinner.

The marginal note for verse 49 shows how foolish some copyists were to add in words from John 19:34 about Jesus being speared *before* His final two of the seven statements He uttered from the cross.[10] He cried out again with a loud voice, as a shout of triumph, and yielded up His spirit. In other words, having borne the wrath of God's judgment against sin, Jesus knew that He had triumphed over Satan and the curse of sin. His heel was "bruised," but the serpent's head had been "crushed" (cf. Gen. 3:15). The yielding of His life was the result of His voluntary surrender of His life for the sake of those who had and would believe in Him. Crucifixion was an ugly business, and the Romans were experts at it. They did it all the time. But this time was different. As their hammers rang out against the rocky cliff of "The Skull," one voice could be heard above them all, "Father, forgive them; for they do not know what they are doing" (Luke 23:34). Here in this awful place, Jesus rose above it all. Here we see no screaming, squirming, squealing victim—no angry, cursing man. We see the Savior in all His greatness, goodness, and compassion. Indeed, we see the King, rejected yet reigning from the cross.

The events immediately following Jesus' death were remarkable indeed. First, the strange darkness miraculously lifted at 3:00 P.M. Second, the curtain of the temple tore from top to bottom. This refers to either the curtain over the entrance to the holy place (which could be viewed from the porch) or to the curtain separating the holy place from the Holy of Holies (cf. Ex. 26:31). The latter is most likely here, especially in view of Hebrews 6:19, 9:3, and 10:20, and symbolizes the permanent opening of God's presence to people and their direct access to God through the atoning death of Christ. Henceforth, all ceremonial services of priests and sacrifices would be done away for the Christian believer.

Jesus' sacrifice was a once and for all atonement, not like that of the Jewish priests who had to offer sacrifices annually on the Day of Atonement. The earth shook as a visible manifestation of God's judgment on those who had wrongly crucified the Lord. The earthquake caused the tombs to be opened, and many bodies of the saints (departed Old Testament believers) were raised. This incident is stated only by Matthew and indicates that the Old Testament believers were resurrected only after His resurrection. Jesus is called "the first fruits of those who are asleep" (1 Cor. 15:20) and "the first-born from the dead" (Col. 1:18). Just as the Feast of First Fruits in the Old Testament (Lev. 23:9–14) signified that the rest of the harvest was soon to follow, so Christ's resurrection has the same ultimate meaning.

Those who were raised up after Jesus' resurrection entered the holy city and appeared to many. Some suppose that they were resurrected from "paradise," or "Abraham's bosom" and taken to heaven by the resurrected Christ (cf. Eph. 4:8–9). Others, with William Hendriksen, hold that "after some small period of time, God took them—now body and soul—to himself in heaven, where their souls had been previously."[11]

The centurion and those who were with him exclaimed, "Truly this was the Son of God!" (v. 54). There is no textual variant here. Some translations have "The Son of God" (KJV, RSV, NKJV, NIV, and NASB), while others do not make "son" definite (NJB and REB). Whether this was an affirmation of genuine faith (based on all they had witnessed) or merely a pagan appreciation of the awesomeness of the circumstances is not clear. However, we dare not minimize the spiritual effect these events could have had on them. Certainly the incident reveals how Jesus' life and character, even in the face of death, rose above the greatest qualities of pagan Rome.

Those who witnessed Jesus' death also included several key women, such as Mary Magdalene. It seems clear that she is the woman out of whom Jesus cast seven devils in the region of Magdala, in Galilee (Luke 8:2–3). This is the Mary who stood weeping at Christ's tomb and thought someone had stolen His missing body (John 20:11–18). Other female witnesses were Mary, the mother of James and Joseph and wife of Clopas (Matt. 27:56; John 19:25); Mary, the mother of Jesus (John 19:26–27); the "other Mary" of verse 61; and the mother of the sons of Zebedee, Salome (cf. Mark 15:40), who was apparently a sister of Mary, the mother of Jesus.[12]

The burial of Jesus' body was undertaken by a rich man from Arimathea named Joseph. In fulfillment of Isaiah 53:9, Jesus made His death with the rich. Joseph was a Sanhedrinist, who had become a disciple. His wealth enabled him to own a tomb at Jerusalem even though he lived nearly twenty miles away. Wealthy people in those days often selected their tombs while they were still living. He asked for the body from Pilate and got it, undoubtedly not without personal risk on his part. With help from Nicodemus, a believing Pharisee (cf. John 3), they took the body from the cross and wrapped it in a clean linen cloth or shroud in the typical burial custom of the day.[13] John 19:39–40 tells us that Nicodemus brought about a hundred pounds (Greek, *litras*) of myrrh and aloes, which they poured on the body and into the cloths as they wrapped the body. This would have made the body covered like an Egyptian mummy, the resinous myrrh and aloes holding the cloths firmly in place.

Jesus' body was then placed in Joseph's own new tomb, hewn out of the rock. The tomb would be above ground, and the entrance would have a great stone, generally rolled in a groove, thus blocking the entrance. The height of many of the tomb openings would be only three and one half to four feet. This explains why John was said to be "stooping" to look into the tomb on resurrection morning (John 20:4). Such a stone would be humanly impossible for one man to roll back by himself from the inside, thus nullifying the ridiculous view that Jesus had only passed out and later "revived" and escaped from the tomb. All such antisupernatural explanations of the text cause more interpretive problems than they supposedly solve. According to Matthew's text, only the two Marys watched the burial of Jesus by Joseph and Nicodemus, and none of the twelve disciples were present. However, Luke 23:55 leaves open the possibility that several other women may have been present on that occasion as well.

Matthew refers to "the next day . . . the one after the preparation." There is some question as to whether this was Saturday (the Sabbath), following a Friday crucifixion. However, John 19:14 and 31 indicate that this "preparation day" was the day before the Passover feast day. This may account for Matthew's not using the term "Sabbath" here. Homer Kent, for example, seems to favor a Wednesday crucifixion, with the burial lasting a full seventy-two hours and taking literally the terms "after three days" and "on the third day."[14] In favor of the Wednesday crucifixion, it should be observed that the text does not specify "Friday," and this view can harmonize all the Sabbath references and resolve the problems of the Jewish leaders meeting with Pilate on the Sabbath and the women preparing spices on the Sabbath.

A Wednesday view of the crucifixion, however, seems to face several insurmountable problems. (1) It would be hard to explain why the women would take Thursday, Friday, and Saturday to prepare spices and not return until Sunday. When Lazarus had been dead four days, they explained "Lord, by this time there will be a stench, for he has been dead four days" (John 11:39). (2) Luke, always concerned with precise chronology says clearly that the women who observed the burial went home to prepare spices, "and on the Sabbath they rested according to the commandment" (Luke 23:56). Only the Saturday Sabbath is covered by "the commandment"—the fourth commandment (Ex. 20:8–11). (3) The two on the road to Emmaus clearly stated that Sunday was the *third* day since the crucifixion of Jesus, not the fourth or fifth. Jews normally counted the day something happened as day one. Thus, one week after the resurrection was termed "after eight days" (John 20:26).[15] It seems that the traditional view, that Christ was crucified on Friday, then rose again "on the third day"—Sunday—is correct.[16] On that day, everything would change forever. The resurrection would become the ultimate proof that Jesus was indeed the Son of God.

Study Questions

1. What did the chief priests do with the thirty pieces of silver when Judas returned the money?

2. What was the Potter's Field called even to the day Matthew wrote his Gospel?

3. Who prophesied what would be done with the thirty pieces of silver?

4. Who was released instead of Jesus?

5. Who suffered many things in a dream because of Jesus?

6. Who carried Jesus' cross? Why do you think the names of this man's two sons are listed in Mark 15:21?

7. What does Golgotha mean?

8. What book contains many of the prophecies concerning the crucifixion that Matthew mentions in chapter 27?

9. From which book and chapter did Jesus quote the words, "My God, My God, why hast thou forsaken me?"

10. What three women are mentioned in chapter 27 as ministering to Jesus?

11. Who begged Pilate for the body of Jesus? What relationship did he have with Jesus?

CHAPTER 28

Resurrection of the King
Matthew 28:1-20

Preview:

The resurrection of Jesus Christ from the dead sets Him apart from all other religious teachers and leaders. Jesus is unique. About a dozen different appearances of Christ after His resurrection are recorded, though Matthew recounts only two of these and the cover-up attempt of the Jewish leaders who had Jesus put to death. Matthew then recounts the Great Commission of Jesus to His disciples. These are the church's marching orders for this age.

Jesus' Resurrection (28:1-8)

The resurrection of Jesus Christ is the most unique event in all the world. There is nothing else to compare to it. The resurrection is the ultimate proof that Jesus is indeed the Son of God and the rightful King of Israel. It is the strongest argument of all for the truth of Christianity. The resurrection separates Jesus from all other religious leaders. He is not just a great teacher. He is a risen Savior. (See also Mark 16:1-20; Luke 24:1-12; John 20:1-29.)

All four gospels essentially agree in reporting the facts of Jesus' resurrection. The variety of details in each account supplement rather than contradict one another. Matthew records that the empty tomb was discovered late on the Sabbath, which agrees with the accounts of the other evangelists. By Jewish reckoning the day ended at sunset on Saturday and the new day began at the same time. Thus Saturday night by our reckoning was actually the beginning of Sunday by their calendar. Accordingly, the resurrection actually occurred sometime during the night, for by the time the women arrived "as it began to dawn," He had already risen from the dead.

The earthquake and the angel (Mark's "young man sitting . . . wearing a white robe," Mark 16:5) who rolled the stone away did not come to let Jesus out of the tomb, but to reveal that it was empty and that He was gone already! It has often been observed that the stone was rolled away not to let Jesus out, but to let us in. The guards were on duty when the angel appeared. They shook and became like "dead men." Their fear was so great at this miraculous event that they practically froze in place. Eventually they made their way back to the Jewish authorities with their amazing story.

The women who came to the tomb with spices were the next to see the angel and become witnesses of the empty tomb. Evidently Mary Magdalene left immediately upon seeing the angel. She hastened to tell Peter and John that Christ was missing from the tomb (John 20:1–2). The angel told the remaining women, "Do not be afraid. . . . He is not here, for He has risen, just as He said." The pronoun "you" is emphatic: "you, you women, do not fear me" (as the guards did, who were paralyzed with terror). Floyd Filson remarks, "They have come to see the grave, drawn there by sorrow, love, and, perhaps, inarticulate hope. For their loyalty and persistent love they hear first the news of the resurrection."[1] The angel said, "Go quickly and tell His disciples." This is one of the major themes of the Gospels—tell the good news of Christ's death, burial, and resurrection to others. The angel then also instructed them to go into Galilee to meet Him. We have no recorded resurrection appearance of Christ to these women in Galilee, unless it is when "He appeared to more than five hundred brethren at one time" (1 Cor. 15:6). Over the next forty days of Christ's ministry on earth before His ascension back to glory, He could have appeared numerous times to others that are not recorded in the New Testament. What is written as inspired truth is only that which is necessary and adequate. Both of these criteria are fulfilled in the resurrection appearances found in the four gospels.

Critics of the Christian gospel are hard-pressed to discount the resurrection story because there were so many eyewitnesses. Each one of the disciples eventually sealed his testimony with his life. The uniqueness of the personal details in the story speak of its authenticity—the despair of the disciples, the confusion of the women when they found the stone rolled away, the panic of the Jewish leaders, the embarrassment of the Roman officials, the assertion by Thomas that the others were deceived.

No one inventing such a story would have told it the way it is told. *Women* saw him first? Their testimony wasn't even admissible in a first-century court of law. The very fact that evangelists admitted the women saw Him first indicates the truthfulness of their record. Based on the gospel accounts, the stone was moved and the body was missing. Matthew 28:2 gives the only valid explanation: "an angel of the Lord descended from heaven and came and rolled away the stone."

Jesus' Reappearance (28:9–15)

Running ahead with fear and great joy, the women actually met Jesus and worshiped Him. We cannot imagine their emotional attitude at this moment when fear and joy gripped them simultaneously. Again, Jesus instructed the women to go tell the disciples to leave for Galilee. Here Matthew's account is considerably briefer and less detailed than the other Gospels (where we have specific accounts of Peter and John running to the tomb; Mary meeting Jesus; the appearance in the upper room; the appearance to more than five hundred believers at once; and the undeniably literal incident on the seashore, John 21). The one addition by Matthew is the falsified report of the guards in verses 11–15. Pilate had put the soldiers at the disposal of the Jewish Sanhedrin, so they reported first to them. If these Jewish leaders had questioned the report, they should have immediately investigated. If honesty had prevailed in their lives, they might have come to faith in Christ. R. C. H. Lenski keenly observes, "God sent the message of Jesus' resurrection to these high priests through their own witnesses, the soldiers they themselves has posted, the most unimpeachable witnesses possible. Nor do the high priests dare to question this witness; they accept it as being entirely true."[2] John Walvoord comments, "The dishonesty and lack of integrity on the part of the scribes and Pharisees, when confronted with the fact of the resurrection of Jesus, all too frequently are found in other forms of unbelief. Liberal scholarship today shows the same incredible blindness to the facts and tends to give credence to any criticism of the scriptural record more than to the Scriptures themselves."[3]

The assemblage gave a large sum of money or a large bribe to the soldiers to hide the truth of the resurrection with the lie that His disciples came by night and stole Him away while the soldiers were asleep, a ridiculous statement in itself. If the Roman guards were actually asleep, they would have had no idea what had happened. Further, if they were really asleep on the job, they could lose their heads. If they were not asleep, the story also does not make sense in view of the disciples' earlier defection in the garden. How could this band of cowards overpower an armed Roman guard? Thus Matthew observed that this explanation was still widely spread among the Jews to the very day that Matthew was writing his Gospel.[4]

Jesus' Recommission (28:16-20)

Matthew's gospel ends with the Great Commission. Instead of sending His disciples back to the house of Israel, Jesus sent into all the world. The kingdom rejected by Jews would now be offered to the Gentiles in accordance with Jesus' earlier parables. This appearance in Galilee is not to be confused with the appearance at Jerusalem and could be the same as the appearance to "above five hundred brethren" (cf. 1 Cor. 15:6), with the eleven being among them. This is further implied by the statement "They worshiped Him; but some were doubtful," which would be unlikely of the Eleven after the earlier appearances and the "doubting Thomas" incident (John 20:28).

This might also imply a difference in Jesus' appearance after His resurrection, as also described by John, His own beloved disciple, who barely recognizes the resurrected-glorified Christ in Revelation 1.[5] Lenski explains, "The context does not point to the resurrection but to the appearance and the identity of him who stood before them as causing the doubt. Was this Jesus, indeed, or was it not? While doubt thus arose in some, it did not continue, it soon vanished."[6]

John Peter Lange adds the further explanation that "were doubtful" (Greek, *distazō*) may also be translated "hesitated," in the sense that while they obviously saw Jesus, they hesitated to offer Him such unbounded worship.[7] Prior to Christ's death and resurrection, His disciples, while recognizing His divine messiahship, did not openly worship Him in the manner that would now become customary. Otherwise, why would Matthew, writing to convince the Jews of Jesus, say so close to the end of his gospel that some "were doubtful"? The more obvious explanation is that as he wrote to the hesitant Jewish community, he was saying he understood their hesitation, for he too was a Jew who had become a Christian.

The Great Commission
Matthew 28:19-20

"Go therefore:

1. *Make disciples of all the nations.*
2. *Baptize them in the name of the Father, the Son, and the Holy Spirit.*
3. *Teach them to observe all that I commanded you.*

I am with you always."

The Great Commission brings the first gospel to its grand finale. Christianity is not represented here as the mere reverential devotion of disappointed people who honor their martyred leader. Here is a far different scene. The triumphant living Lord sends forth His ambassadors to proclaim His gospel throughout the entire world. The Commission is not just an order, but a pronouncement of victory (*mundus regium Christi*) by the risen Savior through His disciples. All authority (Greek, *exousia*) was now in the hands of Christ, in heaven and on the earth. On the basis of that authority and power, the Christian disciple is to carry out the great commission of the church. "Go," William Hendriksen notes, "stands in rather sharp contrast to 'Go not' of 10:5. Cf. 15:24. It is clear that the particularism of the pre-resurrection period has now definitely made place for universalism."[8] "Go" is actually a participle and conveys not a command to go, but the assumption that the listener will automatically be going. The idea expressed in "As you are going, make disciples of all nations" could be translated "convert all Gentiles" or "disciple all nations." Thus the converting influence of the gospel is indicated here as a message of hope for all people.

Reaching the nations is not merely a matter of education, but the full process of discipleship—that is, teaching and training, beginning with conversion. The "all nations" makes it clear that the commission to the church is a worldwide one, encompassing the entire missionary effort.[9] The church is not to be merely "missionary-minded." The church is the vehicle of Christ's mission to the world, and the two (church and mission) are inseparable. Every local church has a mission to its world. To attempt to eliminate this commission from the Church Age (as do the hyper-dispensationalists) would be to leave the church without an assigned purpose from the Lord.

Baptizing the converted disciples is the first step of outward obedience to Christ and brings entrance into the membership of the local congregation. "Baptize" (Greek, *baptizō*) is an English transliteration and means to "dip," or "dunk," or "immerse," thus indicating its proper mode. Nowhere does this term ever indicate "sprinkling" (see the comments on Matthew 3:13–14).[10] These converts are to be baptized "in the name of the Father and the Son and the Holy Spirit." The "name" is singular, followed by an elliptical clause indicating that the one name is the name of each person of the Trinity. One baptismal reference in Acts (19:5) refers to some being baptized in the name of the Lord Jesus, either emphasizing His deity as Savior, or the fact of Christian baptism as opposed to John's baptism. This, however, in no way eliminates the significance of this standard formula given by Christ Himself. Nor do the three persons of the Godhead necessitate a trine immersion in each name.

Furthermore, these baptized converts are to be taught "all things" that Jesus taught. Thus the edifying and exhorting ministry of the church is seen as it develops in the book of Acts. This is the part of the Great Commission that perhaps is the most important relative to each convert. It is a lifelong goal that should be accomplished in the context of the local church.

Christ's promise of His presence, "I am with you always" (v. 28), guarantees the success of the church's mission, because it is really His mission carried out by His called-out disciples. This closing promise, though given to the apostles, is transmitted to every generation of believers (cf. John 17:20). The phrase "even to the end of the age [Greek, *aiōn*]" means that this empowerment of Christ to the church to evangelize the world is available in every age, even unto the end of the Church Age. There is no excuse, then, for failing to exercise that power in our day. No time of apostasy will ever be so great as to nullify the true gospel ministry of the Bible-preaching church. In comparing the Great Commission with Jesus' promise to continually build His church (16:18), we must conclude that He intended His church always to be spiritually militant and evangelistically aggressive as we take His claims of lordship to the entire world of our generation.

Charles Spurgeon said it best when he proclaimed, "Come just as you are, all guilty, empty, meritless and fall before the great King. And see if He will cast you away. Jesus is ready to pardon you . . . never tolerate low thoughts of Him. You may study, look and meditate, but Jesus is a greater Savior than you think Him to be, even when your thoughts are at their highest."[11]

And to that we both would add a simple and emphatic, Amen!

Study Questions

1. What two women went to the tomb at dawn on the first day of the week?

2. What persuaded the soldiers to lie about Jesus' resurrection even though they had witnessed it firsthand?

3. What did the chief priests and elders tell the soldiers to tell the people about the reason for Jesus' empty tomb?

4. How many of Jesus' disciples were present at the giving of the Great Commission?

5. Where did Jesus tell the two Marys to tell the disciples that they would see Him?

6. Who rolled the stone away from the tomb opening, and why?

7. What do you think was the reason why some of Jesus' disciples doubted when they saw Jesus on a mountain after the resurrection? Was there good reason to doubt, or is Matthew just being honest about the incident?

8. Is there a good explanation as to why Matthew does not give an account of the ascension of Jesus? Could it be that he wanted to portray the King as being present with all authority?

9. How many parts does the Great Commission have? Are there three things to do or four? Why?

10. Is it important for people to be baptized once they have trusted in Christ? Why or why not?

BIBLIOGRAPHY

Blomberg, Craig. *Matthew.* New American Commentary. Nashville: Broadman, 1992.

Broadus, J. A. *Commentary on the Gospel of Matthew.* American Commentary Series. Philadelphia: American Baptist Publication Society, 1886.

Carson, D. A. "Matthew." *The Expositor's Bible Commentary.* Vol. 8, Edited by Frank E. Gaebelein. Grand Rapids: Zondervan, 1984.

France, R. T. *Matthew.* Tyndale New Testament Commentaries. Grand Rapids: Eerdmans, 1985.

Glasscock, Ed. *Matthew.* Moody Gospel Commentary. Chicago: Moody, 1997.

Gundry, Robert. *Matthew.* Grand Rapids: Eerdmans, 1992.

Hendriksen, William. *Exposition of the Gospel According to Matthew.* Grand Rapids: Baker, 1973.

Keener, Craig S. *A Commentary on the Gospel of Mattthew.* Grand Rapids: Eerdmans, 1999.

Lenski, R. C. H. *The Interpretation of St. Matthew's Gospel.* Minneapolis: Augsburg, 1961.

MacArthur, John Jr. *Matthew.* MacArthur New Testament Commentary. 4 vols. Chicago: Moody, 1987–89.

Morris, Leon. *The Gospel According to Matthew.* Grand Rapids: Eerdmans, 1999.

Mounce, Robert. *Matthew.* New International Biblical Commentary. Peabody, MA: Hendrickson, 1991.

Noland, John. *The Gospel of Matthew.* New International Greek Testament Commentary. Grand Rapids: Eerdmans, 2005.

Tasker, R. V. G. *The Gospel According to St. Matthew.* Tyndale New Testament Series. Grand Rapids: Eerdmans, 1961.

Toussaint, S. D. *Behold the King: A Study of Matthew.* Portland, OR: Multnomah, 1980.

Walvoord, John F. *Matthew: Thy Kingdom Come.* Chicago: Moody, 1974.

NOTES

Introduction—Background of Matthew

1. W. Graham Scroggie, *A Guide to the Gospels* (Grand Rapids: Kregel, 1985), 267–72. Scroggie's detailed analysis of the biblical contents of the Gospels remains a classic even today. Nothing else comes close to his meticulous detail.
2. Ibid., 246.
3. Michael Wilkins, "Matthew," in *Zondervan Illustrated Bible Backgrounds Commentary,* ed. Clinton E. Arnold (Grand Rapids: Zondervan, 2002), 5.
4. Ibid.
5. Cf. Gary Habermas, *The Historical Jesus: Ancient Evidence for the Life of Christ* (Joplin, MO: College Press, 1996); and F. F. Bruce, *Jesus and Christian Origins outside the New Testament* (Grand Rapids: Eerdmans, 1974).
6. Richard Burridge, *Four Gospels: One Jesus?* (Grand Rapids: Eerdmans, 1994), 4. Cf. also, Markus Bockmuehl, *This Jesus: Martyr, Lord, Messiah* (Downers Grove, IL: InterVarsity, 1994); and Luke Timothy Johnson, *The Real Jesus* (San Francisco: HarperSanFrancisco, 1996).
7. I. Howard Marshall, "The Gospels and Jesus Christ," *Eerdmans Handbook to the Bible* (Grand Rapids: Eerdmans, 1987), 470.
8. Robin Griffith-Jones, *The Four Witnesses* (San Francisco: HarperSanFrancisco, 2001), 6.
9. John MacArthur, *Matthew 1–7,* MacArthur New Testament Commentary (Chicago: Moody, 1985), x.
10. Louis Barbieri, "Matthew," *The Bible Knowledge Commentary* (Wheaton: Victor, 1983), 17.
11. Stanley Toussaint, *Behold the King: A Study of Matthew* (Portland, OR: Multnomah, 1980), 19. Toussaint provides the most thorough examination of the kingdom issue in any commentary on Matthew.

12. John F. Walvoord, *Matthew: Thy Kingdom Come* (Chicago: Moody, 1974),
13. Walvoord, like Toussaint, follows this theme throughout his com-
    mentary.

13. R. V. G. Tasker, *The Gospel according to St. Matthew*, Tyndale New
    Testament Commentaries (Grand Rapids: Eerdmans, 1961), 11.

14. D. A. Carson, Douglas J. Moo, and Leon Morris, *An Introduction to the
    New Testament* (Grand Rapids: Zondervan, 1992), 66.

15. Theodor Zahn, *Introduction to the New Testament*, trans. by J. M. Trout
    (New York: Scribners, 1917), 2:506.

16. George Salmon, *A Historical Introduction to the Study of the Books of the
    New Testament* (London: John Murray, 1891), 152–74. Salmon address-
    es this issue in all its complexity, concluding that the Greek text of
    Matthew is not a translation, but an original composition.

17. R. C. H. Lenski, *The Interpretation of St. Matthew's Gospel* (Minneapolis:
    Augsburg, 1953), 16–17.

18. Walvoord, *Matthew*, 10.

19. See A. M. Farrar, "On Dispensing with Q," in *Studies in the Gospels*, D.
    Nineham, ed. (Oxford: Blackwell, 1955), 223–39.

20. For a thorough discussion of the introductory matters regarding
    Matthew, see Donald Guthrie, *New Testament Introduction* (Downers
    Grove, IL: InterVarsity, 1990), 19–48; 136–208; and Carson, Moo, and
    Morris, *Introduction to the New Testament*, 61–87; Zahn, *Introduction to the
    New Testament*, 2:506–601.

21. Much has been written on this topic across the theological spectrum, but
    see the recent work by Robert L. Thomas, ed., *Three Views on the Origins
    of the Synoptic Gospels* (Grand Rapids: Kregel, 2002), in which the two-
    source view (Markan priority), the Matthean priority view, and the inde-
    pendence view are given full discussion with interaction by the authors,
    Grant Osborne, Matthew Williams, John Niemela, and F. David Farnell.

22. Guthrie, *New Testament Introduction*, 52.

23. Scroggie, *Guide to the Gospels*, 247.

24. Alfred Plummer, *An Exegetical Commentary on the Gospel according to St.
    Matthew* (New York: Scribners, 1910), introduction.

25. B. F. Atkinson, "The Gospel according to Matthew," *New Bible
    Commentary* (Grand Rapids: Eerdmans, 1963), 771.

26. Scroggie, *Guide to the Gospels*, 248.

27. Robert H. Gundry, *Matthew: A Commentary on His Literary and Theological
    Art* (Grand Rapids: Eerdmans, 1982), 606.

28. Ibid. 608ff.

29. Cf. D. A. Carson, "Matthew," *Expositor's Bible Commentary* (Grand
    Rapids: Zondervan, 1984), 8:21, and Craig L. Blomberg, *Matthew*, New
    American Commentary (Nashville: Broadmans, 1992), 42.

30. William Hendriksen, *Exposition of the Gospel according to Matthew*, New
    Testament Commentary (Grand Rapids: Baker, 1973), 87.

31. Toussaint, *Behold the King,* 23.

32. See "Disciple" (*mathētēs*), in Colin Brown, ed., *The New International Dictionary of New Testament Theology* (Grand Rapids: Zondervan, 1975), 1:483–490.

Chapter 1—The Birth of the King

1. R. V. G. Tasker, *The Gospel according to St. Matthew,* Tyndale New Testament Commentaries (Grand Rapids: Eerdmans, 1961) 32.

2. See James A. Borland, "Re-examining New Testament Textual-Critical Principles and Practices Used to Negate Inerrancy," *Journal of the Evangelical Theological Society* 25, no. 4 (December 1982): 499–506.

3. Homer A. Kent, *The Gospel according to Matthew,* Wycliffe Bible Commentaries, ed. C. Pfeiffer and E. Harrison (Chicago: Moody, 1962), 3.

4. For more on the Old Testament appearances of Christ, see James A. Borland, *Christ in the Old Testament* (Ross-shire, UK: Christian Focus, 1999); and Edward Hindson and Edward Dobson, eds., *Knowing Jesus Study Bible* (Grand Rapids: Zondervan, 1999).

5. R. C. H. Lenski, *The Interpretation of St. Matthew's Gospel* (Minneapolis: Augsburg, 1953), 52.

6. W. F. Arndt and F. W. Gingrich, *A Greek-English Lexicon of the New Testament,* 4th ed. (Chicago: University of Chicago Press, 1974), 677.

7. See, e.g., *The Interpreter's Bible,* (New York: Abingdon, 1958) 5:218. It is interesting that the exegetical and homiletical sections of this work are done by different authors, and on the same page the exegete denies that Isaiah is predicting the birth of Christ and the expositor claims that he is!

8. Examples would include G. Cox, *The Gospel according to St. Matthew,* (London: SCM, 1956), 29–30; A. Argyle, *The Gospel according to Matthew,* Cambridge Bible Commentaries on the New Testament (Cambridge, UK: Cambrige University Press, 1999), 28; F. V. Filson, *A Commentary on the Gospel according to St. Matthew* (New York: Harper and Brothers, 1960), 54–55.

9. Arndt and Gingrich, *Greek-English Lexicon,* 632.

10. See G. Knight, *A Christian Theology of the Old Testament* (Richmond: John Knox, 1959), 310. For a thorough discussion of the Old Testament usage of *'almâh* see E. J. Young, *The Book of Isaiah* (Grand Rapids:Eerdmans, 1965) 1:284–291; Young, *Studies in Isaiah* (Grand Rapids: Eerdmans, 1954), 143–198; C. Feinberg, "Virgin Birth in the Old Testament and Isaiah 7:14," *Bibliotheca Sacra* 119:251–258; Edward Hindson, *Isaiah's Immanuel: A Sign of His Times or The Sign of the Ages,* (Grand Rapids: Baker, 1979); and Hindson, "Development of the Interpretation of Isaiah 7:14," *Grace Journal,* 10 (Spring, 1969): 1, 2, 3–15, 19–25.

11. For a discussion of the significance of the virgin birth of Christ, see R. Gromacki, *The Virgin Birth: Doctrine of Deity* (New York: Nelson, 1974);

H. Hanke, *The Validity of the Virgin Birth* (Grand Rapids: Zondervan, 1963); J. G. Machen, *The Virgin Birth of Christ* (reprint, Grand Rapids: Baker, 1965).

Chapter 2—Who Is the King of the Jews?

1. Homer A. Kent, *The Gospel according to Matthew*, Wycliffe Bible Commentaries, ed. C. Pfeiffer and E. Harrison (Chicago: Moody Press 1962), 6.
2. Charles R. Ryrie, *Ryrie Study Bible* (Chicago: Moody, 1976), 8.
3. For much more on the three gifts and their use and significance, see William Hendriksen, *Exposition of the Gospel according to Matthew* (Grand Rapids: Baker, 1973), 171–74.
4. For a good portrait of what the escape and journey to Egypt might have looked like, see Elmer L. Towns' fictional account of the life of Jesus, *The Son: A Novel* (Ventura, CA: Regal, 1999), 53–56.
5. On the significance and reliability of Matthew's quotations of Old Testament prophecies see Robert H. Gundry, *The Use of the Old Testament in St. Matthew's Gospel* (Leiden: E. J. Brill, 1967).

Chapter 3—The Mission of the King

1. R. V. G. Tasker, *The Gospel according to St. Matthew*, Tyndale New Testament Commentaries (Grand Rapids: Eerdmans, 1961), 47.
2. See M. Loane, *John the Baptist*. Grand Rapids: Zondervan, 1968.
3. On the significance of repentance, see H. A. Ironside, *Except Ye Repent* (New York: American Tract Society, 1937).
4. William Hendriksen, *Exposition of the Gospel according to Matthew*, New Testament Commentary (Grand Rapids: Baker, 1973), 249.
5. Homer A. Kent, *The Gospel according to Matthew*, Wycliffe Bible Commentaries, ed. C. Pfeiffer and E. Harrison (Chicago: Moody Press 1962), 10.

Chapter 4—Temptation of Christ

1. Arno C. Gaebelein, *The Gospel of Matthew: An Exposition* (reprint, Neptune, NJ: Loizeaux, 1961), 91.
2. John's Gospel, written after the three Synoptics, consciously supplements their works in some ways. John recounts an early Judean ministry in John 2:13–3:36.
3. John F. Walvoord, *Matthew: Thy Kingdom Come* (Chicago: Moody Press 1974), 39.

Chapter 5—Sermon on the Mount

1. George Lawlor, *The Beatitudes Are for Today* (Des Plains, IL: Regular Baptist Press, 1974), 11.

2. Arthur W. Pink, *An Exposition of the Sermon on the Mount* (Grand Rapids: Guardian Press, 1975), 13.

3. D. Martyn Lloyd-Jones, *Studies in the Sermon on the Mount* (Grand Rapids: Eerdmans, 1967), 1:12–15.

4. James M. Boice, *The Sermon on the Mount* (Grand Rapids: Zondervan, 1972), 9.

5. This great statement is first encountered in Habakkuk 2:4, then repeated three times in the New Testament—Romans 1:17; Galatians 3:11 and Hebrews 11:39.

6. Homer A. Kent, *The Gospel according to Matthew*, Wycliffe Bible Commentaries, ed. C. Pfeiffer and E. Harrison (Chicago: Moody Press 1962), 15.

7. Lawlor, *Beatitudes Are for Today*, 60.

8. Cf. J. Murray, *The Imputation of Adam's Sin* (Phillipsburg, NJ: Presbyterian and Reformed, 1958).

9. Charles R. Ryrie, *Ryrie Study Bible* (Chicago: Moody, 1976), 14.

10. B. F. Atkinson, "The Gospel according to Matthew," *New Bible Commentary* (Grand Rapids: Eerdmans, 1963), 780.

11. Some helpful sources expressing various viewpoints on this topic are: J. Carl Laney, *The Divorce Myth: A Biblical Examination of Divorce and Remarriage* (Minneapolis: Bethany, 1981); and William A. Heth and Gordon Wenham, *Jesus and Divorce: The Problem with the Evangelical Consensus* (Nashville: Nelson, 1984);

12. R. C. H. Lenski, *The Interpretation of St. Matthew's Gospel* (Minneapolis: Augsburg, 1953), 233, but see the entire discussion on pp. 230–35.

13. Ryrie, *Ryrie Study Bible*, 14.

14. Cf. *The Qumran Manual of Discipline* 1QS 1:4: "hate all that he has rejected."

15. Kent, *Matthew*, 19.

Chapter 6—Living by Faith

1. F. V. Filson, *A Commentary on the Gospel according to St. Matthew* (New York: Harper and Brothers, 1960), 92.

2. Some of the best books on prayer are Edward M. Bounds, *Power through Prayer* (reprint, Grand Rapids: Zondervan, 1962); E. M. Bounds, *Bible Men of Prayer* (reprint, Grand Rapids: Zondervan, 1964); and Andrew Murray, *God's Best Secrets* (reprint, Grand Rapids; Zondervan, 1980).

3. D. Martyn Lloyd-Jones, *Studies in the Sermon on the Mount* (Grand Rapids: Eerdmans, 1967), 2:54.

4. Arno C. Gaebelein, *The Gospel of Matthew: An Exposition* (reprint, Neptune, NJ: Loizeaux, 1961), 139.

5. W. F. Arndt and F. W. Gingrich, *A Greek-English Lexicon of the New Testament*, 4th ed. (Chicago: University of Chicago Press, 1974), 296.

6. Rudolph Stier, *The Words of the Lord Jesus* (Minneapolis: Augsburg, 1962) 1:198.

7. John Peter Lange, "Matthew," *Lange's Commentary on the Holy Scriptures* (Grand Rapids: Zondervan, 1960), 8:124.

8. Homer A. Kent, *The Gospel according to Matthew*, Wycliffe Bible Commentaries, ed. C. Pfeiffer and E. Harrison (Chicago: Moody Press 1962), 21.

9. R. V. G. Tasker, *The Gospel according to St. Matthew*, Tyndale New Testament Commentaries (Grand Rapids: Eerdmans, 1961), 75.

10. Filson, *Matthew*, 100–101.

11. Jay Adams, *Christian Counselors' Manual* (Grand Rapids: Zondervan, 1986), 117ff.

Chapter 7—Two Choices

1. D. A. Carson, *The Sermon on the Mount* (Grand Rapids: Baker, 1978), 97.

2. F. V. Filson, *A Commentary on the Gospel according to St. Matthew* (New York: Harper and Brothers, 1960), 104.

3. Ibid., 122.

4. The same use of the present tense in found in 1 John 3:9, "No one who is born of God practices sin, because His seed abides in him; and he cannot sin, because he is born of God." Believer's will sin, but the normal course of their lives must not be to abide in sin and to enjoy it.

5. R. C. H. Lenski, *The Interpretation of St. Matthew's Gospel* (Minneapolis: Augsburg, 1953), 314.

Chapter 8—Power of the King

1. For a helpful understanding of leprosy, see William Hendriksen, *Exposition of the Gospel according to Matthew*, New Testament Commentary (Grand Rapids: Baker, 1973), 388–92.

2. Homer A. Kent, *The Gospel according to Matthew*, Wycliffe Bible Commentaries, ed. C. Pfeiffer and E. Harrison (Chicago: Moody Press 1962), 943; Hendriksen, *Matthew*, 399 also provides a list of believers who were also sick at one time (Elisha, Hezekiah, Dorcas, Paul, Timothy, Epaphroditus and Trophimus). God's healing power is available to all of us but it does not prevent us from getting sick at times.

3. George Eldon Ladd, *A Theology of the New Testament*, rev. ed. (Grand Rapids: Eerdmans, 1993), 143–57, has an excellent treatment of the Son of Man passages, but one has to dismiss his references to Q as a Gospel source.

4. For a recent excursus on demons and exorcism, see Craig S. Keener, *A Commentary on the Gospel of Mattthew* (Grand Rapids: Eerdmans, 1999), 283–86.

Chapter 9–The Case for Christ

1. Michael Wilkins, "Matthew," in *Zondervan Illustrated Bible Backgrounds Commentary*, ed. Clinton E. Arnold (Grand Rapids: Zondervan, 2002), 63.

2. Carl B. Hock Jr., *All Things New: The Significance of Newness for Biblical Theology* (Grand Rapids: Baker, 1995). This is a very helpful and practical work on the New Testament's use of being made "new."

3. Sleep also looks like death. When a three-year-old attended the funeral of her four-year-old playmate, as she peered into the tiny casket, she asked her father, "Is she sleeping, Daddy?" It should be strictly noted that it is only the body that is referred to as sleeping. There is no such thing as soul sleep.

4. B. B. Warfield, *Counterfeit Miracles* (London: Banner of Truth, 1983), 3.

5. William Hendriksen, *Exposition of the Gospel according to Matthew*, New Testament Commentary (Grand Rapids: Baker, 1973), 439.

6. Homer A. Kent, *The Gospel according to Matthew*, Wycliffe Bible Commentaries, ed. C. Pfeiffer and E. Harrison (Chicago: Moody Press 1962), 945.

7. John MacArthur, *Matthew 8–15*, MacArthur New Testament Commentary (Chicago: Moody Press 1987), 117.

Chapter 10–All the King's Men

1. John MacArthur, *Matthew 8–15*, MacArthur New Testament Commentary (Chicago: Moody, 1987), 130.

2. Stanley D. Toussaint, *Behold the King: A Study of Matthew* (Portland, Or: Multnomah, 1980.

3. There are about twelve different names in Scripture that are applied to Satan. For a listing and brief explanation of these see Henry C. Thiessen, *Lectures in Systematic Theology*, rev. ed. (Grand Rapids: Eerdmans, 1979), 141–43.

4. Archibald Thomas Robertson, *Word Pictures in the New Testament* (Nashville: Broadman, 1930), 1:83.

5. William Hendriksen, *Exposition of the Gospel according to Matthew*, New Testament Commentary (Grand Rapids: Baker, 1973), 471. The same usage is in view in Matthew 25:46; Mark 9:47–48; and 2 Thessalonians 1:9.

6. For the theological significance of the cross, see Leon Morris, *The Cross in the New Testament* (Grand Rapids: Eerdmans, 1965); and *The Apostolic Preaching of the Cross* (Grand Rapids: Eerdmans, 1955).

7. MacArthur, *Matthew 8–15*, 227.

Chapter 11—More Than a Prophet

1. William Hendriksen, *Exposition of the Gospel according to Matthew*, New Testament Commentary (Grand Rapids: Baker, 1973), 490.
2. William L. Pettingill, *The Gospel of the Kingdom: Simple Studies in Matthew* (Findlay, OH: Dunham, n.d.), 138–39.
3. See Alva J. McClain, *The Greatness of the Kingdom: An Inductive Study of the Kingdom of God* (Chicago: Moody Press 1959), 319–20. He teaches that the concept of a contingency is the best way to explain John the Baptist being Elijah.
4. Only three Greek manuscripts have "works." The huge majority of Greek, Latin, Gothic, and Armenian manuscripts have "children." Additionally, the earliest sources, the Diatessaron, Irenaeus, Origin, Hilary, and others, all have "children."
5. Michael J. Wilkins, "The Gospel of Matthew" in *Zondervan Illustrated Bible Backgrounds Commentary*, ed. Clinton E. Arnold (Grand Rapids: Zondervan, 2002), 76, notes, "The Pharisees spoke of 613 commandments, and their *Halakot* (binding interpretations) produced an overwhelmingly complicated approach to life." But he adds that "discipleship to Jesus is not essentially a religious obligation. Rather, ours is an intimate relationship . . . discipleship at heart simply means walking with Jesus in the real world and having him teach us moment by moment how to live life his way."

Chapter 12—Who Do You Think You Are?

1. C. I. Scofield, *The Scofield Reference Bible* (New York: Oxford University Press, 1917), 1012, observes, "Jesus here is not so much rejected as *Savior* as the rejected *King;* hence the reference to David" [italics in original].
2. William Hendriksen, *Exposition of the Gospel according to Matthew*, New Testament Commentary (Grand Rapids: Baker, 1973), 515. Hendriksen also notes that Jesus honored the Sabbath in many ways, including attending synagogue services (and participating in them), healing and showing mercy on that day, "resting in the tomb on that day," and "fulfilling its symbolic significance."
3. William L. Pettingill, *The Gospel of the Kingdom: Simple Studies in Matthew* (Findlay, OH: Dunham, n.d.), 149–50.
4. Hendriksen, *Matthew*, 525.
5. Pettingill, *Gospel of the Kingdom*, 150–51.
6. D. A. Carson, "Matthew," *The Expositor's Bible Commentary*, ed. Frank E. Gaebelein (Grand Rapids: Zondervan, 1984), 8:291–92.
7. John MacArthur, *Matthew 8–15*, MacArthur New Testament Commentary (Chicago: Moody, 1987), 321.
8. See W. Graham Scroggie, *Guide to the Gospels* (Grand Rapids: Kregel, 1985), 569–577.

9. The Jews numbered any part of the day an event occurred in their counting; thus Friday, Saturday, and Sunday would be days one, two, and three.

10. Arno C. Gaebelein, *The Gospel of Matthew: An Exposition* (reprint, Neptune, NJ: Loizeaux, 1961), 256–57 asserts that "The return of the unclean spirit with its seven companions will take place during the great tribulation." Pettingill, *Gospel of the Kingdom*, 153, concurs, saying "This points to the time of The Great Tribulation, when Israel shall be found worshiping the Beast and his image, until the Deliverer shall come and turn away ungodliness from Jacob (vv. 43–45)."

11. Craig S. Keener, *A Commentary on the Gospel of Mattthew* (Grand Rapids: Eerdmans, 1999), 369.

12. Homer A. Kent, *The Gospel according to Matthew,* Wycliffe Bible Commentaries, ed. C. Pfeiffer and E. Harrison (Chicago: Moody Press 1962), 951.

13. Hendriksen, *Matthew,* 542.

14. Keener, *Matthew,* 370.

15. Hendriksen, *Matthew,* 542.

Chapter 13—Parables of the Kingdom

1. John F. Walvoord, *Matthew: Thy Kingdom Come* (Chicago: Moody Press 1974), 96.

2. R. V. G. Tasker, *The Gospel according to St. Matthew,* Tyndale New Testament Commentaries (Grand Rapids: Eerdmans, 1961), 134–135.

3. Walvoord, *Matthew,* 101.

4. Homer A. Kent, *The Gospel according to Matthew,* Wycliffe Bible Commentaries, ed. C. Pfeiffer and E. Harrison (Chicago: Moody Press 1962), 45.

5. George Eldon Ladd, *A Theology of the New Testament,* rev. ed. (Grand Rapids: Eerdmans, 1993), 94.

6. For treatments of this passage by pretribulational rapture proponents, see Arno C. Gaebelein, *The Gospel of Matthew: An Exposition* (reprint, Neptune, NJ: Loizeaux, 1961), 274–81, and Walvoord, *Matthew,* 100–101.

7. William L. Pettingill, *The Gospel of the Kingdom: Simple Studies in Matthew* (Findlay, OH: Dunham, n.d.), 158.

8. B. F. Atkinson, "The Gospel according to Matthew," *New Bible Commentary* (Grand Rapids: Eerdmans, 1963), 790.

9. Kent, *Matthew,* 47.

10. H. C. Kee, "Matthew," *Interpreter's Commentary on the Bible* (New York: Abingdon, 1958), 626.

11. H. Stagg, "Matthew," *Broadman Bible Commentary* (Nashville: Broadman, 1969), 159.

12. John A. Broadus, *Commentary on the Gospel of Matthew* (Valley Forge, PA: American Baptist Publication Society, 1886), 310–12.

13. John MacArthur, *Matthew 8–15*, MacArthur New Testament Commentary (Chicago: Moody, 1987), 414.

Chapter 14–Miracles of the Messiah

1. V. Robert Mounce, *Matthew* (Peabody, MA: Hendrickson, 1991), 141.
2. Josephus, *Antiquities* 18.5.4.
3. Josephus confirms these details as well in *Antiquities* 18.5.2 and 117–18.
4. See Harold Hoehner, *Herod Antipas* (Grand Rapids: Zondervan, 1980); and Stewart Perowne, *The Life and Times of Herod the Great* (London: Stock & Sons, 1958).
5. William Barclay, *The Gospel of Matthew* (Philadelphia: Westminster, 1975), 1:341.
6. R. T. France, *The Gospel according to Matthew* (Grand Rapids: Eerdmans, 1985), 235.
7. Cf. F. V. Filson, *A Commentary on the Gospel according to St. Matthew* (New York: Harper and Brothers, 1960), 174.
8. France, *Matthew*, 240.

Chapter 15–Tradition! Tradition!

1. See "Tradition," in *Eerdmans Bible Dictionary* (Grand Rapids: Eerdmans, 1987), 1014–15.
2. Leon Morris, *Gospel according to St. Matthew* (Grand Rapids: Eerdmans, 1977), 147.
3. Archibald Thomas Robertson, *Word Pictures in the New Testament* (Nashville: Broadman, 1930), 1:124.
4. William Hendriksen, *Exposition of the Gospel according to Matthew*, New Testament Commentary (Grand Rapids: Baker, 1973), 618.
5. R. C. H. Lenski, *The Interpretation of St. Matthew's Gospel* (Minneapolis: Augsburg, 1953), 593.
6. Hendriksen, *Matthew*, 439.

Chapter 16–The Great Prediction

1. Robert C. Newman, "Breadmaking with Jesus," *Journal of the Evangelical Theological Society* 40, no. 1 (March 1997): 1–11. This article to all. It was one of the greatest presidential addresses ever delivered at the Evangelical Theological Society. Dr. Newman received a very loud, long, and enthusiastic standing ovation when he concluded.
2. William Hendriksen, *Exposition of the Gospel according to Matthew*, New Testament Commentary (Grand Rapids: Baker, 1973), 439.
3. Ibid., 439.
4. Ibid., 439.
5. John A. Broadus, *Commentary on the Gospel of Matthew* (Valley Forge, PA: American Baptist Publication Society, 1886), 355. He remarks, "As Peter means rock, the natural interpretation is that 'upon this rock' means

upon thee. No other explanation would probably at the present day be attempted, but for the fact that the obvious meaning has been abused by Papists to the support of their theory. But we must not allow the abuse of a truth to turn us away from its use."

6. For convincing arguments that Peter alone is the rock, see Robert L. Saucy, *The Church in God's Program* (Chicago: Moody, 1972), 62–64; and Henry C. Thiessen, *Lectures in Systematic Theology*, rev. by Vernon Doerksen (Grand Rapids: Eerdmans, 1979), 311–12.

7. Benjamin Chapman, *New Testament Greek Notebook* (Grand Rapids: Eerdmans, 1974), 68.

8. Oswald Chambers, *My Utmost for His Highest* (New York: Dodd, Mead & Company, 1959), 346 (December 11).

9. Hendriksen, *Matthew*, 439.

10. See Thomas Ice and Kenneth L. Gentry Jr., *The Great Tribulation: Past or Future? Two Evangelicals Debate the Question* (Grand Rapids: Kregel, 1999).

11. Everett F. Harrison, *A Shorter Life of Christ* (Grand Rapids: Eerdmans, 1968), 163.

Chapter 17—The Glorious King

1. John F. Walvoord, *Matthew: Thy Kingdom Come* (Chicago: Moody, 1974), 128.

2. Homer A. Kent, *The Gospel according to Matthew*, Wycliffe Bible Commentaries, ed. C. Pfeiffer and E. Harrison (Chicago: Moody, 1962), 960.

3. Ibid., 960. See also George N. H. Peters, *The Theocratic Kingdom* (1884; reprint, Grand Rapids: Kregel, 1972), 2:560. Arno C. Gaebelein, *The Gospel of Matthew: An Exposition* (reprint, Neptune, NJ: Loizeaux, 1961), 363–64, and William L. Pettingill, *The Gospel of the Kingdom: Simple Studies in Matthew* (Findlay, OH: Dunham, n.d.), 216–20 agree with this assessment.

4. Pettingill, *Gospel of the Kingdom*, 220.

5. William Hendriksen, *Exposition of the Gospel according to Matthew*, New Testament Commentary (Grand Rapids: Baker, 1973), 671–72.

6. Walvoord, *Matthew*, 131. Walvoord focuses this statement on the supposition that Elijah must be one of the two witnesses in Revelation 11.

7. Gaebelein, *Matthew*, 369.

8. Hendriksen, *Matthew*, 377.

9. Heinrich August Wilhelm Meyer, *Critical and Exegetical Hand-Book to the Gospel of Matthew*, trans. Peter Christie (6th ed. 1884; reprint, Peabody, MA: Hendrickson, 1983), 315.

10. John A. Broadus, *Commentary on the Gospel of Matthew* (Valley Forge, PA: American Baptist Publication Society, 1886), 678.

11. Archibald Thomas Robertson, *Word Pictures in the New Testament* (Nashville: Broadman, 1930), 1:142.

12. Michael Wilkins, "Matthew," in *Zondervan Illustrated Bible Backgrounds Commentary,* ed. Clinton E. Arnold (Grand Rapids: Zondervan, 2002), 110.

13. B. F. Atkinson, "The Gospel according to Matthew," *New Bible Commentary* (Grand Rapids: Eerdmans, 1963), 794.

14. Robertson, *Word Pictures,* 1:144.

Chapter 18—Forgive and Forget

1. B. F. Atkinson, "The Gospel according to Matthew," *New Bible Commentary* (Grand Rapids: Eerdmans, 1963), 794.

2. Archibald Thomas Robertson, *Word Pictures in the New Testament* (Nashville: Broadman, 1930), 1:147.

3. William Hendriksen, *Exposition of the Gospel according to Matthew,* New Testament Commentary (Grand Rapids: Baker, 1973), 692.

4. Ibid., 439.

5. However, only a dozen Greek manuscripts omit this verse while most contain it, supported by the Old Latin, the Vulgate, the oldest Syriac and Armenian versions, the Diatessaron, Hilary, Chrysostom, and Augustine.

6. F. C. Cook, "Matthew," *The Bible Commentary,* (Grand Rapids: Baker, 1981), 94.

7. D. A. Carson, "Matthew," *The Expositor's Bible Commentary,* ed. Frank E. Gaebelein (Grand Rapids: Zondervan, 1984), 8:406.

Chapter 19—Marriage, Divorce, and Money

1. Homer A. Kent, *The Gospel according to Matthew,* Wycliffe Bible Commentaries, ed. C. Pfeiffer and E. Harrison (Chicago: Moody, 1962), 67.

2. However, 1 Corinthians 6:16 points out that "one who joins himself to a harlot is one body with her."

3. See Jay Adams, *Marriage, Divorce and Remarriage.* (Grand Rapids: Zondervan, 1990).

4. John F. Walvoord, *Matthew: Thy Kingdom Come* (Chicago: Moody, 1974), 143.

5. Archibald Thomas Robertson, *Word Pictures in the New Testament* (Nashville: Broadman, 1930), 1:157.

6. David L. Cooper, *Messiah: His Historical Appearance* (Los Angeles: Biblical Research Society, 1958), 19.

7. The NASB note says, "Many mss. read: *a hundredfold.*"

Chapter 20—Is It Really Worth It?

1. R. C. Trench, *The Parables of Our Lord,* (Grand Rapids: Zondervan, n.d.), 169.

2. On the believer's rewards, see Woodrow Michael Kroll, *It Will Be Worth It All: A Study of the Believer's Rewards* (Neptune, NJ: Loizeaux, 1977).

3. Archibald Thomas Robertson, *Word Pictures in the New Testament* (Nashville: Broadman, 1930), 1:163.

4. Homer A. Kent, *The Gospel according to Matthew*, Wycliffe Bible Commentaries, ed. C. Pfeiffer and E. Harrison (Chicago: Moody, 1962), 71.

Chapter 21–Here Comes the King

1. Alfred Edersheim, *The Life and Times of Jesus the Messiah* (reprint, Grand Rapids: Eerdmans, 1962), 2:736.

2. D. A. Carson, "Matthew," *The Expositor's Bible Commentary*, ed. Frank E. Gaebelein (Grand Rapids: Zondervan, 1984), 8:441.

3. Gleason L. Archer, *Encyclopedia of Bible Difficulties* (Grand Rapids: Zondervan, 1982), 335.

4. Homer A. Kent, *The Gospel according to Matthew*, Wycliffe Bible Commentaries, ed. C. Pfeiffer and E. Harrison (Chicago: Moody, 1962), 966.

5. William Hendriksen, *Exposition of the Gospel according to Matthew*, New Testament Commentary (Grand Rapids: Baker, 1973), 775.

6. Ibid., 776.

7. Hendriksen, *Matthew*, 778, summarizes, "The textual evidence showing whether the son who refuses and later repents comes first (as reflected in A.V., R.S.V., Beck, etc.), or whether the order should be reversed (N.A.S.B., Phillips, N.E.B., etc.), is about equally divided. It makes little difference which order is followed."

8. Alva J. McClain, The Greatness of the Kingdom: An Inductive Study of the Kingdom of God (Chicago: Moody, 1959), 295–96.

9. Michael Wilkins, "Matthew," in *Zondervan Illustrated Bible Backgrounds Commentary*, ed. Clinton E. Arnold (Grand Rapids: Zondervan, 2002), 134.

10. Hendriksen, *Matthew*, 787. So also Craig S. Keener, *A Commentary on the Gospel of Mattthew* (Grand Rapids: Eerdmans, 1999), 516, cites Brad Young, *Jesus and His Jewish Parables* New York: Paulist, 1989), 295, who says that "whether Israel, a rock, falls on other nations, which are clay vessels, or the vessels fall on the rock, woe to the vessels."

11. John A. Broadus, *Commentary on the Gospel of Matthew* (Valley Forge, PA: American Baptist Publication Society, 1886), 444.

Chapter 22–Answering the Critics

1. F. C. Cook, "Matthew," *The Bible Commentary*, (Grand Rapids: Baker, 1981), 108.

2. Michael Wilkins, "Matthew," in *Zondervan Illustrated Bible Backgrounds Commentary*, ed. Clinton E. Arnold (Grand Rapids: Zondervan, 2002),

136. Wilkins adds, 137, that "Some estimate that a Jewish family paid approximately 49 percent of its annual income to these various taxes," and he then gives a complete percentage breakdown of the different taxes (p. 137).

3. John F. Walvoord, *Matthew: Thy Kingdom Come* (Chicago: Moody, 1974), 166.

4. R. V. G. Tasker, *The Gospel according to St. Matthew*, Tyndale New Testament Commentaries (Grand Rapids: Eerdmans, 1961), 211.

5. Archibald Thomas Robertson, *Word Pictures in the New Testament* (Nashville: Broadman, 1930), 1:176.

6. It should not be thought that if angels were not "in heaven" that they could somehow manufacture bodies for themselves and become sexual beings. This is never contemplated in the Scriptures, though some have proposed this with regard to the sons of God in Genesis 6. Luke 20:36 indicates that the asexuality of angels is not limited to being "in heaven."

7. Alfred Plummer, *An Exegetical Commentary on the Gospel according to St. Matthew*, 2nd ed. (London: Robert Scott, 1910), 306.

8. Tasker, *Matthew*, 211.

9. Walvoord, *Matthew*, 168.

10. Robertson, *Word Pictures*, 1:177.

11. F. V. Filson, *A Commentary on the Gospel according to St. Matthew* (New York: Harper and Brothers, 1960), 237.

12. William Hendriksen, *Exposition of the Gospel according to Matthew*, New Testament Commentary (Grand Rapids: Baker, 1973), 808.

13. Tasker, *Matthew*, 213.

14. See Alfred Edersheim, *The Life and Times of Jesus the Messiah*, appendix 9, "List of Olde Testament Passages Messianically Applied in Ancient Rabbinic Writings" (reprint, Grand Rapids: Eerdmans, 1962), 2:710–41.

15. So Hendriksen, *Matthew*, 812; Homer A. Kent, *The Gospel according to Matthew*, Wycliffe Bible Commentaries, ed. C. Pfeiffer and E. Harrison (Chicago: Moody, 1962), 969; and R. C. H. Lenski, *The Interpretation of St. Matthew's Gospel* (Minneapolis: Augsburg, 1953), 887.

Chapter 23–Denouncing the Pharisees

1. John F. Walvoord, *Matthew: Thy Kingdom Come* (Chicago: Moody, 1974), 170.

2. Archibald Thomas Robertson, *Word Pictures in the New Testament* (Nashville: Broadman, 1930), 1:178. D. A. Carson, "Matthew," *The Expositor's Bible Commentary*, ed. Frank E. Gaebelein (Grand Rapids: Zondervan, 1984), 8:474, notes, "The peculiar term used here only in the NT has pagan associations ("amulet") and may insinuate that [they] . . . had become like pagan charms."

3. William Hendriksen, *Exposition of the Gospel according to Matthew,* New Testament Commentary (Grand Rapids: Baker, 1973), 829.

4. Carson, "Matthew," 478.

5. Homer A. Kent, *The Gospel according to Matthew,* Wycliffe Bible Commentaries, ed. C. Pfeiffer and E. Harrison (Chicago: Moody, 1962), 970.

6. R. V. G. Tasker, *The Gospel according to St. Matthew,* Tyndale New Testament Commentaries (Grand Rapids: Eerdmans, 1961), 220.

7. Gleason L. Archer, *Encyclopedia of Bible Difficulties* (Grand Rapids: Zondervan, 1982), 338.

8. William L. Pettingill, *The Gospel of the Kingdom: Simple Studies in Matthew* (Findlay, OH: Dunham, n.d.), 284–86, has a nice section on the uses of the word *until* in the New Testament. He says, "Many times in the New Testament this word is thus used to direct our attention to those things not seen as yet but which must shortly come to pass." He lists and explains seven of these occurrences.

Chapter 24–Signs of the Times

1. Homer A. Kent, *The Gospel according to Matthew,* Wycliffe Bible Commentaries, ed. C. Pfeiffer and E. Harrison (Chicago: Moody, 1962), 971.

2. John F. Walvoord, *Matthew: Thy Kingdom Come* (Chicago: Moody, 1974), 182.

3. Josephus, Antiquities of the Jews, 15.11.3; and Wars of the Jews, 5.5.1–6.

4. On the history and destruction of the temple, see Randall Price, *The Temple in Bible Prophecy,* (Eugene, OR: Harvest House, 2005).

5. Walvoord, *Matthew,* 179–95. For a detailed exegesis of the Olivet Discourse, see Tom Ice, thirty articles in *Pre-Trib Perspectives* (1994–2004), and Ed Glasscock, *Matthew* (Chicago: Moody, 1997), 461–94.

6. Walvood, *Matthew,* 181.

7. R. T. France, *The Gospel according to Matthew* (Grand Rapids: Eerdmans, 1985), 338.

8. Kent, *Matthew,* 86. For contrary views see Willoughby C. Allen, *A Critical and Exegetical Commentary on the Gospel according to St. Matthew* (Edingburgh: T & T Clark, 1907), 256, and H. Stagg, "Matthew," *Broadman Bible Commentary* (Nashville: Broadman, 1969), 200.

9. D. A. Carson, "Matthew," *The Expositor's Bible Commentary,* ed. Frank E. Gaebelein (Grand Rapids: Zondervan, 1984), 8:503.

10. William Hendriksen, *Exposition of the Gospel according to Matthew,* New Testament Commentary (Grand Rapids: Baker, 1973), 861–62.

11. See W. Prince, *Jesus' Prophetic Sermon* (Chicago: Moody, 1958), 118ff.

12. *Seventh-day Adventists Believe. . . : A Biblical Exposition of 27 Fundamental Doctrines* (Washington, DC: General Conference of Seventh-day Adventists, 1988), 339–41.

13. John Peter Lange, "Matthew," *Lange's Commentary on the Holy Scriptures* (Grand Rapids: Zondervan, 1960), 8:428.

14. James A. Borland, "The Meaning and Identification of God's Eschatological Trumpets," *Looking into the Future: Evangelical Studies in Eschatology*, ed. David W. Baker (Grand Rapids: Baker, 2001), 69.

15. John F. Walvoord, *Matthew: Thy Kingdom Come* (Chicago: Moody, 1974), 192.

16. Ibid., 192. Kent, *Matthew*, 86, however, views the fig tree as Israel "budding" in the last days as a reborn nation.

17. R. V. G. Tasker, *The Gospel according to St. Matthew*, Tyndale New Testament Commentaries (Grand Rapids: Eerdmans, 1961), 227. G. C. Morgan, *Matthew*, 286, does not even attempt an explanation.

18. E.g., Walvoord, *Matthew*, 192, and R. C. H. Lenski, *The Interpretation of St. Matthew's Gospel* (Minneapolis: Augsburg, 1953), 951.

19. Tom Ice, "Olivet Discourse," Tim LaHaye and Ed Hindson, eds. *Popular Encyclopedia of Bible Prophecy*. (Eugene, OR: Harvest House, 2004), 248–56. Compare also his thirty articles on the Olivet Discourse in *Pre-Trib Perspectives* (1994–2004).

20. Arno C. Gaebelein, *The Gospel of Matthew: An Exposition* (reprint, Neptune, NJ: Loizeaux, 1961), 513–14, holds this view, basing it somewhat on the fact that Luke 16:8 uses the word "generation" to mean "race." He argues that if "this generation" meant those living in Christ's day, then "the events predicted by our Lord *must* have been fulfilled within the life-time of the people living then."

21. W. F. Arndt and F. W. Gingrich, *A Greek-English Lexicon of the New Testament*, 4th ed. (Chicago: University of Chicago Press, 1974), 153.

22. Carson, "Matthew," 507.

23. F. V. Filson, *A Commentary on the Gospel according to St. Matthew* (New York: Harper and Brothers, 1960), 257–258.

24. This is essentially the position of Robert H. Gundry, *The Church and the Tribulation* (Grand Rapids: Zondervan, 1973), 42–43; and Marvin Rosenthal, *The Pre-Wrath Rapture of the Church* (Nashville: Nelson, 1990), 220, 248. These basic posttribulationists still like to maintain the doctrine of the imminency of Christ's coming, no doubt agreeing with Carson ("Matthew," 508), "Moreover it is ridiculous quibbling divorced from the context to say that though the day and the hour remain unknown, we ascertain the year or month."

25. Walvoord, *Matthew*, 193, and Kent, *Matthew*, 88–89.

26. Kent, *Matthew*, 89.

27. John MacArthur, *Matthew 24–28*, MacArthur New Testament Commentary (Chicago: Moody, 1987), 77.

Chapter 25—Parables of the Second Coming

1. Homer A. Kent, *The Gospel according to Matthew*, Wycliffe Bible Commentaries, ed. C. Pfeiffer and E. Harrison (Chicago: Moody, 1962), 974.

2. William Hendriksen, *Exposition of the Gospel according to Matthew*, New Testament Commentary (Grand Rapids: Baker, 1973), 875.

3. B. F. Atkinson, "The Gospel according to Matthew," *New Bible Commentary* (Grand Rapids: Eerdmans, 1963), 801.

4. Alfred Plummer, *An Exegetical Commentary on the Gospel according to St. Matthew*, 2nd ed. (London: Robert Scott, 1910), 347–48.

5. John MacArthur, *Matthew 24–28*, MacArthur New Testament Commentary (Chicago: Moody, 1987), 112.

6. Atkinson, "Matthew," 801.

7. Robert H. Gundry, *The Church and the Tribulation* (Grand Rapids: Zondervan, 1973), 163–68 argues for this judgment to be at the end of the millennium, equivalent to the Great White Throne Judgment, and asserts that older premillennialists such as Alford and Lange held essentially that same position.

8. William L. Pettingill, *The Gospel of the Kingdom: Simple Studies in Matthew* (Findlay, OH: Dunham, n.d.), 297.

9. Arno C. Gaebelein, *The Gospel of Matthew: An Exposition* (reprint, Neptune, NJ: Loizeaux, 1961), 545.

10. John F. Walvoord, *Matthew: Thy Kingdom Come* (Chicago: Moody, 1974), 201.

Chapter 26—Rejection of the King

1. See "Excursus: Historical Tradition in the Passion Narrative," in Craig S. Keener, *A Commentary on the Gospel of Mattthew* (Grand Rapids: Eerdmans, 1999), 607–11.

2. John F. Walvoord, *Matthew: Thy Kingdom Come* (Chicago: Moody, 1974), 208.

3. H. Stagg, "Matthew," *Broadman Bible Commentary* (Nashville: Broadman, 1969), 231.

4. H. C. Kee, "Matthew," *Interpreter's Commentary on the Bible* (New York: Abingdon, 1958), 640.

5. J. Walther, "Chronology of Passion Week," *Foundations of Biblical Literature*, 1958, 116ff.

6. Homer A. Kent, *The Gospel according to Matthew*, Wycliffe Bible Commentaries, ed. C. Pfeiffer and E. Harrison (Chicago: Moody, 1962), 97–109.

7. See B. F. Atkinson, "The Gospel according to Matthew," *New Bible Commentary* (Grand Rapids: Eerdmans, 1963), 803).

8. Alfred Plummer, *An Exegetical Commentary on the Gospel according to St. Matthew*, 2nd ed. (London: Robert Scott, 1910), 371.

9. A. B. Bruce, "The Synoptic Gospels," *The Expositor's Greek Testament*, ed. W. Robertson Nicoll (reprint, Grand Rapids: Eerdmans, 1961), 1:315.

10. F. V. Filson, *A Commentary on the Gospel according to St. Matthew* (New York: Harper and Brothers, 1960), 280.

11. Archibald Thomas Robertson, *Word Pictures in the New Testament* (Nashville: Broadman, 1930), 1:214.

12. See F. W. Krummacher, *The Suffering Savior: Meditations on the Last Days of Christ* (Chicago: Moody, 1947), for more on the meaning of these events.

13. For a devotional discussion of these matters, see James Stalker, *The Trial and Death of Jesus Christ: A Devotional History of Our Lord's Passion* (1884; reprint, Grand Rapids: Zondervan, 1961). On the theological significance of Christ's death, see James Denney, *The Death of Christ*, rev. and enlarged ed. (London: Hodder and Stoughton, n.d.); Leon Morris, *The Cross in the New Testament* (Grand Rapids: Eerdmans, 1965); and George Smeaton, *The Apostles' Doctrine of the Atonement*, (1870; reprint, Grand Rapids: Zondervan, 1957).

Chapter 27–Crucifixion of Christ

1. A. W. Tozer, *Knowledge of the Holy* (New York: Harper & Row, 1961), 101. Cf. also, J. I. Packer, *Knowing God* (Downers Grove, IL: InterVarsity, 1973).

2. Archibald Thomas Robertson, *Word Pictures in the New Testament* (Nashville: Broadman, 1930), 1:223.

3. William Hendriksen, *Exposition of the Gospel according to Matthew*, New Testament Commentary (Grand Rapids: Baker, 1973), 948.

4. For much more on this particular problem, see Edward J. Young, *Thy Word Is Truth* (Grand Rapids: Eerdmans, 1965), 172–75, where he gives five answers to this problem, any one of which is possible, and then says that we still may not know the real answer. Nevertheless, we are certain that God's Word is totally truthful.

5. Alfred Plummer, *An Exegetical Commentary on the Gospel according to St. Matthew*, 2nd ed. (London: Robert Scott, 1910), 386.

6. Michael Wilkins, "Matthew," in *Zondervan Illustrated Bible Backgrounds Commentary*, ed. Clinton E. Arnold (Grand Rapids: Zondervan, 2002), 173.

7. See comments by A. H. McNeile, *The Gospel according to St. Matthew* (London: Macmillan, 1915), 413.

8. Plummer, *Matthew*, 393.

9. Wilkins, "Matthew," 179.

10. The manuscripts in question are those most relied on by Westcott and Hort and many of the modern versions today: Aleph, B, C, and L.

Fortunately, the great majority of manuscripts do not contain this false imported text.

11. For a brief discussion of a wide range of views on this see John Peter Lange, "Matthew," *Lange's Commentary on the Holy Scriptures* (Grand Rapids: Zondervan, 1960), 8:528. Whether the saints were long ago dead, such as Abraham, Isaac, Jacob, Joseph, Daniel, and Ezekiel, or those only recently passed away who would be known to those in Jerusalem, it is useless to speculate. Lange concludes, "It was a supernatural and symbolic event which proclaimed the truth that the death and resurrection of Christ was a victory over death and Hades, and opened the door to everlasting life."

12. Hendriksen, *Matthew*, 977–78, has a good discussion of who these women were, how many there were, and how they are to be distinguished.

13. On the possible legitimacy of the shroud of Turin, see Kenneth Stevenson and Gary R. Habermas, *Verdict on the Shroud: Evidence for the Death and Resurrection of Jesus Christ* (New York: Dell, 1982).

14. Homer A. Kent, *The Gospel according to Matthew*, Wycliffe Bible Commentaries, ed. C. Pfeiffer and E. Harrison (Chicago: Moody, 1962), 984. By contrast see B. F. Atkinson, "The Gospel according to Matthew," *New Bible Commentary* (Grand Rapids: Eerdmans, 1963), 805, who favors a Friday crucifixion based on Jewish "inclusive reckoning" of any part of a day equal to a full day.

15. For more on the chronology of the day of the crucifixion, see James A. Borland, *A General Introduction to the New Testament*, rev. ed. (Lynchburg, VA: University Book House, 1995), 94–96; and Harold W. Hoehner, *Chronological Aspects of the Life of Christ* (Grand Rapids: Zondervan, 1977).

16. See "Chronology of the Crucifixion" chart and the detailed discussion and diagrams in W. Graham Scroggie, *A Guide to the Gospels* (Grand Rapids: Kregel, 1985), 568–77.

Chapter 28—Resurrection of the King

1. F. V. Filson, *A Commentary on the Gospel according to St. Matthew* (New York: Harper and Brothers, 1960), 302.

2. R. C. H. Lenski, *The Interpretation of St. Matthew's Gospel* (Minneapolis: Augsburg, 1953), 1161–62.

3. John F. Walvoord, *Matthew: Thy Kingdom Come* (Chicago: Moody, 1974), 241. See also, Robert L. Thomas and F. David Farnell, *The Jesus Crisis: The Inroads of Historical Criticism into Evangelical Scholarship* (Grand Rapids: Kregel, 1998), who explore this issue more fully.

4. On the theological significance of the resurrection, see Gary R. Habermas, *The Resurrection of Jesus, An Apologetic* (Grand Rapids: Baker, 1980); Josh McDowell, *The Resurrection Factor* (San Bernadino, CA: Here's Life Publishers, 1981); G. Ladd, "The Resurrection of Jesus Christ," in

Christian Faith and Modern Theology, ed. Carl F. H. Henry (New York: Channel Press, 1964), 261–284; Merrill C. Tenney, *The Reality of the Resurrection* (New York: Harper & Row, 1963).

5. D. A. Carson, "Matthew," *The Expositor's Bible Commentary*, ed. Frank E. Gaebelein (Grand Rapids: Zondervan, 1984), 8:593, asserts that, "'The most that can be said for this interpretation is that others passages show that Jesus in his postresurrection appearances was not always instantly recognized." He reasons, "Perhaps it is best to conclude that, especially if the 'some' refers not to the Eleven but to other followers, the move from unbelief and fear to faith and joy was for them a 'hesitant' one" (594).

6. Lenski, *Matthew's Gospel*, 1169.

7. John Peter Lange, "Matthew," *Lange's Commentary on the Holy Scriptures* (Grand Rapids: Zondervan, 1960), 8:556.

8. William Hendriksen, *Exposition of the Gospel according to Matthew*, New Testament Commentary (Grand Rapids: Baker, 1973), 999.

9. The gospel of Christ is exclusivistic—that is, one must believe in Christ to be saved and have any hope of eternal life. For a clear presentation of this, see James A. Borland, "A Theologian Looks at the Gospel and World Religions," *Journal of the Evangelical Theological Society* 33, no. 1 (March 1990): 3–11.

10. For further reading on baptism, see G. R. Beasley-Murray, *Baptism in the New Testament* (Grand Rapids: Eerdmans, 1962); E. Hulse, *Baptism and Church Membership* (London: Carey, 1972), R. E. O. White, *The Biblical Doctrine of Initiation* (Grand Rapids: Eerdmans, 1960).

11. Charles Spurgeon, quoted in R. Lee and E. Hindson, *No Greater Savior* (Eugene, OR: Harvest House, 1995).

ABOUT THE AUTHORS

Dr. Ed Hindson is the assistant chancellor, distinguished professor and dean of the Institute of Biblical Studies at Liberty University in Lynchburg, Virginia.

He has authored thirty books, including *Isaiah's Immanuel* and *Revelation: Unlocking the Future*. He also served as general editor of the Gold Medallion and Angel Award-Winning *Knowing Jesus Study Bible*, plus numerous other reference books, including the *Popular Encyclopedia of Bible Prophecy* and the *Popular Bible Prophecy Commentary*.

Dr. Hindson is a Life Fellow of the International Biographical Association of Cambridge, England, and serves as the speaker on *The King Is Coming* international telecast. He holds degrees from several institutions: B.A., William Tyndale College; M.A., Trinity Evangelical Divinity School; Th.M., Grace Theological Seminary; Th.D., Trinity Graduate School; D.Min., Westminster Theological Seminary; D.Phil., University of South Africa. He has also done graduate study at Acadia University in Nova Scotia, Canada.

Dr. James Borland is professor of Biblical Studies at Liberty University in Lynchburg, Virginia and serves on the executive committee of the Evangelical Theological Society, of which he is a past president.

Dr. Borland holds the following degrees: B.A., Los Angeles Baptist College; M.Div., Los Angeles Baptist Seminary; Th.M., Talbot Theological Seminary; Th.D., Grace Theological Seminary. He is the author of *Christ in the Old Testament* and *Introduction to the New Testament*. With more than thirty years of teaching experience, Dr. Borland specializes in biblical theology and New Testament studies.

About the General Editor

Mal Couch was founder of Tyndale Seminary in Ft. Worth, TX. and served as president there for eighteen years. He is now president of Scofield Ministries in Clifton, TX. He holds the following degrees: B.A., John Brown University; Th.M., Dallas Theological Seminary; M.A., Wheaton Graduate School; Th.D., Louisiana Baptist Seminary. He serves as general editor, along with Dr. Hindson, of the Twenty-First Century Biblical Commentary Series.® His other publications include *A Bible Handbook to Revelation* and the award-winning *Dictionary of Premillennial Theology*.